SUPERVISOR SAVVY

LaVerne L. Ludden, Ed.D.
and
Tom Capozzoli, Ed.D.

jist
Publishing

Supervisor Savvy

© 2000 by JIST Works, Inc.

Published by JIST Works, Inc.
8902 Otis Avenue
Indianapolis, IN 46216-1033

Phone: 1-800-648-JIST   Fax: 1-800-JIST-FAX
E-mail: editorial@jist.com   Web site: www.jist.com

Other books by LaVerne L. Ludden:

Best Jobs for the 21st Century
Job Savvy: How to Be a Success at Work
Franchise Opportunities Handbook, Revised Edition
Back to School: A College Guide for Adults
Luddens' Adult Guide to Colleges and Universities (with Marsha Ludden)
Mind Your Own Business (with Bonnie Maitlen)

Other books by Tom Capozzoli:

Kids Killing Kids: Managing School Violence
Managing Violence in the Workplace

See the back of this book for additional JIST titles and ordering information.
Quantity discounts available.

Development Editor: Erik Dafforn
Cover Designer: Michael Nolan
Layout Technician: Katy Bodenmiller
Proofreader: Rebecca York

Printed in the United States of America

05 04 03 02 01 00   9 8 7 6 5 4 3 2 1

ISBN 1-56370-669-5

Contents at a Glance

Table of Contents

V

About This Book

Sandi watches as Mitch sprays water on the lettuce a half hour before the Food Depot opens. Just three weeks ago, she had been promoted to produce supervisor. Sandi thinks about asking Mitch whether he needs time off to attend his high school prom. Just then, Whitney walks past Mitch and he playfully sprays her with water.

Their laughter is interrupted by Sandi yelling at them. "What kind of stupid stunt was that? Get that water mopped up before someone slips."

Mitch's face turns red and he says, "You don't need to scream at us."

"Well, if you're going to act like little kids, that's the way I'll treat you," Sandi replies.

"That's it," Mitch retorts, "I've had about as much of you as I'm going to take. I'm out of here." With that statement, Mitch stalks off, leaving Sandi perplexed and angry.

Sandi turns to Whitney and says, "Don't just stand there, get that water cleaned up." Whitney glares at Sandi, and without saying anything, turns to get the mop.

Two days later, Sandi's manager calls her aside to tell her Whitney just called; she found a better job and won't be coming to work anymore.

This incident illustrates some problems common in many organizations. Mitch is like many young, inexperienced workers—unsure about what is appropriate behavior on the job. Whitney doesn't voice her feelings about Sandi's treatment and quits her job on short notice. Neither employee displayed good communication skills—skills that a good supervisor could help them develop.

Sandi's poor human relations skills resulted in the Food Depot losing two employees. Organizations face a labor shortage, and employee retention is a major concern. The Food Depot needed Mitch and Whitney. But is this situation entirely Sandi's fault? If her experience is like most other new supervisors, she was given little or no training on how to supervise employees.

Be a Better Supervisor

The purpose of this book is to help supervisors do a better job and avoid the types of mistakes Sandi made. You might wonder why, since there are many other books about supervision, you should pick this specific text. Quite simply, this one is different.

Two themes intertwine throughout this book to make it unique. First is the philosophy that the most important tasks of a supervisor are training, coaching, leading, motivating, counseling, and communicating with employees. If people are truly the most important asset of an organization, supervisors should invest their time in developing this resource.

The second theme focuses on the type of worker commonly employed in many organizations today—organizations that face a major labor shortage. Competition for workers has forced many organizations to hire workers with little or no job experience and few skills. Many newly-hired workers lack the basic skills that employers want and expect. This book is a guide for supervisors who want to develop those inexperienced, low-skilled workers into valuable and productive employees.

What's So Special about *Supervisor Savvy?*

This book is grounded on organizational research and theory. But it isn't a boring ivory tower book. Both authors have worked in the trenches as first-line supervisors. We've also been professors at a major university. This background has led us to believe that supervisors need to be grounded in theory but equipped with practical, down-to-earth techniques that make these theories work. This belief has framed how we've gone about writing this book. We'd like to provide you with an overview of what this book is all about.

Reading this section is useful because many people aren't going to read an entire book like this. It is more likely that they will browse through it and pull out tidbits that are useful for a particular situation. This section can help this type of reader focus in on the material that is most relevant to the situation. There are some people who will want to read this book in its entirety—and you are dear to our hearts. The following synopsis of the book helps organize your thinking and provides an understanding of where the book is going to take you.

- Chapter 1, "The Changing Workplace," sets the stage by examining the modern organization and the many changes it faces. The workforce is changing and becoming more diverse. Women, ethnic groups, and workers who span a wide age range are participating in greater numbers than ever before. As this change takes place, organizations are redefining work and occupations are evolving. Supervisors need to be aware of these changes and understand how to facilitate change in organizations.

- Chapter 2, "Workplace Expectations," looks at expectations that employers have about workers that they hire, as well as what workers should expect in return. The most important assets employees bring to an organization are their skills. This chapter describes the skills that employers consider to be basic work skills. These skills are important because throughout the book you will discover ideas about how supervisors can develop these skills in their employees. Another important topic covered in this chapter are the laws that govern employer/employee relationships.

- Chapter 3, "The Supervisor at Work," examines the role of a supervisor. A supervisor is someone who gets work done through other people. This is accomplished through planning, organizing, delegating, leading, and controlling. All of these activities make a supervisor an important part of any organization. We've also added some information in this chapter that you won't find in most books about supervision. We also include a list of the primary skills and abilities supervisors need based on research done by the U.S. Department of Labor.

- Chapter 4, "Motivating Employees," considers the topic of motivation. It reviews the major theories and concepts that have been developed to explain behavior in the workplace. The chapter provides supervisors with a basic understanding about what can be done to create a work environment that motivates employees.

- Chapter 5, "Communications—Getting the Point," introduces the subject of communication. The communication skills that are reviewed are important for supervisors to understand before moving on to other chapters in the book. The chapter explains how a supervisor can become a better communicator in face-to-face, written, and electronic communications. It also considers the issue of how men and women communicate in the workplace and how this can be improved.

3

- Chapter 6, "Employee Socialization," explains how a supervisor can make the process of employee socialization easier. Socialization gradually converts a new employee from an outsider to an insider in the organization. We discuss functions such as preparing for a worker's first day and orientation of new workers. In addition, the chapter looks at how you can help employees learn very basic skills such as attendance, timeliness, dress, hygiene, and getting along with coworkers.

- Chapter 7, "Training Employees," presents the skills a supervisor needs to train employees. It examines the role of supervisor as instructor and explains basic concepts of adult learning. You will also discover how to develop a training program, conduct classroom learning programs, and implement on-the-job training. This chapter also contains the basic knowledge a supervisor needs to help his or her employees become lifelong learners.

- Chapter 8, "Leadership," furnishes you with insight into what it means to be a leader—the importance of goals and vision. We consider several leadership models and offer practical ideas on how to apply the models in the workplace. The chapter concludes with a review of "followership" and proposes ways that you can prepare your employees to be good followers.

- Chapter 9, "Teamwork—Reaching the Goal," looks at the ways organizations are structured and how a supervisor develops organizational competence. Most organizations are practicing the use of teams and this chapter offers many insights into creating, developing, and using teams effectively. Two important functions of teams are to engage in problem solving and apply creative thinking to organizational needs, and both of these topics are reviewed.

- Chapter 10, "Improving Employee Performance," examines how the supervisor can have the most positive effect on employee performance. The chapter gives a systematic method for analyzing performance and an explanation of how to coach, counsel, and discipline employees. It concludes by considering four special problems supervisors often face: sexual harassment, racial harassment, dating, and workplace violence.

- Chapter 11, "Developing Ethical Behavior," concludes the book by considering the supervisor's part in developing ethical behavior in employees. Organizations face enormous losses, both economically and intrinsically, when employees engage in unethical behavior. Supervisors frequently respond to ethical problems, but this chapter describes and urges the proactive stance of encouraging ethical behavior in employees. We review basic ethical models and provide some very practical guidelines that you can teach employees to use when they must decide how to respond to ethical dilemmas.

You'll find a feature throughout the book called "Quick Tips." These are ideas and techniques that you can use to apply the concepts explained in the chapter. The tips focus on improving supervisory practices for the emerging workforce. We consider the emerging workforce to consist of the following groups of workers:

- Younger workers—This group includes workers between the ages of 14 and 19 with little or no work experience and very little life experience in general. Younger workers present a challenge to supervisors because they may lack basic work skills most often acquired through experience.

- Older workers—Older workers have many skills and often a large amount of work experience. In this book, we focus on situations supervisors encounter with older workers who are moving into a new job. They enter this job with basic skills and many transferable skills but may lack some specific job skills and knowledge of an organization.

- Welfare-to-work employees—The welfare reform changes that were initiated in 1996 were bolstered by the Welfare-to-Work program. The focus of this program is to help welfare recipients move from the Temporary Assistance to Needy Families program to permanent employment and economic self-sufficiency. Virtually all welfare recipients are mothers with children. They bring a unique set of needs to the workplace that supervisors must meet in order to develop productive and satisfied workers.

- Immigrant workers—Any person who has moved from another country to the United States and is of working age fits into this group. The difference in cultures and limited English-speaking abilities of many immigrants are challenges driving supervisors to develop new skills and techniques in managing a workforce.

- Disabled workers—This group includes anyone with a physical or mental impairment substantially limiting one or more major life activities. The courts are still in the process of defining exactly who fits into this definition. However, specific tips about supervising people with disabilities should help clarify what is considered a disability.

- Contingent workers—The definition of contingent workers varies. The U.S. Department of Labor's definition includes temporary workers, independent contractors, workers provided by contract firms, and on-call workers. We have also included in this group part-time workers. These are workers that supervisors have to manage for shorter periods of time than permanent employees.

- Ex-offenders—This term can apply to anyone convicted of a crime regardless of whether they serve time. However, this book concentrates primarily on issues affecting individuals recently released from prison or jail. Their incarceration results in circumstances occurring in the work-place that supervisors must be able to handle.

These groups of workers are often entering their first job—at least in the United States economy. They are inexperienced, have unique needs and problems, and typically require a supervisor to respond with a high level of human relations skills. Supervisors who work in organizations employing a large number of entry-level workers will find this information very useful.

We hope that as a result of reading this book, you develop a deeper appreciation for employees and the contribution they make to the success of every organization. Investing your time in helping employees become all they can be is a worthwhile, fulfilling endeavor. We also hope that this book provides the knowledge, tools, and skills you need to become a better supervisor.

In the back of the book, you'll find a bibliography. We didn't want to fill the text with a lot of footnotes and references—these can be distracting. However, we wanted you to know where we found many ideas and facts included in the book.

Chapter 1

The Changing Workplace

Work is changing in many ways. The labor force, the workplace, and the business environment are all changing. Being a supervisor in this changing world is more difficult than ever. This chapter puts into perspective the many developments that are taking place in the world of work. Both new and experienced supervisors will have already observed many of the trends described here. The chapter should help organize your thoughts in a more structured way and assist you to better understand the forces affecting your job. Other transformations affecting work will be new and the chapter may provide insights that will help you more effectively manage today's work-force. In this chapter, we'll look at how the labor force, occupations, the workplace, and the structure of work are evolving.

The Labor Force, 2006

The labor force refers to people who are available and want to work. Anyone who is looking for a job or working at a job is a member of the labor force. You'll be a more effective worker if you understand some of the changes that the U.S. Bureau of Labor Statistics indicates are occurring in the labor force.

1. **The labor force is growing more slowly than before.** The labor force grew by 16 million workers between 1986 and 1996. But it is expected to grow by only 15 million workers between 1996 and 2006. This slower rate of growth will create more demand for workers in business. The percent of unemployed workers is expected to be lower than at any time since the 1960s. It will be particularly difficult for many businesses to find workers for minimum wage jobs.

This trend may spur higher participation of younger workers (16 to 19 years old) in the workforce. Today, about 52 percent of this age group is in the labor force. Many businesses now recruit 14- and 15-year-olds because they are willing to work for minimum wage. There won't be much competition for jobs that require little education and offer lower wages. Supervisors will be challenged to retain workers that can easily find a job with another organization. In addition, they will need to concentrate on providing basic work skills that young workers need to be successful on the job.

Younger workers—Almost 70 percent of workers between the ages of 16 and 19 are employed part-time. They typically work while finishing high school or starting college. The highest percentage of younger workers are employed as ski patrol workers, lifeguards, dining room helpers, private child care workers, cashiers, food counter workers, waiters and waitresses, stock and material movers, ushers, ticket takers, and counter and rental clerks. Supervisors who manage workers in these occupations are likely to find that almost 50 percent or more of the workers are in this younger age group.

The higher demand for workers is also likely to increase the recruitment of immigrants. There is a groundswell of support among employers to increase the number of immigrants—particularly those with skills that are in demand in the U.S. economy. In this situation, workers often have difficulties speaking and understanding spoken English and are not always aware of some behavioral expectations in American culture. Supervisors will need to focus on their communication skills so that instructions and tasks are clearly understood by workers new to the United States. In addition, orientation to the workplace should accommodate cultural differences.

Immigrant workers—Immigration trends tell us to expect 820,000 immigrants to arrive annually in the United States. Two out of three will be working age upon their arrival. By 2050, it is projected that immigration will have increased the U.S. population by 80 million people. Fully two-thirds of the projected U.S. population increase will be due to net immigration. There were

14,524,000 immigrants employed in the workforce—about 10 percent of the workforce—in 1997, according to the U.S. Census Bureau. In California, one out of every four workers is foreign born. Clearly, supervisors need to be prepared to effectively manage this group of workers.

2. **More women are entering the workforce.** Women are expected to account for almost 48 percent of workers in the labor force by 2006. This is a dramatic change from 1969, when the Department of Labor reported only 38 percent of the workforce was female. This change has been referred to as the "feminization" of the labor force. There are also more women supervisors today, both in number and percentage, than any other time in history.

Women's participation in the workforce has had a great impact on businesses. They have become more concerned about child care, family leave, flextime, job sharing, sexual harassment, and other issues. The changing view of women in the workplace also has changed how many organizations view the role of men within the family. This has created a demand among female and male workers for "family-friendly" employment practices. Supervisors have had to adjust to the conversion of the workplace to a more family-friendly place. Most of these adjustments have made a supervisor's job more difficult because it requires balancing more factors in scheduling workers and tasks. However, many positive changes have resulted from the increased participation of women in the workplace, and this trend is likely to continue.

Ex-offenders—The combined federal, state, and local adult correctional population grew by 163,800 men and women during 1998 to reach a new high of 5.9 million people, the Justice Department's Bureau of Justice Statistics (BJS) recently announced. This includes incarcerated inmates and probationers and parolees in the community, BJS said. Almost 3 percent of the nation's adult population, or about 1 in every 34 adults, were incarcerated or on probation or on parole at the end of last year. Current trends indicate that almost 1 out of every 20 individuals will serve a prison term sometime in their life. It is not reasonable for organizations to exclude ex-offenders from employment because it limits the potential to recruit a significant portion of the population.

3. **The labor force is aging.** The Baby Boom generation makes up a large portion of the labor force. By 2006, this group will be 42 to 60 years old. Workers in this age group typically are the most productive. It's likely that the graying of the workforce will force businesses to rethink outmoded retirement policies and to find new ways to use workers regardless of age. In her book *New Passages,* Gail Sheehy states that because this generation will be the healthiest and most vital group of older workers in history, we may alter views about changing careers later in life and about how long people should work. Supervisors are going to be challenged to develop strategies that take advantage of the aging workforce experience. In addition, they will need to accommodate the needs of older workers.

Older workers—Currently there are almost 4 million workers 65 years of age and over who are employed. This number is likely to increase in the next 20 years. According to studies reported by the American Association of Retired Persons (AARP), many older people continue to work after retirement because they need the income. One study indicates that almost one-fourth of all Baby Boomers say they will need to continue working because of income needs. Many older workers often change careers when they enter retirement. Often they choose to work at a lower paying job that provides them flexibility and less responsibility than they had before retiring. Supervisors should recognize that this group of employees brings significant experience to the workplace but this experience may not be directly related to their current job.

4. **The workforce is showing greater ethnic diversity.** According to the U.S. Bureau of Labor Statistics, the percentage of all minority ethnic groups in the population will increase by the year 2006, and this increase will be reflected in the workforce. Hispanic Americans are expected to comprise almost 12 percent of the workforce; African Americans 11 percent; Asians 3 percent; and Native Americans 1 percent. Together, these groups will represent more than one in four workers. Companies have responded to this trend by creating ethnic diversity programs to help workers understand and appreciate cultural differences. This mix of cultures in the workplace will bring new perspectives to solving business problems. Supervisors can tap into ethnic diversity to create a team of workers with a broad range of perspectives. It becomes increasingly important for a supervisor to understand ethnic differences and work to create a blended workplace where all workers feel comfortable.

5. **Workers with disabilities are finding a more accessible workplace.**
   The Americans with Disabilities Act has made employers more aware
   of the need to create a workplace that accommodates the needs of
   people with disabilities. The definition of disability is somewhat
   complex. However, a general definition is that it is a condition,
   impairment, limitation, or inability that interferes with normal everyday life or with work- specific tasks.

Disabled workers—Fifty percent of working-age people
with disabilities are unemployed. A 1994 Harris Poll found
that of the 15 million or so unemployed people with disabilities, nearly 12 million want to work. Labor force participation
rates for individuals with disabilities increased in the 1980s, but
have not significantly changed since 1990. However, persons with
disabilities due to neurotic disorders, multiple sclerosis, arthritis, and
benign tumors experienced an increase of 40 percent or more in
participation rates from 1983 to 1994. This indicates that it is possible to accommodate disabled persons in the workplace and employers
should consider disabled persons a valuable resource to overcome
the labor shortage. In fact, studies have found that on average, it
costs less than $500 per person to accommodate a disabled worker.

The U.S. Bureau of Labor Statistics reports that 16 percent of the workforce—that is, about 1 person in 6 from ages 20 to 64—consists of workers with moderate or severe disabilities. The percent of workers
with disabilities is much higher in service occupations and operator and
fabricator occupations than for the general population. As the economy
makes it more difficult to find workers, it becomes more important to
recruit and retain workers. Supervisors need to learn how to make adap-
tations in the workplace to accommodate people with disabilities. It is
important to understand how to communicate with disabled workers
about their needs and respond appropriately.

The workforce of the future will represent a broader range of gender, ages,
ethnicities, and other differences. At the same time, the recruitment and retention
of workers is becoming increasingly difficult. The supervisor's role—never an
easy one to fill—is going to become increasingly important as businesses strive
to adapt to the new labor market. Interpersonal skills are going to be particularly
vital to a supervisor's success.

Organizations and Work

In the U.S. economy, most workers—71 percent, in fact—are employed by service-producing organizations. (The remaining portion of the workforce—the other 21 percent—is employed in goods-producing organizations, agriculture, and self-employment.) As shown in the following table, service organizations include a wide variety of businesses—not just fast-food franchises, which is the first thought many people have when they hear the words "service economy." The type of organization is listed in the first column of the table. The second column shows the percentage of workers employed by each sector in 1996. The third column shows the projected employment in 2006.

Type of Organization	*1996*	*2006*
Transportation, Communications, Utilities	4.7	4.7
Wholesale Trade	4.9	4.8
Retail Trade	16.3	15.8
Finance, Insurance, and Real Estate	5.2	5.1
Specialized Services	25.4	29.7
Government	14.7	14.0
Total Service-Providing Workers	71.2%	74.1

As you can see in the table above, all of the growth in service jobs falls under the "specialized services" area. This category includes health services, business services, and social services, where the highest rates of growth are projected. The goods-producing sector of the economy has had a declining share of employment for the past several decades, and continued decline is expected. The next table shows current and projected employment for these businesses.

The goods-producing businesses will decline from almost 18.5 to 16.2 percent by the year 2006. Supervisors were once considered to be primarily responsible for blue-collar workers. Today, however, most supervisors are responsible for white-collar workers.

Not only are most workers employed in service-producing fields, but 84 percent are working for smaller organizations—those with fewer than 1000 employees.

In fact, 66 percent of workers in the U.S. are employed by organizations with 250 or fewer employees. Smaller organizations are less likely than larger ones to provide their workers with training. This means most supervisors must provide on-the-job training and coach their workers about other ways to improve their skills.

Type of Business	1996	2006
Mining	.4	.3
Construction	4.1	3.9
Manufacturing	13.9	12.0
Agriculture	2.8	2.4
Private Household Workers	.7	.5
Self-Employed	6.8	6.8
Total Goods-Producing Workers	28.7	25.9

Occupational Trends

The book *Best Jobs for the 21st Century* (see Bibliography) examines the best jobs based on annual earnings, growth rate, and annual number of job openings using data from the U.S. Bureau of Labor Statistics. Of the top 25 best-paying jobs, 23 require at least a four-year college degree. The fastest-growing jobs in the labor market are also typically ones that require a high level of skills—16 out of the top 25 require postsecondary vocational training or a college degree.

Those jobs with the most annual openings offer a contrast because they require few skills. In fact, of the jobs with the most openings per year, 19 of the top 25 require only short-term, on-the-job training. However, the average pay for those 25 jobs is a little under $20,000 per year, compared with an average for all jobs, which is over $29,000.

This occupational trend helps explain why a person's level of education has such a dramatic affect on his or her earnings. The following table illustrates the relationship between education and earnings. The third column shows the percentage of difference in average earnings over the earnings of a high school drop-out.

Level of Education	Avg. Annual Earnings	Difference
Professional Degree	71,700	264
Doctorate	62,400	217
Master's	50,000	154
Bachelor's	40,100	104
Associate	31,700	61
Some College	30,400	54
High School	26,000	32
Less Than H.S.	19,700	

Welfare-to-work employees—Businesses that don't hire welfare workers are missing an opportunity to increase their recruiting potential; more than 7 million families were receiving welfare in 1999. The federal government has developed a Welfare-to-Work program that encourages welfare recipients to move into jobs. However, a survey done in 1998 found that over 60 percent of companies do not hire welfare applicants or not have a well defined program to recruit and train welfare recipients. Yet this potential pool of workers has been found to have good employees. A survey conducted by the Welfare-to-Work Partnership in 1999 found that companies that hire welfare recipients consider them a good investment. More than three-fourths of the executives for these companies reported that workers hired from welfare programs are good and productive employees.

The difference in earnings over a lifetime is staggering. Let's assume that a high school drop-out begins working full-time when he is 16 and retires 49 years later, at age 65. His total life earnings would be about $925,000. The college graduate who begins working at age 23 and retires at age 65 works for 42 years, but earns about $1.8 million—almost double the earnings of the high school drop-out. Earnings and employment opportunities for less educated workers declined significantly in the last decade, and that trend is likely to increase in the future. There's truth to the old adage that education pays. It's also important—in fact, in today's economy, it's necessary—to continue learning once you're on the job.

There are two major trends affecting occupations that impact organizations and supervisors. First, an increasing number of jobs require a high level of skills. This trend will require supervisors to continue to improve their skill level. In addition, it compels supervisors to create a learning environment where employees can continue to develop existing skills and obtain new ones as a technique to promote both retention and motivation.

Second, the skills required for a job change significantly over time. For example, it is estimated that nearly half the knowledge of computer engineers becomes obsolete within their first year of employment. It is important for workers to recognize the importance of lifelong learning. Supervisors should look for ways to assist employees in their lifelong learning efforts.

The Structure of Work

The structure of work is changing, and that affects the way jobs are organized. Most organizations recognize the need to have a flexible workforce. This flexibility allows a business to keep its workforce as small as possible, thus saving money. Full-time permanent workers form the foundation of an organization's workforce. However, to provide for flexibility, more work is now organized into projects, which are then contracted out or assigned to workers that are hired in a non-conventional arrangement. These non-conventional workers are called a *contingent workforce*. Some experts believe the use of contingent workers is redefining jobs. They believe the structure of today's workforce is an indicator of this trend.

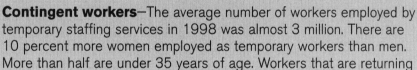

Contingent workers—The average number of workers employed by temporary staffing services in 1998 was almost 3 million. There are 10 percent more women employed as temporary workers than men. More than half are under 35 years of age. Workers that are returning to the workforce often use temporary staffing services to test their skills and try out prospective employers. Many organizations use temporary staffing as a tactic for screening and evaluating new workers. Supervisors can observe the worker's performance as a temporary employee and offer them full-time employment if they are satisfied with their work. In fact, the National Association of Temporary and Staffing Services reports that 72 percent of temporary workers go on to permanent jobs. The strategy of hiring temporary employees to evaluate their skills and work ethics appears to work well for both organizations and workers.

The workforce that exists today is composed of workers that typically fall into two broad categories: core employees and contingent employees. This latter group consists of independent contractors, on-call employees, temporary hires, and contract company workers.

15

■ **Core employees** are hired by an organization to work full-time or part-time on a permanent basis. "Permanent" doesn't mean guaranteed lifetime employment. Rather, it implies that the employment is expected to last until the employer or employee determine there are significant reasons to terminate it. Core employees have a basic loyalty to the organization and understand both its short-term and long-term goals. They usually are provided with benefits like vacation time, holiday pay, health insurance, and other fringe benefits. In fact, the fringe benefits make them more expensive than most other types of employees. Core employees often coordinate or lead projects for an organization, and their work is supplemented by contingent workers. This is still the bulk of the workforce.

■ **Independent contractors** are private business owners—including self-employed individuals—who provide services to an organization, such as cleaning, maintenance, payroll, accounting, security, computer programming, telecommunications, and printing. Subcontractors or their employees typically are paid a fee for completion of a task rather than a wage. Their services may be used for a specific project and their work ends when the project is completed. Many workers who have lost jobs to corporate restructuring in recent years have become self-employed. Independent contractors make up 6.7 percent of the workforce.

The IRS scrutinizes workers hired as independent contractors. It is important that these individuals are truly different from a regular employee. They must maintain genuine independence from the organization when it comes to work arrangements. If they must work in an office, follow the same work schedule as regular employees, and are otherwise treated much like regular employees, the IRS doesn't consider them independent contractors. A supervisor should understand the guidelines established by the IRS and follow them when directing the activities of independent contractors.

■ **On-call employees** are hired by a company to work whenever they are needed. This may be for a single day or several weeks in a row. Substitute teachers, nurses, truck drivers, and construction workers are the most common examples of on-call employees. About 1.6 percent of the workforce consists of on-call workers.

An on-call job arrangement is quite desirable for an organization. However, it is difficult to recruit quality employees for on-call work because of inconsistent earnings. On-call employees are a challenge to supervise because they have sporadic communication with the supervisor and others within an organization.

■ **Temporary workers** are hired by an organization for a short time or obtained through a temporary employment service. Many organizations prefer to use a "temp service" because it reduces their paperwork, administrative tasks, and recruitment efforts. Temporary workers may be hired to work on a specific project, and their employment ends when the project is completed. Temporary workers also are hired when the work load increases beyond the capacity of core employees, in which case there may be no specific date when the work is completed. Rather, the organization stops using the worker's services when the work load decreases. Temporary workers comprise about 1 percent of the labor force.

Temporary employees often have no fringe benefits—unless they are provided by the temp service—and their work can be terminated with no advance notice. The supervisor has several challenges when working with temporary workers. More frequent turnover may necessitate more time for orientation and on-the-job training of employees. Also, some employees may be less motivated when they know that they can request a reassignment to another organization by the temporary employment agency.

■ **Contract company workers** make up .6 percent of the labor force. These people work for a company that provides employees under contract to an organization. They provide many of the advantages obtained by using temporary employees. However, they are used when an organization needs workers for an ongoing task that is done daily. In essence, the organization hires an entire workforce rather than a single individual. They simply contract with a company to supply workers. These workers are much like core employees when it comes to supervision. The company that supplies the workers instructs them to follow the direction of a supervisor and that failure to do so will result in termination. However, the loyalty of these workers may not be as high as what you find among core employees.

So, what does all this mean for you? It means that supervisors function in a more complex world of work than their predecessors did. Your job as a supervisor is going to require more skills to handle this complexity. This book is designed to help you acquire these skills. It is specifically focused on managing a diverse workforce in a changing workplace.

Managing Change

Amidst the uncertainty that surrounds many organizations, there is one thing that is certain: change. In fact, due to workers redefining their roles, evolution in workplace culture, and technological advances, businesses face rapid change more often now than they ever have. Successful supervisors are able to identify, cope with, and manage change. Sometimes, the supervisor even initiates change. Change is a part of progress and progress is a very important part of business. Change may be sudden or it may be gradual, but it will always be continual. Change can be classified into one of three different categories:

- **Internal change** involves structural alterations within the organization. An example of this type of change might be the merging of two departments within the organization.

- **External change** involves forces outside of the organization that affect the organization in some manner. An example might be a change in consumer wants or needs that forces the organization to change the way it provides its main product or service.

- **Technological change** involves some type of automation, computerization, or robotics that affects the organization. An example might be the automation of a production line that eliminates several jobs.

People in organizations usually resist change of any type. The types of resistance are:

- **Logical resistance** based on disagreement with the facts, rational reasoning, or logic.

- **Psychological resistance** based on emotions, sentiments, or attitudes. Psychological resistance is internally "logical" to employees based on their attitudes and feelings about the change. Many employees fear the unknown and they mistrust management's leadership. They may also feel that change threatens their security. Common fears that employees have about change include:

  ◆ Losing their jobs

  ◆ Losing status

  ◆ Losing pay—taking a wage or salary reduction

  ◆ Losing power or influence

  ◆ Fear of the unknown

  ◆ Changes in relationships

  ◆ Personal adjustments that must be made

- **Sociological resistance** is a logical resistance when it is seen from the aspect of group interests, norms, and values. Social values are very powerful forces in an environment and must be considered. Groups often band together to resist change to protect their common needs.

Because people resist change does not mean that in the long term it will not be accepted if the change is introduced properly and human factors are given proper consideration.

A supervisor plays an important role in helping change occur smoothly in an organization. The amount of change that takes place in the typical organization today makes this role a critical one. A supervisor can use some simple strategies to facilitate change.

- **Keep employees informed.** Share information with employees about changes that are expected. Some organizations resist communicating planned changes with employees and may restrict your access to information or require that you keep it confidential. When there are restrictions on information sharing, let employees know that as soon as you're allowed to discuss the changes, the employees will be told about them. This strategy helps maintain trust between supervisors and their employees. However, keep in mind that employees' trust usually diminishes during times of change.

- **Discuss concerns.** Encourage employees to share their concerns and discuss them with you. This alerts you to the fears that are causing employees to resist change. This information can be used to plan ways to reduce the fear and encourage change. In addition, it helps identify rumors—a major problem during change.

- **Provide islands of stability.** Supervisors should look for specific parts of an operation that don't need to change and keep them stable. Also, encourage social activities, such as lunches once a month at a special restaurant or going out together after work to celebrate employee birthdays. These regular events give employees an anchor in a sea of change and provide some psychological comfort.

- **Personal support.** Supervisors can take the lead on supporting change or destroying it. Your primary responsibility is to support the organization and promote activities essential to its success. When a board of directors and/or management have decided to make a change, they consider it to be crucial to the organization's success. A supervisor doesn't have to agree with the action but does need to support it by working to accomplish the change. Supervisors should communicate and demonstrate their support to employees. If a change is made that you absolutely can't support, you need to give serious thought to resigning your position or perhaps terminating your employment with the organization.

■ **Concentrate on positives.** Every change has some negative aspects and employees usually point them out quickly. It is important that they also recognize the positives. An optimistic viewpoint can help employees consider benefits that may come through change.

■ **Involve employees.** Get your employees involved in helping to implement change. Typically, details in any change must be worked out at the first-line level of an organization. Employees who can help make decisions about these matters are more likely to support the overall change.

■ **Provide training.** Employees are sometimes concerned about having the skills needed to do a job and fear they'll lose their jobs if they fail. Training can help overcome this fear because it provides employees with the ability to perform a new task, operate a new piece of equipment, deal more effectively with customers, and so on.

■ **Promote employability.** Employability encompasses a person's knowledge, skills, abilities, and experiences as they relate to the workplace. People with a high level of employability are more valuable in the labor market and have a higher probability of getting a job when they leave their current one. The more you can help employees feel employable, the less fear they'll have about change occurring in an organization. Supervisors can develop a person's employability by giving them assignments to practice old skills and develop new ones. You can also provide them opportunities to participate in training programs.

Changing economic conditions, labor markets, work structures, technology, and other factors cause organizations to change. Encourage your employees to watch for these changes and be aware of the ways it may affect their jobs. Then help them understand that organizations must successfully adapt to these changes. Supervisors should be prepared to help the organization and its employees move forward in implementing change.

Summary

In today's changing workplace, the key word is flexibility. As the economy continues to shift from goods-producing to services-producing, new and different skills are needed. And as companies rely more on subcontractors and temporary workers, finding new ways to sell your skills (and learning new skills) is crucial to a supervisor's long-term success. The effective supervisor, both now and in the future, is one who can adapt to changes, guide employees through the process of change, and work in a variety of work situations.

Chapter 2

Workplace Expectations

The workplace is an interesting mixture of employer and employee expectations. The supervisor has often been pictured as the person in the middle. On one side, you have owners and management setting goals, objectives, and strategies. On the other side, you have employees who expect you to express their views and interests to management. This chapter examines some of the assumptions that underlie the expectations of both employers and employees.

In this chapter you'll get to know more about the basic skills that employers need, reasons that people work, and legal protections that employees are afforded. An understanding of these topics is critical to a supervisor. The supervisor's primary resource is people and it is necessary to understand the issues that impact your ability to effectively use this resource to meet your employer's expectations.

Business Basics

Three basic expectations govern the actions of most businesses. A successful organization strives to:

1. **Provide a product or service of high quality.** Consumers want quality in whatever they buy. Organizations today place great emphasis on quality. The U.S. government even recognizes companies for their emphasis on quality with the Malcolm Baldridge National Quality Award. An emphasis on quality keeps customers coming back. Just think about the image of quality the names Sony, Mercedes, Godiva, and Hewlett Packard convey in the minds of most consumers. Companies want their customers to perceive the quality of their goods or services in the same way.

2. **Satisfy the customer's needs and wants.** An organization depends on the good will of its customers. Excellent quality can't succeed on its own merit. A restaurant with the highest quality and best tasting food in the world won't prosper without good customer service. Ken Blanchard has written an excellent book on customer service—*Raving Fans*. Customers who receive a high quality product along with superior service will become raving fans. They will remain loyal to the business and even recommend it to other people. Conversely, a bad experience will be talked about with friends, family members, acquaintances, coworkers, and complete strangers for many years to come.

3. **Make a profit.** Product quality and customer satisfaction have to be provided at a cost that allows a business to make a profit. There's no reason for the owners or stockholders to continue the business if they could invest their money elsewhere and receive a higher rate of return.

Even government and nonprofit agencies must stay within a budget. Nonprofit agencies must earn enough money to pay all their expenses. Although they can't distribute earnings greater than their expenses to stockholders, government and nonprofit agencies are expected to operate as efficiently as profit-making businesses.

An employer expects all employees to help the organization accomplish the three essentials of a successful operation. Employees are expected to work hard, help when asked, please customers, and do it for a wage that allows the organization to make a profit and stay in business.

Human resources are a key to achieving these goals in any organization. The human resources are often thought of as the organization's employees. However, they also might be vendors, contractors, consultants, and temporary workers—we'll refer to these collectively as workers or employees. The function of a supervisor is to achieve the organization's goals through the accomplishments of other workers.

Human Resource Needs

It is important for an employee to have job-specific skills. For example, an automotive mechanic must be able to repair or replace parts, such as pistons, rods, gears, valves, and bearings. However, employers want employees who have more than just job-specific skills. They look for employees with a broader base of skills, called adaptive or self-management skills, that help employees adjust to the workplace. For example, getting along with coworkers and listening to a supervisor's instructions are adaptive skills.

In 1976, the Advisory Council for Technical-Vocational Education in Texas compiled a list of skills surveyed employers wanted in their employees. (Other surveys in the past two decades have supported their findings.) In the survey, employers were asked to identify areas in which their employees needed to improve. The following list shows the order in which employers ranked the ten items.

1. Concern for productivity

2. Pride of craftsmanship and quality of work

3. Responsibility and ability to follow through on assigned tasks

4. Dependability

5. Good work habits

6. Positive attitudes toward company and employer

7. Ability to write and speak effectively

8. Ability to read and apply printed matter

9. Ability to follow instructions

10. Ambition/motivation/desire to get ahead

Even though these results were collected almost 25 years ago, they continue to be echoed in more recent studies. Many of these studies are summarized in the U.S. government report, *21st Century Skills for 21st Century Jobs.* Some of these studies are explained in more detail throughout the rest of the chapter.

Workplace Basic Skills

The U.S. Secretary of Labor created a commission to "define the know-how needed in the workplace." The Secretary's Commission on Achieving Necessary Skills (SCANS) was made up of people from business, education, and government who identified the skills that are needed to succeed in highly-skilled, highly-paid jobs. They listed three foundational skills and five workplace competencies. The foundation skills include:

- **Basic skills**, including reading, writing, mathematics, speaking, and listening

- **Thinking skills**, including the ability to learn, reason, think creatively, make decisions, and solve problems

- **Personal qualities**, including individual responsibility, self-esteem, self-management, sociability, and integrity

The commission listed five workplace competencies—skills needed for workers to be productive:

- **Resources,** including the ability to allocate time, money, materials, space, and staff

- **Interpersonal skills,** including the ability to work on teams, teach others, serve customers, lead, negotiate, and work with people from diverse cultural backgrounds

- **Information,** including the ability to acquire and evaluate data, organize and maintain files, interpret and communicate, and use computers to process information

- **Systems,** including the ability to understand social, organizational, and technological systems; monitor and correct performance; and design or improve systems

- **Technology,** including the ability to select equipment and tools, apply technology to specific tasks, and maintain and troubleshoot equipment

The SCANS report demonstrates an important fact: Different, higher-level skills are needed in today's labor market than were required 20 years ago. This report is supported by the *Workplace Basics* study conducted by the American Society for Training and Development (ASTD).

The ASTD asked employers throughout the United States what basic skills their employees need. The study found that most employers want their employees to possess *the workplace basics*, including these:

- **Knowing how to learn.** The concept of lifelong learning is common in the business community. Employers spent approximately *$61 billion* in 1998 on formal employee training. It is estimated that three to four times this amount is spent for informal or on-the-job training. Employees who don't have good learning skills will be unable to take advantage of this investment and may soon find their skills obsolete.

- **Reading, writing, and computation.** People who are weak in these skills will have trouble in most jobs. The Hudson Institute has noted that virtually all occupations requiring lower levels of reading, writing, and mathematics are declining in number. Conversely, occupations requiring higher level language and mathematical skills are growing in number.

- **Listening and oral communication.** According to the ASTD study, "The average person spends 8.4 percent of communications time writing,

13.3 percent reading, 23 percent speaking, and 55 percent listening." Communication is as critical to success on the job as the three Rs.

■ **Adaptability.** Organizations must be flexible to adapt and keep pace with advances in technology, changes in the marketplace, and new management practices. Employees who are creative problem-solvers are essential to today's businesses.

■ **Personal management.** This category covers self-esteem, goal-setting and motivation, and personal and career development. For businesses to succeed, employees must take pride in their work and be able to formulate and achieve goals. Finally, employees must know how to advance within an organization, and how to transfer skills to another business. As more businesses engage in participative management, these skills will become increasingly necessary.

■ **Group effectiveness.** Individualism is a thing of the past in most jobs. It is far more important that workers understand and practice teamwork, negotiation, and interpersonal skills. People who understand how to work effectively in groups are the foundation of a successful enterprise.

■ **Influence.** Each employee must establish his or her own influence in order to successfully contribute ideas to an organization. Employees must understand the organizational structure and informal networks in order to implement new ideas or to complete some tasks.

The studies about skills employees need are important to supervisors for two reasons. One reason is that it helps you understand the skills you personally need to do a credible job. Another reason is that it provides a basis for understanding how to create a productive workforce in the unit under your supervision. These skills serve as a foundation for this book. They guided us in the selection of topics and in deciding the amount of emphasis to put on the knowledge and skills described. In the same way, they can guide you in the emphasis and development of skills in the workers you supervise.

Reasons for Working

We've been looking at the needs of an organization from the perspective of owners and managers. Now the focus is turned toward the needs and rights of employees. As a supervisor, attention to these needs will improve your relationship with workers. In turn, employees are more likely to achieve the level of performance that you desire.

No one can expect a job to satisfy all of their expectations and values. Many people work at jobs they don't want until they can get the education or experience necessary to start the career they do want. However, a large number of people continue to seek a job that does satisfy most of their primary needs. A supervisor can improve employee retention by creating an environment that allows employees to fulfill their needs.

Many studies have asked what American workers consider their most important job values and expectations. A 1993 study, reported in *The Wall Street Journal*, asked people the reasons they considered "very important" in deciding to take their current jobs. The reasons given by 50 percent or more of the people are shown below. (By the way, salary or wages were cited by only 35 percent.)

Reason Workers Like Their Work	*Percentage of Workers*
Open Communication	65
Effects on Family/Personal Life	60
Nature of Work	59
Management Quality	59
Supervisor	58
Control over Work Content	55
Gain New Skills	55
Job Security	54
Coworker Quality	53
Job Location	50
Stimulating Work	50

A 1995 survey reported in *HR Magazine* asked human resource professionals to rank the most pressing concerns of their employees. Notice that the responses in this survey differ somewhat from the those in *The Wall Street Journal* survey. Two factors may account for the differences:

- The first survey questioned employees, while the second questioned human resource managers.

- The first survey asked about major concerns *before taking a job,* while the second reported concerns of employees *on the job.*

Whatever the reason for the differences, it's important to note there are also similarities.

Items	Highest Rank
Job security	1
Compensation	2
Benefits costs	3
Job satisfaction	4
Career advancement	5
Recognition	6
Dependent care	7
Work environment	8
Job training	9
Vacation time	10

In *Human Relations: A Job-Oriented Approach,* Andrew DuBrin suggested there are both external factors and internal causes that affect job satisfaction. The employer has some control over the external factors. In fact, these factors are the ones that most organizations concentrate on to improve employee satisfaction. However, more organizations have begun to create programs and systems that also satisfy the internal factors. As a supervisor, you play an important role in creating an environment where employees are relatively content.

External Factors	Internal Causes
Mentally challenging work	Interest in the work itself
Reasonable physical demands	Work fitting one's job values
Meaningful rewards	Positive self-image
Contact with customer/end user	Good personal adjustment
Helpful coworkers and superiors	Positive expectations about the job
	A feeling of self-esteem reinforced by the job
	Optimism and flexibility

In addition to basic employee expectations, the federal and state governments place certain requirements on all employers. The following section reviews these requirements.

Understanding Employee Rights

The law requires an employer to do several things for employees, many of which are listed throughout this section. Keep in mind that these explanations are quite general. Labor law is continually changing as new laws are passed by federal and state governments. It's further complicated by court decisions as to how these laws should be interpreted.

A supervisor should work closely with the human resources department (some organizations still use the term *personnel department*) to determine how the business interprets these laws and applies them in the workplace. This is because many policy and procedure decisions must be made as an organization responds to state and federal laws.

A number of laws and regulations affect workers on the job. Since it's difficult to provide a summary of all regulations for every state, we decided to list only the federal regulations for each topic. If you'd like to know more about these laws, we recommend two good books you might want to read. *The Employer's Legal Handbook* by Fred S. Steingold approaches the law from an employer's perspective. *Job Rights & Survival Strategies* by Paul H. Tobias and Susan Sauter examines the laws from the viewpoint of an employee. Another good source is the Department of Labor's Web site called e-laws at www.dol.gov/elaws. This site advises employers and employees about their responsibilities and rights.

Compensation and Benefits

Supervisors are typically not involved in establishing wage and compensation policies for employees—although they usually make recommendations for raises. However, supervisors are responsible for scheduling employees. Be aware of laws and organizational rules governing overtime when scheduling an employee's work time. The following federal laws govern compensation and benefits for workers that supervisors need to know about.

- **The Fair Labor Standards Act (FLSA)** governs the minimum wage, working hours, and child labor laws. The specifics of this law are changed frequently. Employees covered by the FLSA generally are entitled to overtime pay for all hours worked over 40 in one workweek. Overtime pay must equal at least 1.5 times an employee's regular rate of pay. There is no limit to the number of hours per day or days per week an adult employee may be required to work.

- **The Work Hours Act of 1962** extends the application of FLSA, including provisions for paying employees time-and-a-half.

- **The Equal Pay Act of 1972** established equal payment for overtime work, regardless of gender.

- **The Walsh-Healy Act** governs the minimum wage to be paid for federal government suppliers of equipment, materials, and supplies.

- **The Davis-Bacon Act** governs the minimum wage to be paid by contractors for federally funded construction projects.

- **The Employee Retirement Income and Security Act (ERISA)** regulates an organization's pension plans, retirement plans, profit sharing plans, medical insurance plans, and severance pay policy.

Welfare-to-work employees—Workers that are in the process of making the transition from welfare to work usually have two major concerns—child care and transportation. Most employers expect workers to resolve these issues on their own accord. However, the success of many welfare-to-work employees is dependent on employers becoming actively involved in helping workers solve these problems. Some companies have established hotlines where these employees can call to get assistance in dealing with these problems.

Supervisors can take the initiative in helping workers overcome these problems. Sit down with the worker and discuss their transportation needs. Less than 10 percent of welfare recipients have automobiles. This means that they either rely on public transportation or have someone else drive them to work. One possible solution is to help match the work with another employee who could give them a ride when their primary method for getting to work fails. Some supervisors report giving workers a ride in case of emergencies. Also, assist the worker in finding a dependable child-care provider and a backup. You can ask other employees for advice in identifying child-care providers. The more you assist in a worker with solving these problems, the more likely they are to have good attendance and be punctual.

Most employers—92 percent, according to one study—are required to pay workers at least the minimum wage. Motor carriers and farms are among the organizations exempted from the minimum wage and overtime provisions. This wage varies according to federal regulations. Some states have minimum wage laws that require employers to pay a higher wage than the federal minimum. In a few cases, counties and cities have established their own minimum wage laws.

Equal Opportunity

Supervisors must understand that they cannot discriminate against workers. Discrimination might take the form of hiring, firing, promoting, assigning work, or general treatment based on a worker's age, sex, ethnicity, or disability. Treat all employees fairly and equitably. In later chapters, you'll discover that this isn't important just because of the law but research shows that this treatment results in a more productive group of employees. The following is a list of laws that govern equal opportunity in the workplace.

■ **The Age Discrimination in Employment Act of 1967** prohibits firms with 20 or more employees from discriminating against workers 40 years of age and older.

Older workers—One study of older workers explored the reasons they accepted a new job. The following reasons were given and are ranked in order of importance.

■ Desire to feel useful

■ Earn additional income

■ Meet people

■ Want a challenge

■ Need for a change—to do something different

■ Obtain fringe benefits

■ Receive medical insurance

This list provides some insight for supervisors on how to manage older workers. For many older workers, their primary expectation is to feel useful on the job. This is relatively easy to accomplish even when the work environment doesn't consist of many jobs demanding a high skill level—for example cashier, stock clerk, and janitor. Build on the experience of older workers by using them as mentors and coaches for younger workers. This is usually very rewarding because it contributes to the development and success of another person. Another effective technique is to seek the advice of older workers before making a decision. Ask them if they have experience with a similar problem and what their solutions were. Use the people skills that many older workers have developed to provide special assistance to customers. Acknowledging and using the experience, knowledge, and skills of older workers is a sure way to make them feel useful.

■ **The Equal Employment Opportunity Act of 1972** prohibits firms with 20 or more employees from discriminating against workers because of their race, gender, religion, or national origin.

■ **The Pregnancy Discrimination Act of 1978** requires that pregnant women be entitled to benefits related to sick leave that would be given for other medical reasons.

■ **The Vocational Rehabilitation Act of 1973** prohibits employers with federal contracts of $2500 or greater from discriminating against persons because of physical or mental impairments.

■ **The Vietnam Era Veterans' Readjustment Act of 1974** prohibits firms with federal contracts of $10,000 or more from discriminating against Vietnam-era veterans.

Quick Tip

Immigrant workers—The expectations of immigrant workers in the workplace can often be quite different from American workers because of cultural differences.

Supervisors need to be sensitive to the possible conflicts that this can cause. American workers would respond positively to a supervisor who "pitched in" to help get a job done on schedule. This gives the supervisor an image of being "one of them." However, this same action would be interpreted negatively by many Asian workers. They would consider this behavior an insult and think that the supervisor didn't think they could do their work correctly. Doing this frequently could result in an Asian worker quitting. Supervisors can avoid this problem by learning about the culture of workers they supervise. Also, frequently talk to immigrant workers about their expectations and ask them if they have any concerns.

■ **The Immigration Reform and Control Act of 1986** requires employers to verify U.S citizenship or an Immigration and Naturalization Service authorization for an immigrant to legally work in the U.S. The law also prohibits an employer from discriminating against aliens who have authorization to seek work in the U.S.

■ **The Americans with Disabilities Act (ADA)** prohibits employers from discriminating against workers because of physical or mental disabilities.

An employer cannot discriminate in pay, promotions, training, or in any other way because of race, gender, age, disability, national origin, or religion.

Disabled workers—Workers who have learning disabilities are protected under the ADA. Learning disabilities can be identified in employees in a variety of ways. Not following instructions that are given more than once may indicate that the worker can't "sequence." A supervisor can help the worker by developing job aids that help sequence a task. Providing a list of steps to complete a task, placing numbers on equipment or parts, or mounting a chart at a workstation are just some examples of job aids that can be used to help overcome the difficulty of sequencing.

Some learning disabilities make it difficult for a person to interpret vague terms. Telling a worker with this type of disability that they need to reduce the number of mistakes setting up tables doesn't convey any meaning. Instead a supervisor should provide very specific instruction. For example, you should tell the worker to set a placemat, spoon, knife, fork, and water glass in front of each chair.

Another type of learning disability makes it difficult for a person to pick up on social cues. The comment "Have a nice weekend"—meant as a farewell—might meet with a lengthy response telling you everything the person plans to do over the weekend. An appropriate response by a supervisor is to tell the person that the comment was made as a farewell statement. Workers who don't respond correctly to social cues should be informed specifically how to react appropriately. Learning disabled workers usually don't require physical accommodation—like those sometimes needed by other disabled workers. Instead they require a supervisor to recognize that some social behaviors considered inappropriate are in fact connected with learning disabilities and these workers need extra coaching.

Child Labor Laws

Employers are expected to abide by child labor laws and supervisors are usually responsible for the day-to-day conformance with these laws. Generally speaking, child labor laws prevent businesses from employing anyone under the age of 14. Workers ages 14 and 15 are limited in the number of hours and the time of day they can work, and they are excluded from work in manufacturing, mining, and hazardous jobs. Workers ages 16 and 17 also are excluded from employment in hazardous jobs. Employers are responsible for obtaining proof of age from the young people they hire. Some states require employers to have work permits on file for workers under the age of 18. High school counselors can advise students about how to obtain a work permit.

Youths aged 16 and 17 may work at any time for unlimited hours in all jobs not declared hazardous by the Secretary of Labor. Hazardous occupations include: working with explosives and radioactive materials; operating certain power-driven woodworking, metalworking, bakery, and paper products machinery; operating various types of power-driven saws and guillotine shears; operating most power-driven hoisting machines such as non-automatic elevators, fork lifts, and cranes; most jobs in slaughtering, meat packing, rendering plants, and the operation of power-driven meat processing machines when performed in wholesale, retail or service establishments; most jobs in excavation, logging, and sawmilling; roofing, wrecking, demolition, and shipbreaking; operating motor vehicles or working as outside helpers on motor vehicles; and most jobs in the manufacturing of bricks, tiles, and similar products. Exemptions from some of the hazardous occupations orders apply for apprentices and students in vocational education programs.

Youths aged 14 and 15 may work in various jobs outside school hours under the following conditions: no more than 3 hours on a school day with a limit of 18 hours in a school week; no more than 8 hours on a nonschool day with a limit of 40 hours in a nonschool week; and not before 7 a.m. or after 7 p.m., except from June 1 through Labor Day, when the evening hour is extended to 9 p.m.

Minors who are 14 and 15 years old may not work in the following jobs: manufacturing, mining, most processing work, and all occupations declared hazardous by the Secretary of Labor; operating or tending most power-driven machinery; public messenger service; and work connected with warehousing, storage, transportation, communications, public utilities, and construction (except office and sales jobs when not performed on transportation vehicles or on construction sites).

Youths under 14 may work only if their jobs are exempt from the child labor standards or not covered by the FLSA. Exempt work includes: delivery of newspapers to consumers; performing in theatrical, motion picture, or broadcast productions; and work in a business owned by parents of the minor, except in manufacturing or hazardous occupations.

All states have child labor laws; when both state and federal child labor laws apply, the employer must observe the more stringent law.

Federal law does not require age certificates or work permits. Employers may protect themselves from unintentional violations of the child labor laws by keeping on file an age certificate or work permit for each minor employed. Certificates and permits issued under most state laws are acceptable for this purpose.

Worker Safety

A supervisor should consider the health and safety of employees to be one of his or her most critical responsibilities. It is important that the law be followed and the first-line supervisor is in the best position to ensure that all health and safety policies and procedures are followed. In addition, employees are motivated to do a better job when they are in a safe working environment. The following list describes laws that encompass workplace safety.

Younger workers—Workers 17 years old and younger are nearly twice as likely to be injured on the job than older workers. Between 1992 and 1997, 403 workers in this age group were killed on the job. Forty percent of these occurred in the agriculture industry. However, the service and retail industries—the jobs that employ almost 75 percent of workers age 15 to 17—had 87 deaths. Homicides accounted for 68 percent of these deaths while 18 percent died in transportation accidents. Most homicides occurred during robberies, while most transportation accidents happened to newspaper carriers.

Supervisors need to be alert to dangers that may occur in the workplace due to the inexperience of young workers. Spend extra time training younger workers how to do a job. Review safety procedures—including plans on how to respond to robberies—with young workers. Don't assign younger workers to late-night shifts; that increases their danger of being involved in a robbery. Take time to acquaint yourself with the provisions of the child labor laws and don't allow young workers to operate equipment that they are prohibited from using. Put stickers on equipment that warns younger workers not to operate the equipment. Some employers even use different colored uniforms for workers under 18 so that all employees quickly know when a worker shouldn't be operating dangerous equipment.

■ **The Occupational Safety and Health Act of 1970 (OSHA)** places several requirements on employers to provide safe working conditions for employees and protects from dismissal employees who report unsafe working conditions.

■ **The Hazard Communication Standard** (an addition to OSHA) prescribes a system for informing employees about health hazards and how to respond to exposure from such hazards.

As you can see, many federal and state laws govern employee safety. As the employer's representative, a supervisor is expected to ensure that a work area is both safe and clean. You should also make sure employees wear proper safety equipment such as eye protectors, hard hats, or steel-toed shoes. In addition, all employees should be informed about any hazardous materials they may work with, as well as what to do in case they are exposed to hazardous materials. Again, youth under 18 years of age are restricted from working in any hazardous occupation. The matter of employee safety and health is so important that we discuss it throughout the book where appropriate.

Contingent workers—The advantage of nontraditional work for some workers is the added flexibility that helps balance work with family and other responsibilities. For example, in 1997, slightly more than half of women independent contractors combined their work arrangements with their work at home raising children. Roughly 25 percent of independent contractors, 20 percent of temporary help agency workers, and 53 percent of on-call workers worked part time, as compared to 18 percent of traditional workers. Many individuals in alternative employment relationships report satisfaction with their arrangements. Supervisors find that contingent workers also provide them flexibility in meeting workforce needs. You can use them to make more efficient use of the staff resources assigned to your department.

Labor Relations

The major federal laws governing labor relations have been in effect for over 50 years. The organization's executives and human resources department are responsible for negotiating collective bargaining agreements with unions. However, a supervisor should be aware of that there are some important things to consider when working in a unionized organization.

If the organization doesn't have a union, supervisors and managers are not to hinder union activities. You should not express your opinion to employees about unionization efforts. Even more importantly, don't single out or mistreat employees active in union activities. Collective bargaining agreements often place stipulations on work assignments and schedules that supervisors must follow. You should avoid violating any provisions of the agreement because this can cause significant labor problems. Finally, keep in mind that when a supervisor takes

35

disciplinary action against an employee, a union representative normally must be present to represent the employee. The following list describes laws that pertain to labor issues.

- **The Wagner Act of 1935** guarantees employees the right to organize and participate in union activities.

- **The Taft-Hartley Act of 1947** balances the rights of employers and unions.

- **The Landrum-Griffin Act of 1957** guarantees union members certain rights within the union itself.

Employers are required by federal law and some state laws to allow employees to participate in lawful union activity. As a supervisor, you should remain neutral in collective bargaining activities.

Several states also have right-to-work laws, which ensure that employees aren't *required* to join a union. However, in states without this provision, employees may be required to pay union dues even if they don't join, because they benefit from the collective bargaining. Union dues vary and are usually handled as automatic deductions from paychecks.

Fair Treatment

Many of the laws that follow govern the personnel policies of an organization. The decisions about how to follow these policies are usually made by executives and the HR department. A supervisor should keep employees informed about established policies and be consistent in following them.

Employment-at-will is a legal term that means an employer can fire you at any time for any reason, but the termination cannot be in violation of federal or state law. The application of this law has been changed over the years by many state courts and some state legislatures. Instead they have promoted the concept of *wrongful discharge*. This concept says that an employee should be dismissed only for *just cause*, which places the burden of proof on the employer to show that the employee has done something serious enough to justify termination. Wrongful discharge cases have diminished—but not eliminated—employment-at-will laws.

The law related to dismissals varies from state to state and is undergoing a great deal of change. The only way a worker can be sure he or she was unfairly dismissed is to obtain the services of an attorney, which is often prohibitively expensive and time-consuming. The following list contains additional laws regarding fair treatment.

■ **The Worker Adjustment and Retraining Notification Act (WARN)**
requires employers to provide 60 days' advance warning for major layoffs
or plant closings. The law covers only certain employers.

■ **The Family and Medical Leave Act of 1993** covers organizations with
50 or more employees and applies to employees who have worked for
the organization at least one year and for at least 1250 hours in the 12
months before the leave is requested. The law requires that employers
give employees unpaid leaves for up to 12 weeks for family and medical
reasons. An employee given this leave must be allowed to return to the
same job or a similar one.

■ **The Civil Rights Act of 1964** prohibits sexual harassment, including
unwelcome sexual advances, requests for sexual favors, and verbal or
physical conduct of a sexual nature that creates a hostile or abusive work
environment. Some states have passed laws defining and prohibiting sexual harassment.

■ **The Employee Polygraph Protection Act** restricts the use of polygraph
(lie detector) tests. In general, an employee cannot be required to take a
lie detector test. An exception to this rule is provided if the employer is
investigating theft, embezzlement, or other injuries to the business.

■ **The Consumer Credit Protection Act** states that employees can't be
terminated for having their wages garnished. It doesn't protect an employee that has multiple garnishments.

■ **The Juror Protection Act** protects workers from being fired for serving
jury duty.

■ **The Uniformed Services Employment and Reemployment Rights
Act of 1994** protects workers from being fired because of any obligations
they have to the armed forces reserve units. Also, an employer is restricted from terminating an employee without just cause within a year after
the worker returns from active duty.

■ **Anti-Retaliation Provisions**—Most of the federal laws prevent an
employer from treating employees unfairly because they report an
employer for violation of a law. This not only applies to terminating
the employee but ensures that the employee is not unfairly reassigned
to other duties or given duties that aren't assigned to other workers with
similar job titles and responsibilities. Supervisors need to guard against
unfair actions that might be taken against any employee they are
responsible for.

Ex-offenders—The Federal Bonding Program provides employers with an incentive to hire ex-offenders. It is possible to get a bond for ex-offenders (usually they are not eligible for fidelity bonding under private programs) through the State Employment Service or One Stop Career Center in your area. This bond is provided free of charge and insures the employer for any type of theft, forgery, larceny, or embezzlement committed by the worker. It requires little or no paperwork by an employer to obtain this bond.

Supervisors should not assume that because an employee is bonded that they can relax in applying reasonable protections against theft or embezzlement. Reducing the opportunities for theft is both reasonable and fair to the employee. Many organizations realize that opportunities for theft are unfair to employees because they create an unnecessary temptation. Monitor the actions of your employees and implement procedures to guard against theft.

Resolving Employee Rights Issues

Many employers provide procedures for employees to express their belief that they are not being treated in accordance with a law. The following list illustrates a typical procedure that an employee is expected to follow:

■ Employees are first expected to discuss any problem with their supervisor to correct a situation that they feel violates their rights. When an employee approaches you about this matter, remain calm, don't be judgmental, and gather as many facts as you can. You may be able to immediately clarify the situation and the employee may be assured that there really is not a problem. When you're unsure about what action to take, indicate to the employee that you will look into the matter, contact the appropriate managers, and keep them informed about the process. Always get the appropriate counsel on how to handle grievances. The first person to discuss it with is the manager you report to. It is usually a good idea to ask the human resources department to consult with you about the complaint.

■ If the supervisor doesn't correct the problem or provide an explanation that satisfies the employee, that employee may contact the HR department or the company owner. (Personnel handbooks usually describe the process to follow when appealing a supervisor's actions.) At this point, your role as a supervisor is to provide the facts that management needs to resolve the problem. It is important that you not let emotions control your actions during the appeal process. Attempt to treat the employee in the same manner you would have treated him or her had there been no complaint filed.

■ If the company doesn't correct a problem, the employee can contact a government agency responsible for seeing that the law is enforced. From this point on you are likely to have little direct responsibility over the employee or the situation. The human resource department and legal representatives for the organization take over. You should cooperate in providing whatever information is needed by company officials. Find out what the company expects you to do when contacted by federal or state investigators.

In many cases, an organization will not want you to talk with investigators without legal representation present. However, keep in mind that attorneys furnished by the business are working for its interest and not yours. In most cases, the actions of a supervisor are considered to be the responsibility of the organization, and the law protects you from legal prosecution or civil action. However, this is not always the case. When an employer requires you to violate the law, you are not protected from legal responsibility for subsequent actions. A good rule to follow is to abide by all laws. If company policy or a manager directs you to break the law, you should personally follow the appeal process just outlined.

Summary

A good supervisor can balance the expectations of employers with those of employees. Employers want to provide a high quality product with excellent customer service that results in a profit. To achieve these objectives, an organization needs skilled employees. As a supervisor, you need to help identify new employees with the skills that a company needs and develop the skills in current employees.

Look for ways that you can help satisfy the needs of employees in your work group. Communicate their needs to management and attempt to create a positive work environment. Keep in mind that a good work environment begins with concern for protecting workers' rights under federal and state laws.

Chapter 3

The Supervisor at Work

Most supervisors are promoted to their jobs because they were a successful worker. Management often notices workers who perform well in their jobs, identifies workers who are dependable, and promotes these workers to supervisory positions. Once a person is appointed as a supervisor, a major transition takes place. The job skills that got them the promotion are no longer critical in doing their job. In fact, the U.S. Department of Labor defines a supervisor as a person who spends at least 80 percent of his or her time supervising rather than doing the same work as people he or she supervises.

A good supervisor is one who can accomplish major tasks and achieve objectives by directing the efforts of other workers. This chapter describes some of the key components of a supervisor's role. In addition, we include a unique feature about supervision. This section relies on information from the U.S. Department of Labor and describes the most important skills, abilities, and work activities for supervisors. And finally, we list typical job descriptions for supervisors.

A Supervisor's Basic Role

As a supervisor, you will be required to perform many tasks. The term *supervision* comes from a Latin word that means to oversee. You will oversee employees in order to get work done. In some organizations, participative management has such an emphasis that the term *oversee* would be unfashionable. Instead, these organizations might use the terms *lead, coach,* or *coordinate.* However, in almost every organization, a supervisor is held accountable for the accomplishments of the group. In this sense, the supervisor still "oversees" the group.

Three major factors distinguish a supervisor's role from that of other workers:

- **You must use independent judgment.** The organization establishes policies and procedures but these are somewhat like theories. It is necessary for the supervisor to decide how to implement policies in a practical manner. Also, some situations arise in every organization that are not anticipated and thus not covered by existing policies or procedures.

- **You must exercise authority.** This is a difficult function for some newly-appointed supervisors. In most cases, a person becomes friendly with coworkers. A promotion to supervisor sometimes requires you to set aside friendships and ensure that workers complete a task regardless of their wishes and desires.

- **Your work will be primarily mental rather than physical.** This means that a stock clerk promoted to supervisor no longer spends much time stocking inventory. Instead, the supervisor schedules workers, plans the work, monitors work other employees are doing, and so on.

A supervisor is required to carry out four primary functions:

- **Planning** is a process that involves setting objectives, looking ahead for improved performance, solving problems, and making decisions.

- **Organizing and delegating** involves scheduling work to be performed, assigning responsibilities, and assigning authority to accomplish the responsibilities.

- **Leading** is a process that comprises creating an environment in which employees are willing to motivate themselves to ensure objectives are achieved and providing the resources needed to achieve the objectives.

- **Controlling** involves ensuring your work unit is meeting the objectives that have been set by comparing actual results with expected results and evaluating whether or not the objectives have been met.

Younger workers—Younger employees are limited in the time that you can schedule them to work. The Fair Labor Standards Act limits youth 14 and 15 years old to no more than 3 hours of work on a school day and 18 hours in a school week. They can work 8 hours on a non-school day—but no more—and 40 hours on a non-school week.

Work must be performed between the hours of 7 a.m. and 7 p.m., except from June 1 through Labor Day, when evening hours are extended to 9 p.m.

There are no limits on hours that can be worked for employees that are 16 years of age or older. However, studies indicate that employers may want to limit the number of hours worked by all children under the age of 18 during the school year. Students younger than 18 who work 20 hours or more per week experience significant problems. They are less likely to progress as far in school, and they are more likely to use illegal drugs, partake in other deviant behavior, and get insufficient sleep and exercise. Supervisors would be well advised to limit the hours of all workers who are still in school.

To fulfill a supervisory role, there are three skill areas that must be developed.

- **Technical skills** encompass specific knowledge, methods, procedures, or techniques required to perform a specific job. For example, a supervisor of computer network administrators must understand the physical operation of computers, cables, and routers that connect the computers, along with networking software. Almost all supervisors excel in technical skills—this is why they were promoted in the first place.

- **Conceptual skills** help the supervisor understand how a work unit fits into the total organization. For example, suppose that management for a hotel sets a goal to improve customer satisfaction. A housekeeping supervisor needs to be able to work with management to determine how this goal can be achieved by establishing specific objectives related to room cleanliness. Most new supervisors do not have well-developed conceptual skills because they often aren't required to use them in other jobs.

- **Human skills** help a supervisor understand, communicate with, and interact effectively with employees. For example, a supervisor who encourages workers to produce more electrical motors by regularly praising and encouraging them is practicing human skills. Many workers have good human skills in relating to coworkers. However, the skills used to lead a work group often need additional development.

Many supervisors fail because they are not trained in the skills required to be a supervisor. Some organizations put employees in supervisory positions but never give them training on how to be effective in the role. Some supervisors fail because they have an unwillingness to deal with situations that involve conflict or discipline. Here are some basic concepts that can help you succeed as a supervisor.

The Planning Function

Planning is the best "guess" at what may happen in the future. In different terms, planning is the process of setting objectives and determining in advance what resources, activities, and tasks are needed to achieve the objectives.

Objectives are specific accomplishments to be obtained within a given time period and they define the desired end result. The objectives you set should be:

- **Specific, measurable, and quantifiable.** The question to ask yourself is whether management, workers, or you can know for sure when or if an objective has been achieved.

  Examples
  Not Specific: The agency will help more clients find jobs than last year.
  Specific: The agency will help 10 percent more clients find jobs than last year.

- **Difficult but attainable.** This is a judgment call on the part of the supervisor. It is important that the objective challenges workers but not discourages them as being "next to impossible." For the following examples, let's assume that a department has had a 50 percent turnover in the number of employees each year for the last five years.

  Examples
  Too Easy: The annual turnover rate of employees will be reduced to 45 percent.
  Too Difficult: The annual turnover rate of employees will be reduced to 10 percent.
  Probably Achievable: The annual turnover rate of employees will be reduced to 35 percent.

- **Consistent with the goals of the organization.** The supervisor usually wants to set departmental objectives that are going to help the organization achieve its overall objectives. Objectives specific to the work unit may sometimes be needed, but these should not distract the unit from supporting organizational objectives. For the purpose of these examples, assume that an automotive parts manufacturer sets an objective to increase sales by 10 percent for the year.

  Examples
  Doesn't Support Organization's Objective: The department will reduce product waste by 5 percent.
  Indirectly Supports Organization's Objective: The department will reduce absenteeism by 20 percent.

Supports Organization's Objectives: The department will increase the number of parts produced by 10 percent.

Types of Plans Supervisors Use

You may use four different plans as a supervisor:

- **Operational plans** facilitate the accomplishment of everyday activities. An example is a plan for keeping check-out lines moving quickly.

- **Daily plans** structure your actions for a particular day. For example, a daily plan might include a meeting, checking inventory, reviewing monthly sales reports, and so on.

- **Contingency plans** act as an alternative if unexpected events occur and the plans you have made cannot be used. An example might be the substitution of another menu item if the daily special runs out at a restaurant.

- **Standing plans** are policies, procedures, and rules that are developed for handling recurring and predictable situations. These plans are usually developed by upper management—often with the involvement of supervisors—and it takes upper management to change them. For example, a specific amount of supplies are ordered for a hospital each week based on the number of patients admitted.

Older workers—When you develop a work schedule for older workers who receive Social Security benefits, you should consider limits that they have placed on these benefits. Workers who receive Social Security retirement benefits have limits placed on the amount of money they can earn while receiving benefits. Workers under the age of 65 can earn up to $9600 with no reduction in their Social Security benefits. If they earn more than that, $1 in benefits is withheld for every $2 they earn over $9600. Workers age 65 through 69 can earn up to $15,500 with no reduction in their Social Security benefits. If they earn more than that, $1 in benefits is withheld for every $3 they earn over $15,500. There are no limits on earnings for workers 70 or older. (These amounts are based on 1999 regulations. You can find the most current information on these limits by calling the Social Security Administration's information line at [800] 772-1213, or on the Internet at www.ssa.gov.)

Supervisors should discuss these earning limits with older workers. Calculate the number of hours that they can work during the year based on their hourly pay. It is usually best to discuss the work schedule based on an annual schedule. This is because older workers often plan their work around leisure activities that vary with the seasons. For example, workers who enjoy golfing or gardening prefer to work fewer hours during those times of the year so that they can engage in these activities. Older workers also may prefer not to work as many hours during winter months. Supervisors who take time to discuss the preferences and plans of older workers for an entire year find that there will be fewer problems with scheduling.

Types of Plans Supervisors Make

In addition to using plans that already exist, most supervisors are responsible for creating specific types of plans. Learning to develop good plans is important to a supervisor's success.

- **Human resource plans** help to plan the number of employees required to do the work at the present and in the future. You should know the skills, knowledge, and abilities an employee needs to get the job done.

- **Material resource plans** help you determine the quantity of material and supplies required to do the job. You will also have to plan the use of both facilities and equipment required to produce the product or service.

- **Financial resource plans** aid in planning your budget to make sure you spend your financial resources in an effective manner. You will also have to plan the time you will need to produce the product or service, even if it means planning overtime.

The Organizing Function

Organizing is the process of grouping activities to be performed in a manner that enables you to easily supervise them. The organizing function follows, and in some instances, overlaps the planning function. Organizations have both a formal and informal structure.

Formal Organization Structure

The formal structure of an organization is defined by an organization chart, which shows:

- The division and type of work.
- The chain of command or reporting structure.

- The levels of management in the organization.

- The departmentalization of the organization or how specific tasks are grouped into departments. They are most commonly grouped by function but they may also be grouped by product, customer, geography, or process.

The Informal Organization Structure

The informal structure develops from the social interactions of employees in the organization. It usually has a leader who comes from the ranks of employees and it can be a very powerful influence in the organization. As a supervisor, you must be aware of the informal structure and who has the most influence as far as leadership.

It is often important to identify informal leaders for several reasons. An informal leader can gather and refine ideas about plans and activities. Informal leaders can convince other workers to support objectives and related tasks. It is also a good idea to use informal leaders as key people in delegating tasks. They can take the lead and encourage other employees to assist in the task. Informal leaders should also be considered for future promotion to supervisory positions.

The Delegating Function

Delegating is the process a supervisor uses to invest authority in an employee to act on behalf of the supervisor. It is sometimes called "empowerment." Delegating includes giving employees the responsibility (obligation) and authority (power) to carry out a task or accomplish an objective. Delegating tasks to employees helps a supervisor develop employee skills, demonstrates trust and confidence in workers, frees up time for the supervisor to do other tasks, and helps create a motivating environment.

You should try to delegate routine tasks, repetitive tasks, and tasks that help develop employee skills. Tasks that you should not delegate are tasks that have been delegated to you by your superior, human resource matters, and anything that could develop into a crisis. Many times supervisors do not delegate to employees because they do not trust them or because they feel by delegating tasks to employees threatens their status as a manager.

Supervisors need to have a good understanding of their departments to delegate effectively. Among the things a supervisor needs to know are the strengths and weaknesses of each employee, resources available to employees, and potential support from other workers. Supervisors also need to have self-confidence. This includes a willingness to let others receive recognition and rewards for a job well done. When delegating tasks to employees, keep these guidelines in mind:

- Explain to the employee why you delegated a particular task to him or her.

- Explain the purpose for delegating the task.

- In cooperation with the employee, set objectives for the task.

- Define the scope of the employee's authority.

- Establish a deadline for the task to be completed.

- Identify resources that are available to accomplish the task including money, materials, equipment, people, and so on.

- Indicate how frequently you want to be updated about progress in getting the task done.

- Once the employee has agreed to the task, hold the employee accountable. This means the person shouldn't be given the opportunity to have you or another employee complete the task. There are, of course, reasons that this is sometimes necessary but it only should be done in exceptional circumstances.

It is important for you to follow through with delegated tasks. Monitor the employee's progress. Make sure that the person makes periodic reports as agreed. Voice your support and encouragement about the work being done— when appropriate. Once a task is complete, review with the employee what was learned and how the task might be done better in the future.

Disabled workers—Workers who suffer from mental illness sometimes have a lack of stamina that results from low energy levels or medication. This also may apply to workers with other disabilities. A supervisor might initially think that the person's drowsiness on the job is due to a lack of sleep or laziness. It is important to seek the root cause of the problem. Talk with the worker about when the periods of low energy start or when the person needs to take medication. Discuss whether the person would like to reduce the number of hours he or she works each day. Also, determine if there is a better time of the day to schedule the person for work—perhaps after the side effects of the medication have diminished. It is possible to keep a good worker when a supervisor is willing to accommodate an employee's needs.

The Leading Function

Leading is the ability to influence employees to accomplish goals and objectives willingly, while at the same time you gain their respect, cooperation, and loyalty. Leadership, unlike management, is earned, not given. It involves developing a vision, conveying the vision to others, and motivating them to achieve the vision. Several leadership models are used by organizations today and are listed here:

- **Trait Theory.** This model suggests that personality traits were strongly associated with people's perception of leaders. It is then necessary to identify these traits and help leaders understand how to use them more effectively.

- **Style Theory.** The style model is different from the trait approach because it focuses on the behaviors of leaders rather than their personality characteristics. Researchers propose that leadership is essentially composed of two kinds of behaviors: *task behaviors* and *relationship behaviors*. Leaders must have the knowledge to complete important tasks and understand relationships with employees who can help accomplish the tasks.

- **Situational Leadership.** The basic premise of the situational leadership model is that different situations should be approached with different leadership styles. It suggests that employees' behavior on the job is affected by two factors—level of commitment and competence. Leaders must learn how to adapt to situations by appropriately balancing worker's commitment and competence.

- **Leader-Member Exchange Theory.** This philosophy pays attention to the differences that might exist between leaders and each of their followers. In every organization, one group of employees is willing to assume responsibility and initiative to complete a task. Another group approaches their jobs in a formal contractual manner only doing what they are required to do. A strong leader must identify those employees that fall into the first group because they are crucial to the successful accomplishment of a goal. At the same time, the leader should encourage other employees to grow and assume more responsibility and initiative.

- **Transformational Leadership Theory.** This model proposes that leaders need to transform employees by developing core values, ethical principles, and attention to organizational goals.

■ **Path-Goal Leadership Model.** The underlying premise of this model is that human behavior is goal-oriented. It describes how leaders motivate employees to accomplish specific goals. A leader's challenge is to use a leadership strategy that best meets the employee's motivational needs.

■ **Contingency Model.** This theory also builds on the distinctions between task and employee orientation and it suggests that the most appropriate leadership style will depend on whether the overall situation is favorable or unfavorable or in an intermediate state of favor for the leader. This state is based on the leader's relationship with employees, the task that must be accomplished, and the leader's power and authority. As this situation changes, the requirements of the leader also changes.

We consider leadership to be such an important supervisory function that Chapter 8 is devoted entirely to leadership and factors beyond those that have been presented above.

Contingent workers—Supervisors that haven't used contingent workers in the past need to prepare for them. Because these workers may be on the job for only a few days, it is important to carefully plan their work. Develop the schedule you expect them to follow during the entire time that they will be at your work site. Make sure that all supplies, materials, equipment, and other items vital to completing the work are all available. This avoids the organization paying temps or contract workers for down time.

The Controlling Function

Controlling is the function of comparing actual performance with planned performance, and taking appropriate action to correct a situation where actual performance does not measure up to planned performance. When setting standards, remember they must be both realistic and fair to employees and not so high that they are unattainable. The controlling process has four steps:

1. Determining the quantity of work you expect an employee to produce in a given time period. Quantity is easy to measure and evaluate. Example: A car wash crew is expected to clean a minimum of 20 cars an hour.

2. Setting the standards of quality to be produced by an employee. Quality is a relative term and at times, you may have difficulty measuring it. However, arrive at a definition that you and employees can agree on. Example: A bakery employee is expected to produce cookies that are

cooked the proper amount of time, have a consistent texture and taste, and are the same approximate size.

3. Creating deadlines for tasks to be completed. Time is another standard that you can easily measure. Example: A grocery store employee may be expected to stock an entire section of breakfast cereal within 90 minutes.

4. Determining the amount of money or resources it takes to perform a task properly. Example: An extra large pizza should contain approximately 25 pieces of pepperoni.

Once the standards have been set, you must communicate them to all employees so they know what level of performance is expected from them. It is your responsibility as a supervisor to communicate the standards to employees.

To monitor the standards, you have to monitor the performance of employees. You should monitor critical points in the work process and gather data at these points on a timely basis. Once you have the data, you should compare it to the standard to see if there is a variance between the standard and the performance. Once you have compared the data to the performance, you should give the employees feedback on their performance as quickly as possible. For example, to monitor whether employees are using the right number of pepperoni pieces, you might compare the number and size of pizzas ordered during the day with the beginning and ending inventory counts for pepperoni pieces.

Welfare-to-work employees—Supervisors need to take some special considerations into account when scheduling welfare-to-work employees. Many welfare recipients have school-aged children. Usually it is possible for them to find child care for these children either before or after school. However, it is difficult to locate or pay for someone to care for the children both before and after school. You should discuss each worker's needs in this area and base their work schedule on the individual worker's situation.

Welfare recipients are expected to meet with their caseworker on a regular basis to retain their Medicaid, food stamps, and other benefits. You should be flexible in allowing them time to do this and not make them feel bad about it. Making this a big issue can hurt the worker's motivation and may in fact stigmatize them if you say anything about it to other workers. Keep in mind that these workers are making an effort to become independent and self-reliant. Supervisors should encourage this effort and assist in any way possible.

What Supervisors Control

Most supervisors oversee the first line of operations in an organization. This affects the activities and resources that must be monitored. Some of the items supervisors are typically responsible for controlling include the following:

- **Time**—You must be sure that schedules are followed and met.

- **Costs**—The amount of money that is spent must be monitored.

- **Employee behavior**—The conduct of the employee at work.

- **Materials**—The amount of material to produce a product.

- **Equipment**—The efficient and effective use of equipment used in the production process.

- **Processes**—The process used to transform the material into products.

- **Quantity**—The correct amount of a product must be produced in a timely manner.

- **Quality**—The standard of the product.

Methods of Control

To be effective, controls must focus on organizational objectives, be cost effective, provide accurate data, and be accepted by the people who are involved with the control method. Supervisors can use different types of control methods to assure that they are being successful in meeting goals and objectives:

- **Preliminary or input controls** are controls put in place before a product is manufactured or a service is performed. They are directed at the resources that are coming into the organization such as people and material. Example: Every new employee at an amusement park must go through a 20-hour training period.

- **Transformation or concurrent controls** are controls used to prevent problems in the transformation of the material or in the service being provided. These are controls used to prevent problems in the manufacturing process. Example: A scanning system is used for checking out purchases in a hardware store to reduce potential entry errors by a cashier.

- **Post or output controls** are used after a product has been manufactured or a service has been performed. This is really not a good time to use a control because this type of control usually results in some type of rework or added cost to the product or service. Example: A crew tightens a bolt that may not be properly installed during the assembly of a lawn mower.

Within the methods of control there are different control techniques:

- **Budgets** are a method of planning costs and then comparing them to actual costs. Budgets are linked very closely to the planning process and in some organizations you, as a supervisor, may not actually be responsible for setting the budget but you will be responsible for controlling the expenditures so the budget can be met. Most organizations develop a specific set of techniques for budgeting. Supervisors usually follow the procedures that are established by the department responsible for budgeting procedures. For budgeting to work well, a supervisor must be able to control expenditures and receive regular reports on expenditures—no fewer than once a month.

- **Audits** are a method of examining activities or records to determine their accuracy or effectiveness. The methods of auditing include internal audits where the organization audits itself using employees of the organization. Some organizations prefer external audits, in which an outside organization audits its activities.

Controlling Quality

One of the primary responsibilities you will have is to produce a quality product and/or service, whether the product or service is used by an internal customer or external customer. Quality has a significant effect on an organization's profitability when work has to be redone or scrapped, or when a customer is lost because of poor service. Quality control can be divided into two main categories:

- **Prevention methods** are designed to prevent nonconforming or low-quality products and services from reaching the customer. This includes systems, procedures, policies, or techniques designed and implemented prior to production or service delivery. Examples are process control systems, information systems, or employee training to use these systems. The prevention method is the most effective method of controlling quality by giving the customer a product that is defect-free and it will reduce costs and increase profitability.

- **Appraisal methods** are designed to detect unsatisfactory quality before it reaches the customer. These methods are implemented after production but before a good or service is delivered to the customer. Examples are: tests and inspections of equipment or data gathering about product or service output. This is a method familiar to most manufacturing organizations. They build the product and then test it to see if it is satisfactory.

 Ex-offenders—Workers who are ex-offenders often have issues that need to be considered when scheduling their work times. Some may be in a halfway house that assists ex-offenders in making the transition from prison to civilian life. Determine whether the person is expected to be in residence at certain hours in the halfway house. Other ex-offenders may have regularly scheduled times to meet with their parole or probation officers. Supervisors should develop schedules for ex-offenders that account for these special needs.

O*NET Analysis of Supervisors

We've reviewed the basic role and functions of a supervisor. The appendix at the end of this book concentrates on specific skills and tasks performed in the workplace. The U.S. Department of Labor identifies and analyzes all occupations—a total of 1122 jobs—found in the U.S. economy. Each occupation is analyzed on almost 500 characteristics, including skills, abilities, knowledge, general work activities, interests, and workplace conditions. Each of these characteristics can be rated on a scale of importance from 0 (low) to 100 (high). This information is collected in a database called the Occupational Information Network (O*NET).

The O*NET identifies 25 occupations designated as supervisory jobs. (We've included these job descriptions in the appendix.) In order to help you better understand the supervisor's job, we have provided information from the O*NET. First, we analyzed the skills, abilities, and general work activities that are important for a supervisor's job, and we present that analysis in three tables.

Out of the 36 total skills analyzed in O*NET, the first table displays the 14 skills in which the supervisory jobs scored an average importance of 60 or greater.

Skills and Their Level of Importance to a Supervisor

Skill	All Jobs	Supervisors
Coordination	38	80
Management of personnel resources	18	79
Speaking	47	74
Time management	31	73
Problem identification	52	68

Skill	All Jobs	Supervisors
Implementation planning	33	66
Judgment	43	65
Critical thinking	42	65
Active listening	47	64
Instructing	23	63
Reading	54	61
Identifying key causes (changes needed to meet goals)	40	60
Information gathering	52	60
Writing	44	60

Immigrant workers—Workers from other cultures often have holidays that are as important to them as Thanksgiving, Christmas, and New Year's Day are to many Americans. Make an attempt to know when these holidays take place. Whenever possible, avoid scheduling employees for work on their culture's holidays. Most workers will appreciate this considerate behavior. In addition, you don't have workers failing to show up at work when scheduled.

The next table displays 7 abilities—from a total of 52 analyzed in the O*NET—that have an average score of 60 or greater for all supervisory occupations.

Abilities and Their Level of Importance to a Supervisor

Ability	All Jobs	Supervisors
Oral expression	51	85
Oral comprehension	51	71
Problem sensitivity (sensing a problem exists)	49	64
Written comprehension	53	62
Speech clarity	40	61
Information ordering (following a set of rules)	53	60
Written expression	43	60

The final table displays 9 general work activities—from a total of 42 in the O*NET—that have an average score of 60 or greater for all supervisory occupations.

General Work Activities and Their Level of Importance to a Supervisor

General Work Activity	All Jobs	Supervisors
Getting information needed to do the job	71	78
Communicating with other workers	46	78
Coordinating work and activities of others	25	78
Monitor processes, material, surroundings	57	71
Guiding, directing, and motivating subordinates	15	69
Making decisions and solving problems	48	68
Identifying objects, actions, and events	59	67
Scheduling work and activities	21	67
Organizing, planning, and prioritizing	39	61

Summary

Technical skills usually get a person promoted to the position of supervisor. However, the key to success as a supervisor is the development of conceptual and human skills. This is critical. A supervisor's main functions include planning, organizing, leading, and controlling. A more specific idea of the skills and tasks performed by supervisors can also be found by reviewing supervisor job descriptions found in the U.S. Department of Labor's O*NET System. There is a purpose in understanding the skills a supervisor needs—it allows you to identify and develop skills that you need to be a successful supervisor.

Chapter 4

Motivating Employees

Motivation is something that is very frequently talked about in organizations but is also very misunderstood. Over the years, there have been numerous definitions of motivation. Here is one definition:

*Motivation is the willingness of an employee to do something with the anticipation that in doing the action, it will result in the fulfillment of a **need** for the employee.*

In this chapter, you'll discover some of the theories of how to create an atmosphere to motivate employees. Actually, a supervisor can't motivate an employee—a person can only motivate herself or himself. What a supervisor can do is control the environment and conditions that motivate an employee. This chapter discusses theories about motivation and provides you with some practical ideas about how to apply them in the workplace. This chapter is a little different than most of the chapters in the book because motivation is a complex subject and no one person or theory has all of the answers. There are times you are likely going to see that a theory applies well in trying to motivate an employee. At other times, it may not seem to offer the right solution. And, even if you look at every theory of motivation, it might not explain why a specific person motivates herself or himself. This is the problem with most theories. However, motivation theories are beneficial in providing some general guidelines that need to be balanced by a supervisor's practical experience.

The Needs Theory of Motivation

The needs theory of motivation is actually a group of theories about motivation which are sometimes called **content theories** of motivation. These theories attempt to explain what motivates employees to behave in certain ways, and they focus on the needs of employees as requirements for survival and well being. A basic assumption of need theories is that to motivate an employee, a supervisor must first determine what needs the employee is trying to satisfy on the job and then create an environment where the employee can satisfy these needs.

Younger workers—Teen workers are going through a difficult transition in their lives—moving from childhood to adulthood. They are trying to develop a personal identity separate from their parents. This means that their ego needs assume a primary role during this period of their lives. Supervisors often find it difficult to deal with teen workers during this transition period because they sometimes act like children but still expect to be treated like adults. However, you can help teens to become productive workers through proper motivation.

Treat younger workers with respect. Recognize that they have skills needed by your organization and point these skills out to them. Acknowledge their ideas and respond to them in an appropriate manner. Listen carefully when younger workers explain an idea. When they have a good idea, try to implement it, because this reinforces their ego needs. If their idea isn't a good one, explain why it may not work instead of using the tiresome and demeaning expressions, "We've tried that before and it didn't work" or "You're too young to understand." Treating teens like adults satisfies their self-esteem needs and keeps their motivation high.

Maslow's Hierarchy of Needs

Abraham Maslow was a psychologist who proposed that human beings have five universal needs that they seek. He also proposed that these needs are not of equal strength, they emerge in a definite sequence, and the various need levels are interdependent and overlapping. Maslow indicated that sound motivational theory assumes people are in a continuous motivational state. Although Maslow did not develop the theory specifically for work, the implications of the theory for work were recognized. Maslow looked at the fact that people are in a continuous motivational state and the nature of their motivation is fluctuating and complex. He also proposed that humans are seldom in a state of complete satisfaction for a long time period because as soon as one need is satisfied, another one rises to takes its place. Maslow proposed that needs are ordered in a hierarchical manner with the lower needs being primary and the higher needs secondary.

Order	Level	Description	Examples
Highest	Self-actualization	The need to realize one's full potential	Using one's skill and ability to the fullest and striving to achieve one's maximum potential
Higher	Esteem needs	The need to feel good about oneself and capabilities, to be respected by others, and to receive recognition and appreciation	Receiving a promotion or being recognized for accomplishments on the job
High	Belonging needs	Need for social interaction, love, friendship, and affection	Having good relations with coworkers and supervisors and becoming a member of a cohesive work group
Low	Safety needs	Need for security and a safe environment	Receiving job security, adequate medical benefits, and safe working conditions
Lowest	Physiological needs	Basic needs such as water, food, air, and shelter	Receiving enough pay to buy food, clothing, and shelter

Immigrant workers—In some cultures there is a high value placed on job security. This value is so strong that it would appear that Maslow's hierarchy simply doesn't apply to these cultures. Workers from these cultures are going to be more motivated when supervisors attempt to satisfy their security needs. Countries where there is a strong emphasis placed on avoiding uncertainty include most Central and South American countries, Mexico, Japan, Greece, Israel, Italy, Portugal, Spain, and South Korea.

Applying Maslow to the Workplace

According to Maslow, unsatisfied needs are the prime motivators of a person's behavior, and the lower-order needs (physiological and safety) take precedence over higher-order needs (belonging, esteem, and self-actualization). Maslow's theory has often been misinterpreted to mean that lower-order needs must be satisfied before the higher-order needs begin to operate. Maslow indicated that higher-order needs can and will emerge before the lower-order needs have been completely satisfied and individuals may also reorder the needs. This is seen in situations where a lower-paid employee might be more satisfied receiving praise—esteem needs—from a supervisor rather than a slight pay raise that would satisfy physiological needs.

By specifying which needs contribute to an employee's motivation, Maslow's theory helps a supervisor determine what will motivate any given worker. However, you as the supervisor must remember that workers differ in the needs they try to satisfy at work and what motivates one person may not motivate another. To have a motivated workforce, you must identify which needs each employee is attempting to satisfy and ensure these needs are satisfied when a person exhibits the desired behaviors. *You must also remember that a need that has been satisfied will not be as strong a motivator as a need that is unsatisfied.* For example, let's assume a new collective bargaining agreement is signed that guarantees a year's notice prior to a plant closing. The safety need for job security is satisfied and no longer becomes a motivator. As a supervisor, you must explore other ways to satisfy an employee's needs.

The age of employees may have some effect on the needs they are trying to satisfy. For example, younger workers just entering the work force may be concentrating on satisfying the primary needs of physiological and safety for the first few years on the job. They may be unmarried and not have a lot of responsibility, or have a desire to work hard to prove to others that they are competent and can be successful. They may also experiment with different jobs and move around but they are probably going to be in the lower income bracket. This is the time they may try to find a mentor to help them in their pursuit of higher-order needs.

The person who has been in the workforce for a number of years may be more interested in satisfying the higher-order needs of belonging and esteem. This person may be ready to find a significant other and make major purchases in establishing a home. They may also look to be rewarded for the contributions they are making on the job. During this time, they may find that they have one last chance to make it big in their career. Some of their ability to satisfy their belonging needs may come from activity in the community. As the employee moves through this stage, money will eventually begin to be less important.

In contrast to these two types of employees, people who might have 30+ years in the workplace might want to retire and do something they have always wanted to do. They may start to soften and start to look at everyday joys and triumphs. As they look at retirement, their future plans will include pensions, endowment checks, and in some cases, security may even become a concern. These employees will want to move on and attempt to become "self-actualized."

Older workers—Studies have indicated there are three primary factors for motivating older workers. These are financial security, social affiliation, and the opportunity to make a contribution to the organization. Supervisors need to talk with each older worker and observe the person's behavior to identify the particular dominant need(s). Older workers who place a high degree of importance on financial security need assurance that their job is secure and that they can work the number of hours needed to meet their financial goals. If they place a high value on affiliation needs, assign them tasks that involve a large amount of contact with other workers and customers. Finally, for older workers who are motivated by the need to contribute, assign tasks that are meaningful. Take time to explain the importance of the task and how it contributes to the organization.

Examining How Needs Shift As Circumstances Change

Employees might also move between these stages of needs depending on their particular situation, for example:

George was an employee of the Acme Products Company. He was hired by the company when he was 23 years old and had 28 years of service when in 1989 the company decided to move to the southern region of the U.S. George was not invited to go along in the move. He was planning to retire in four years and open a small engine repair shop—something he had wanted to do since high school— and he had even taken classes at the local vocational technical school to prepare for the day he would open the shop.

Two of George's five children still lived at home when the plant moved. George had no real skills, other than small engine repair, so he was out of a job with no income, no health benefits, and no job prospects. Most of George's needs had been satisfied by the time he was 51. He had a family, he was respected at the plant, his home was almost paid for, and he thought he was secure. George went without a job for two years. Unemployment insurance lasted for six months and when it was exhausted, he couldn't find a job that even came close to paying what he had been making at the plant. He used up all the savings that he was going to use to start the small engine repair business.

In George's case, he went from his dream of becoming self-actualized to almost starting over and needing to fulfill his physiological and safety and security needs. In time, George did find another job, but not at the same rate of pay he had at the plant. He didn't retire at 55 and open his small engine repair shop, and he may be lucky to retire when he reaches 65. George is an example of how people can continuously move through the needs hierarchy.

Even though Maslow's theory has been around for a number of years and is very well known, it has not been confirmed by research.

Alderfer's ERG Theory of Motivation

In seeking to improve on Maslow's Needs Hierarchy, Clayton Alderfer proposed a modified needs hierarchy with just three levels. His model was termed the **Existence-Relatedness-Growth** (ERG) theory of motivation. The ERG model places less emphasis on the hierarchical order and indicates that more than one need may operate at one time and the satisfaction of a need may or may not lead to the progression to the next higher need. The ERG model is much less restrictive than Maslow's theory; however, they both agree that satisfying human needs is an important part of creating a motivating environment. The model has three basic factors:

1. **Existence needs** concern the physical needs of the person. They include such basics as food, clothing, and shelter and the means provided by work to attain these things. Pay, fringe benefits, and working conditions are examples.

2. **Relatedness needs** are interpersonal needs that are satisfied through interactions with others on and off the job.

3. **Growth needs** are personal development and improvement needs that are met by developing the abilities and capabilities that are important to a person.

The ERG model also contains a **frustration-regression** dimension. Alderfer said that if higher-order needs are not satisfied, employees will demand greater satisfaction of the lower-order needs. For example, if an employee is unable to satisfy his or her relatedness need for more social interaction, the result tends to be an increase in the desire for more money or better working conditions.

A supervisor usually has the ability and resources to satisfy the relatedness and growth needs of an employee. Later in the book you will discover some very practical ways that you can help an employee satisfy their relatedness and growth needs.

Herzberg's Two-Factor Model

On the basis of research with accountants and engineers in the 1950s, Frederick Herzberg developed what is known as the **Two-Factor Model** of motivation. He asked the subjects of his research to think of a time when they felt especially good about their jobs, a time when they felt especially bad about their jobs, and to describe the conditions that led to those feelings. He found that those involved in the study described different types of conditions for good or bad feelings.

From the study, Herzberg concluded that two separate factors really influenced motivation. The factors that dissatisfied employees are called hygiene factors or maintenance factors, and the factors that satisfied employees were called motivational factors or motivators. The maintenance factors will not cause employees to motivate themselves, but if they are absent or insufficient, they may cause employees to be less motivated because they are dissatisfied. These factors do not stimulate the growth or development of people. Maintenance factors are primarily related to job context—the environment surrounding the job, such as pay, working conditions, job security, status, and company policy. Motivators are related to job content, which is related to the work itself, advancement, recognition, achievement, responsibility, and possibility of growth.

The difference between job context and job content is similar to the differences between extrinsic motivators and intrinsic motivators. Extrinsic motivators are those external rewards that occur apart from the work and provide no direct satisfaction at the time the work is performed. Intrinsic motivators are those internal rewards that people feel when they perform a job satisfactorily and there is a direct connection between the work and the reward they receive. Herzberg's model provides a distinction between maintenance factors, which are necessary to a point but not sufficient to improve employee behavior, and motivators that have the potential for improving employee behavior.

According to Herzberg, job satisfaction is produced by building motivating factors into the job. This process is known as job enrichment. When the motivating factors are present in a job, they can lead to superior effort and job performance by employees. Motivating factors can lead to a challenge for people to grow and contribute to an organization. These factors also directly influence the way people feel about their work.

One of the problems with Herzberg's model is that it may not be universally applicable because it was based on studies made on professional and upper-level white-collar workers and it is more concerned with job satisfaction than motivation. For this reason, the two-factor model may not be useful as a guide for your supervisory decisions that you make on a day-to-day basis. However, it has been primarily responsible for encouraging organizations to redesign work to make it more intrinsically interesting and challenging for employees.

Welfare-to-work employees—Welfare recipients have been stereotyped as lazy and lacking motivation. In the past, many were motivated to stay on welfare because they were provided with health care, food stamps, and could stay at home to care for their children. However, welfare reform now limits the number of years that a person can receive welfare assistance. Welfare-to-work employees are entering the labor force with security needs at a high level. They must replace the assistance they receive on welfare with sufficient income and fringe benefits to counterbalance the reduction in assistance.

Supervisors should be sensitive to this need. Talk with workers about what they need to do to keep their job. Explain how they can advance and receive more pay. Inform them about what they must do to qualify for fringe benefits. Then provide workers with regular feedback about their job performance so they aren't concerned about whether they are doing a good job. In this way, supervisors can create a work environment that motivates them to become good employees.

Comparing the Three Need Theories of Motivation

	Maslow	*Alderfer*		*Herzberg*
	Self-actualization	Growth		Work itself
Higher-	Esteem		**Motivational**	■ Responsibility
Order	Belongingness	Relatedness	**Factors**	■ Advancement
Needs				■ Growth
				Achievement
				Recognition

	Maslow	Alderfer		Herzberg
Lower-	Safety			Quality of interpersonal working relationships
Order	Security	Existence		
Needs	Physiological		**Hygiene**	Job security
			Factors	Working conditions
				Salary

Motivational Drives

According to David McClelland of Harvard University, people tend to develop certain motivational drives as a product of their cultural environment and these drives affect the way employees view their jobs. All employees possess these motivational drives but to varying degrees. These are the drives that McClelland identified:

- **The Need for Achievement (n Ach)**—Employees who have a high n Ach think about ways to do a better job, how to accomplish something important, and their career progress. These employees will work harder when they perceive they will receive personal credit for what they have done, there is only a moderate risk of failure, and they are given specific feedback on their performance. They also perform well in nonroutine and challenging situations. To motivate employees who are high in n Ach, give them nonroutine, challenging jobs with clear and attainable objectives. Also give them increased responsibility for new tasks they are given.

- **The Need for Power (n Pow)**—Employees who are high in n Pow like to influence people, change situations, control the situation, and engage in competition they can win. They also like to have positions of authority and status such as supervisory and managerial positions. To motivate employees who are high in n Pow, let them plan and control their jobs as much as possible, include them in decision making (especially if the decision affects them directly), give them an entire task rather than just part of it, and let them work alone if possible.

- **The Need for Affiliation (n Aff)**—Employees who are high in n Aff, like to relate to people on a social basis. These employees seek close relationships with other employees, they want to be liked by others, they enjoy social activities, and they seek to belong. To motivate employees who are high in n Aff, let them work as part of a team, give them lots of praise and recognition, and give them responsibilities for orienting or training new employees (they make good mentors).

65

Theory X–Theory Y and Motivation

In 1960 Douglas McGregor wrote a book titled *The Human Side of Enterprise,* in which he proposed the **Theory X–Theory Y** view of human nature and motivation. McGregor built on Maslow's Needs Hierarchy. According to McGregor, management's view of people in the workplace, or **Theory X,** is based on assumptions that people are motivated by lower-order needs:

1. Employees inherently dislike work and will avoid it whenever possible.

2. Since employees inherently dislike work, they must be coerced, controlled, or threatened with punishment to get them to work.

3. Employees will shirk their responsibilities and will seek formal direction whenever possible.

4. Most employees place security above all other factors and they will display little ambition.

In contrast to the negative views of Theory X, McGregor set out four other assumptions he called **Theory Y:**

1. Employees may view work as being as natural as play or rest.

2. Employees will exercise self-direction and self-control if they are committed to the objectives.

3. Employees can and will learn to accept and even seek responsibility.

4. The ability to make good decisions is not limited solely to management and can be made by employees if given the opportunity. Their imagination, ingenuity, creativity, and the ability to use these qualities can also be used to help solve organizational problems.

According to McGregor, employees should be treated differently according to whether they are motivated by lower-order needs or higher-order needs. He indicated that the assumptions of Theory X were for employees who are motivated by lower-order needs and the Theory Y assumptions are for employees who are motivated by higher-order needs. McGregor proposed that such ideas as participative decision making, responsible and challenging jobs, and good group relations would maximize the employee's job motivation. He also believed that since most people have had their lower-order needs satisfied, Theory Y was typically more appropriate.

There is no evidence that either set of assumptions is valid or that accepting Theory Y assumptions will lead to motivated employees. Using either Theory X or Theory Y assumptions may depend on the individual employee and his or her behavior. However, many managers use Theory Y without questioning its validity or assessing the individual behavior of their employees. A wise supervisor is one who observes the results of using Theory Y—when appropriate—and adjusting subsequent actions based on the results. For example, if employees are given an opportunity to participate in decision making, they should have a positive attitude toward the organization and supervisor. When employees fail to respond in the expected manner, you should do one of two things. First, make sure that the lower-order needs of employees have been satisfied, and second, determine whether McGregor's theory is applicable to your work environment.

Disabled workers—Studies suggest that individuals with learning disabilities may find it difficult to process information needed for effective social interaction. Learning-disabled people sometimes have difficulty communicating with others, using humor appropriately, dealing with change, handling pressure, and interpreting the feelings and moods of others. These problems can be complicated when the learning disabled are mistreated by others because of their disability.

Learning disabilities are more noticeable in an educational setting. Therefore, many people with learning disorders often struggle to complete homework assignments and take tests. Sometimes they have undergone severe teasing by other students. When these individuals enter the workplace, they often have high self-esteem needs. Supervisors should look for opportunities to praise and encourage employees with learning disabilities. They sometimes have difficulty accepting criticism, so be more cautious in the way you phrase comments about their work. Try to avoid using the term "you" in an accusatory way when discussing the appropriate method for completing a task.

For example, instead of saying, "You didn't stack those boxes the right way," you might say, "These boxes aren't stacked the way we need it done. Let me show you the way we do it." Provide frequent encouragement to workers with learning disabilities. These activities will reinforce their self-esteem needs and help motivate them to be productive employees.

Behavior Modification and Motivation

Behavior modification is based on the premise that the behavior of an employee depends on the consequences of the behavior. It is then possible for you to affect employee behaviors by manipulating their consequences. Behavior modification relies on the **Law of Effect,** which comes from the work of social scientist, B.F. Skinner. The law says that a person will tend to repeat behavior that is accompanied by favorable consequences (reinforcement) and they will not repeat behavior that is accompanied by unfavorable consequences. The Law of Effect comes from **learning theory,** which suggests people learn best in pleasant surroundings. Behavior modification indicates that external consequences tend to determine behavior. Two conditions need to be present for behavior modification to be successful:

1. The supervisor must be able to identify some consequences that are perceived as important by the employee.

2. The supervisor must be able to administer the consequences in a manner that will show the employee the connection between the behavior affected and the consequences.

Behavior modification places emphasis on the use of rewards in modifying behavior and alternative consequences to sustain the behavior. When using behavior modification you must decide whether you want an employee to continue the behavior they are exhibiting or decrease it. Once this has been determined, you must decide what type of consequence should be used—positive or negative—and whether to apply it or withhold it. You can use four alternative consequences:

- **Positive reinforcement** is a favorable consequence that encourages the behavior to be repeated and should be contingent on the employee's correct behavior. For example, if an employee meets her production consistently, you can give her recognition for her accomplishment. If she likes the recognition, she will continue the behavior.

- **Negative reinforcement** occurs when an unfavorable consequence is removed. For example, if an employee wears safety glasses, they prevent the chance of an item striking or lodging in his eye, thereby removing the unfavorable consequence—injury.

- **Punishment** is the administration of an unfavorable consequence that is intended to discourage specific behavior. For example, an employee who does not wear a hard hat on a consistent basis may be given a reprimand for exhibiting this behavior. One of the problems with this method of behavior modification is that although it does discourage undesirable behavior, it does not directly encourage the desirable behavior unless the employee understands the correct behavior.

■ **Extinction** means reinforcing behavior by making the employee repeat it. If there is no reinforcement by the supervisor, the behavior tends to diminish because of the lack of reinforcement. Sometimes it is possible to simply extinguish behavior by ignoring. However, it would be a naïve assumption to think that just ignoring undesirable behavior will cause it to go away. It is possible that other rewards reinforce undesirable behaviors.

The major benefit of behavior modification is it makes you become a conscious motivator. It will encourage you to analyze an employee's behavior, explore why it occurs, how often and what consequences will help change the behavior. Some of the general guidelines of behavior modification are in the following list:

■ Identify the exact behavior you want to change.

■ Make sure the employee has the abilities and skills to change.

■ Determine what rewards the employee values.

■ Determine how large the reward will have to be for the employee's behavior to change.

■ Clarify that there is a connection between the desired behavior and the reward.

■ Use positive reinforcement when possible.

■ Use punishment for exceptional circumstances.

■ Ignore minor undesirable behavior to allow it to be extinguished.

■ Minimize the time between the correct behavior and the reward.

■ Provide reinforcement frequently and use a schedule of reinforcement.

In applying various types of consequences, you should use a schedule of reinforcement to modify the employee's behavior. The schedule of reinforcement may be either continuous or partial.

Continuous reinforcement occurs when a reinforcer accompanies each correct behavior you want from the employee. This type of reinforcement may be desirable to encourage quick learning but in most work situations, it is not always possible to reward an employee for every correct behavior. An example of continuous reinforcement is a piece rate payment plan. A piece rate payment plan is where an employee is rewarded for the number of pieces produced over and above a set number of pieces.

Partial reinforcement occurs when only some of the correct behaviors are reinforced. The employee may learn slower under partial reinforcement than with continuous reinforcement but the learning does tend to be retained longer. Some types of partial reinforcement are:

- Time intervals

  - ◆ **Fixed interval**—reinforcement is given after a certain time period. For example,the employee is given a paycheck every week.

  - ◆ **Variable interval**—reinforcement is given after a certain variety of time periods. The employee is given a safety talk twice every month on a random basis.

- Ratios

  - ◆ **Fixed ratio**—reinforcement is given after a certain number of correct responses. The employee is given a free dinner for every ten subscriptions they sell over the phone.

  - ◆ **Variable ratio**—reinforcement is given after a variable number of responses. All employees who have perfect attendance for one year are given a lottery chance to win a television set.

Contingent workers—Many workers choose some form of contingent work because it fits their lifestyle needs. However, some surveys show that almost 60 percent of these workers would prefer a permanent, full-time job. Part of the reason for this is that only a small percentage of contingent workers receive fringe benefits like vacations, sick days, pensions, and health insurance. This means that many contingent workers have high security needs. Also, keep in mind that contingent work often fails to satisfy affiliation and achievement needs.

Supervisors should focus on the security needs of contingent workers to motivate them. Hire contingent workers when permanent jobs become available. This encourages other workers to perform at a high level of productivity in an effort to obtain job openings. When contingent workers perceive little or no opportunity for permanent jobs, their performance is usually sufficient to just "get by." Inform new contingent workers about their prospects for permanent jobs and what they must do to get them. This can create the environment that workers need to be highly motivated.

Goal Setting and Motivation

Goals are objectives set to encourage the performance of employees in the near future. Goal setting, developed by Edwin Locke and his colleagues, works as a motivational process by creating a discrepancy between current and expected performance. This will result in a feeling of tension in employees that they can reduce through the attainment of future goals. Meeting future goals helps to satisfy employees' self-esteem and stimulates their needs of personal growth.

A major factor in goal setting is the concept of **self-efficacy.** This is the internal belief of an employee that they have the capabilities and competencies to perform a task. Employees with a high self-efficacy tend to set higher personal goals because they believe those goals will be attainable. It is a good idea for you as a supervisor to help employees build their self-efficacy. The following table lists some good ideas to help build employees' self-efficacy.

Do	Don't
Ask them for their input	Talk down to them about their job
Praise them for their efforts	Imply to them that they are incompetent
Listen carefully to their input	Find fault with their results
Share positive feedback with them	Criticize them in front of their peers
Provide recognition for their achievements	Make their job seem insignificant

Often supervisors tell employees to "do your best." However, according to goal setting theory, it is better for them to have specific goals that are difficult to achieve—but attainable. Employees should also receive feedback on how they are doing. In addition, if employees are given the opportunity to participate in setting goals, they may try even harder to achieve the goals. The reason for this is that employees will be more committed to what they take part in rather than something that is forced on them. Here are some rules to help you with goal setting:

- Make the goals specific.
- Make the goals challenging.
- Set specific time limits to accomplish the goals.
- Let the employee help you to determine the goals.
- Provide the employee feedback on his or her performance.

71

Consider the following example: Joy is a supervisor in a bank. She was having problems with employees not meeting the quarterly goals that she set for them. In fact, her employees were meeting only about 50 percent of the goals she set. Joy attended a class at the local university, and one of the discussion topics was goal setting and how to help employees set goals they can meet. The next time Joy had to set goals for her department, she had each employee sit down with her to help establish the goals. They set specific goals, made them challenging, and set specific time limits to accomplish the goals. At the end of the quarter, Joy was surprised to find that instead of only meeting 50 percent of the goals, the employees met an average of 80 percent of the goals *they* had helped set. Joy was encouraged with this and decided to use the process again.

Equity Theory and Motivation

Fairness and Equity, introduced by J. Stacy Adams, are concepts that have relevance to the motivation of employees. Workers are sensitive to the relative differences in the rewards they receive and the rewards that other employees receive. Employees perceive what they get from a job situation (outcomes) in relation to what they put into it (inputs), then they compare their ratio of outcome to input with the those of other employees (a reference group) who may be doing similar work. Inputs are all of the things an employee brings to the job, such as education, seniority, work experience, loyalty and commitment, time and effort, and job performance. Outcomes are those rewards they perceive they get from their job and employer, such as pay, fringe benefits, job security, and social and psychological rewards.

If employees perceive they are over-rewarded for what they do, this theory predicts that they will feel the imbalance and try to restore the balance by working harder. Conversely, if employees feel they are under-rewarded for what they do, they may try to restore this balance by lowering their productivity and not working as hard.

Employees may have several different reference groups they compare to, both inside and outside of the organization. Employees may also shift the basis of comparison to the standards that are the most favorable to them. For example, an employee with a bachelor's degree may inflate the importance of her degree to compensate for her lack of experience in the industry. Some employees may also compare themselves with groups that are in a higher economic category than they are. This makes it difficult to predict when equity or inequity will occur. Also, evidence suggests that employees who are over-rewarded can accept this condition with much less difficulty than if they perceive they are under-rewarded.

For example, Jan is an employee in the final assembly department of the plant in which she works. She has been an employee for 15 years, has not missed a day during that time and she has always met her production schedule. On the other hand, Joe, who is also an employee in the final assembly department, has only been on the job for six months, frequently misses work, and on some occasions has not met his production schedule. The supervisor of the department talks to Jim every day and seems to spend a lot of time with him. He has also appointed Joe to the quality committee that meets once a week. Jan has observed that she is not being treated fairly—with equity—and decides that if Joe can get by with what he is doing and still be a favorite of the supervisor, she will quit working as hard. If she feels like taking a day off, she will.

Ex-offenders—Older offenders were more successful at work release than younger offenders. Whites were more successful than Hispanics and blacks. More than 40 percent of Hispanic and black work releasees were returned to prison compared with 25 percent of white offenders. Offenders with no prior criminal record were more successful than those with a prior record. Almost two-thirds of inmates with no prior record were successful compared with fewer than half the offenders with a prior conviction. Offenders convicted of person crimes (for example, robbery and assault) were more successful than offenders convicted of property or drug crimes.

Expectancy Theory of Motivation

One of the most widely accepted theories of how motivation takes place is the **Expectancy Theory**, developed by Victor H. Vroom and expanded on by Porter and Lawler. According to this theory, the likelihood that an employee will act in a certain way depends on how certain the employee is about three things:

1. Whether the employee is capable of performing the assigned task

2. Whether or not the performance of the task be will followed by an expected outcome

3. Whether that outcome will be attractive to the employee

The theory explains that motivation is a product of three distinct factors:

■ **Valence**—How much the reward is wanted. Since employees may have either a positive, negative, or no preference for a reward, valence can be a range of –1 to +1. For example, if an employee has no preference for a reward, the valence could be 0 to –1; if they have a strong preference for it, the valence could be +1.

73

■ **Expectancy**—One's estimate of the probability that the effort exerted will result in successful performance. One of the forces that contributes to expectancy is self-efficacy or the ability an employee has to perform a task successfully. Employees who have high self-efficacy are more likely to believe that if they exert effort, they will have satisfactory performance. Employees who do not have high self-efficacy may have self-doubt and feel they are not capable of high performance. Since expectancy is the probability of a connection between effort and performance, the value may range from 0 to +1. If an employee expects that their effort will not lead to satisfactory performance the value is 0, and if they expect effort will lead to satisfactory performance, the value is +1.

■ **Instrumentality**—One's estimate that successful performance will result in receiving the reward. The employee makes a subjective judgment about the probability that the organization will value their performance and make the reward available to them. The value of instrumentality ranges from 0 to +1. If an employee believes that promotions are based solely on performance, the instrumentality could be +1. If they see that promotions are not based on performance, but on subjective information management uses, the instrumentality could be 0.

The product of valence, expectancy, and instrumentality is motivation. The relationship is stated in the following formula:

Motivation = Valence × Expectancy × Instrumentality

The three factors in the expectancy model can result in a variety of combinations; here are some of the possibilities:

Valence	Expectancy	Instrumentality	Motivation
High positive	High	High	Strong motivation
Positive	High	Low	Moderate motivation
Positive	Low	High	Moderate motivation
Positive	Low	Low	Weak motivation
Negative	Low	Low	Weak avoidance
Negative	High	Low	Moderate avoidance
Negative	Low	High	Moderate avoidance
High negative	Low	Low	Strong avoidance

The connection of the effort and reward is often uncertain because there are so many causes and effects in any given situation, and an employee may never be certain that the desired reward will follow a given action. There are also primary outcomes and secondary outcomes. Primary outcomes result directly from the action and secondary outcomes follow the primary outcomes. For example, an employee goes to school to prepare for a promotion. Eventually he receives the promotion. The promotion may also include a raise, which will give him the ability to purchase more and raise his status in the community.

Supervisors can use the expectancy model by strengthening both the actual value of the reward and the formal connection between the effort and performance and between performance and reward. This will allow employees to see that their effort will result in performance and performance will result in the reward. Supervisors also need to recognize employees' perception of the reward and whether or not they think it is of some value to them. If employees don't perceive the reward as having value to them, they will probably not make the efforts needed to attain the reward. This requires you to find out employee perceptions by communicating with employees and determining the following things:

- Which of the rewards that are available to them do employees value the most?

- Do employees believe their effort will result in successful performance?

- Do employees believe that if they perform well that the desired reward will be received?

The expectancy model is valuable to you as a supervisor because it helps you think about the mental processes that occur in order for an employee to be motivated. Using this model, you can see that employees do not act just because of unmet needs, but they are thinking individuals whose beliefs, perceptions, and probabilities influence their behavior. However, there are also some problems with the expectancy model. It may be too complex for supervisors to use so they will only use general parts of it. Also, for employees in lower-level jobs it may not be applicable because these jobs have limitations imposed by work methods and company policies; thus limiting a supervisor's options for motivating them.

Attribution Theory and Motivation

The **Attribution Theory** was first developed by Fritz Heider and later expanded by Harold Kelley. Attribution is the process by which employees perceive and assign causes for their own and others' behavior. It is the way employees explain their successes or failures, the successes or failures of others, and how it affects their feelings and subsequent behaviors. Attributions can be made to an internal source (something that is within the employee's control) or an external source (something outside of the employee's control). For example, if an employee attributes a promotion to hard work or ability, the person is citing an internal control. However, if the promotion is attributed to the seniority system, the employee is citing an external control.

The attribution patterns typically differ among employees. Employees who are achievement-oriented will attribute their success to ability and their lack of success to not putting forth enough effort. On the other hand, failure-oriented employees will attribute their lack of success to their inability and this may cause them to develop feelings of incompetence.

For you as a supervisor, the attribution model can help you assess an employee's behavior as functional or dysfunctional by observing the person and identifying these three factors:

1. **Consistency**—whether the behavior the employee exhibits is stable or unstable across time.

2. **Distinctiveness**—the degree to which the employee behaves the same way in other situations.

3. **Consensus**—the extent to which the employee's peer group behaves in a similar manner in the same situation.

For example, you have been getting complaints from quality control about Joyce and the job she is doing serving customers. You have not received complaints about other employees (low consensus). You talk with Joyce and find that she received complaints about customer service at other jobs she has worked at (low distinctiveness). The complaints have been coming in consistently for about three weeks (high consistency). In this situation, you would probably make an internal attribution and conclude the complaints must stem from Joyce's work performance. The combination of low consensus, low distinctiveness, and high consistency leads to the conclusion of internal attributions, something that is under Joyce's control. Thus, upon explaining the problem to Joyce and getting her agreement to improve her behavior, you would expect her customer service to improve.

Another situation might be different and produce external attributions. Suppose you have an employee, Brad, who is performing very poorly on meeting his shipping schedules. You find that Brad is not the only one of your employees who is having problems making shipping schedules (high consensus) and he is performing the rest of his job very well (high distinctiveness). You also find that he has only been performing this aspect of the job poorly for a short period of time and most of the time he handles the job quite well (low consistency). This indicates that there is probably an external attribution responsible for the poor performance. It may be that inventory supplies are inadequate to fill all orders in a timely manner.

Attributions are subjective assessments and one important factor is whether we are assessing our own behavior or someone else's. In general, employees will tend to exhibit a self-serving bias when interpreting their situation. They will claim undue credit for success and minimize their own responsibility for problems. They overestimate the influence of internal factors (their personal traits) when assessing their successes and assign external attributions (the work situation) for their failures. For example, Jack was promoted to supervisor over his department and he attributed the promotion to the fact that he worked very hard and gave his best effort to the job he had been doing.

The opposite situation is the fundamental attribution bias when employees attribute other employees' success to luck or easy jobs and that assume others fail because they didn't try hard enough or they didn't have the ability to succeed. Gerri did not get the promotion to supervisor in her department and Jack attributed it to Gerri's inability to get along with people and that she didn't work as hard as he had worked.

The way employees interpret the events around them has a strong influence on their behavior. You as a supervisor must determine the causes of behavior and a perceived source of responsibility. Attribution Theory can help explain how performance judgments differ and how to gain predictability and control over future behavior.

Machiavellianism and Motivation

In 1513, Niccolo Machiavelli wrote a book entitled *The Prince*. In the book, he outlined a ruthless strategy for public officials to seize and hold power. His approach was straightforward; people, he asserted, can be used and manipulated by sticking to a few basic rules:

- Arrogance is much more effective when dealing with people and one should never show humility.

- Powerful people can lie, cheat, and deceive whenever it suits their purpose because morality and ethics are for the weak.

- It is much more beneficial to be feared than to be loved.

- Ends justify the means.

Most supervisors do not adopt Machiavelli's principles, but some do. Those who do are sometimes referred to as **Machs**. They use intimidation, manipulation, and fear to get employees to do what they want. Fear is a motivator that most people will respond to, at least in the short term. In the long term, fear is not an effective motivator because the fear of something happening will eventually dwindle and turn to dislike for the person using the fear tactic. For example, if a supervisor threatens employees with discipline or discharge to get them to work effectively, employees will respond in the short term. If the threat continues for very long, employees will become angry, begin to dislike the supervisor, and adopt the attitude that the supervisor can do whatever he or she wants. Employees eventually arrive at the point where they don't fear the supervisor any longer and they don't care what the supervisor does to them.

A growing economy makes using of Mach behavior even more counterproductive. Employees can more readily find other jobs in a strong economy and will leave an organization where such behavior exists in supervisors. This creates even more frustration for the supervisor who then must get work done with fewer and less experienced workers.

Summary

Of all of the theories of motivation presented in this chapter, none of them is perfect. Each has its own strengths and weaknesses. When people join organizations, they bring with them certain drives and needs that will affect their on-the-job performance. Sometimes the drives and needs will be immediately apparent, but many times they are difficult to determine and satisfy because they will vary greatly from one employee to another.

The final word on motivation has not been written and may never be written. Theorists continue to investigate this extremely complex topic and there will be many disagreements among those theorists as to what is or is not a motivator, and why people do or do not motivate themselves. As the supervisor, you must draw on the theories available and apply them effectively with your subordinates. Discover the ideas that best fit your personality and situation. Not every theory or factor will apply to every employee in all situations; however, many of the factors we have discussed in this chapter will help you in your everyday dealings with employees.

Chapter 5

Communications— Getting the Point

Herman is a supervisor in a small manufacturing plant. On Monday morning, he prepared to give Shawna instructions on what to do with a large box containing some disposable material and some material that needs to be saved for reuse.

Herman approached Shawna and said, "Some of this material is bad and some good; we need to get rid of it. Take it out to the dumpster."

Shawna asked if she should do it right away, and Herman said "yes."

Shawna took the box, thinking that all of it belonged in the dumpster, and she got rid of it just in time for the refuse company to pick it up. Later that afternoon, Herman asked Shawna where the good material from the box was.

Shawna replied, "You told me to get rid of all of it."

"I told you to get rid of the bad material, not the good," Herman said.

Shawna replied, "But I asked you if you wanted me to get rid of all of it in the box, and you said yes!"

Clearly, a miscommunication has taken place.

As this example illustrates, communication in the workplace is very important. When communication fails, problems result. This chapter examines how supervisors can send their messages more clearly, have them understood, and get the results that they expect.

Values and Communication

As a supervisor, you are responsible for working with many different types of employees—young, old, part-time, immigrants and many other people who make up the workforce in your organization. They may have different values than you have but you still have to work with them, communicate with them, and get them to do the job they were hired to do. Values affect our perceptions, which in turn affect our communication with each other. Social psychologists have studied the value differences based on age and suggest that these differences explain why there are sometimes conflicts and problems in communication between supervisors and workers. The following table explains some of the values of today's workers.

Time They Entered the Workforce	Approximate Age Today	Work Values
Late 1950s to early 1960s	55+	Hard work, conservative, loyalty to the organization, will probably only work for one organization during their lifetime
Mid 1960s to mid 1970s	45–55	Quality of life, nonconformance, loyal to themselves rather to an organization, may job hop
Mid 1970s to mid 1980s	35–45	Success, achievement, ambition, hard work, loyalty to their careers, will probably job hop
Mid 1980s to present	18–35	Flexibility, job satisfaction, leisure time, loyalty to relationships, may find the place they want to live and then find a job to support themselves

Keep in mind, as a supervisor, you also fall into one of these categories and you may have employees who fall in all of the categories. You need to communicate with all of these employees even though they have values different than yours. You need to be aware that their responses to words and actions are different than your reactions. You need to consider how you can successfully communicate with them.

Younger workers—It is important to take more time when communicating with young people and other inexperienced workers. Messages are often distorted because a supervisor uses words, lingo, or acronyms that the employee isn't familiar with. A simple instruction by a supervising nurse like telling an aide to show some "TLC" when helping patients, is easily distorted. While many people know that the acronym stands for "tender loving care," others aren't aware of this. The young worker may go through the entire day trying to figure out what TLC is and how to show it to patients.

A simple way to avoid this communication problem is to think back to the time when you first started at the organization. What words, terms, sayings, acronyms, and other concepts were strange to you? Make sure when you communicate with a young employee that you take the time to define exactly what you mean. Don't do this is a manner that "talks down" to the employee. Just casually ask if the person knows what you mean. Avoid settling for a simple "yes" answer. Ask the worker to define what it means. Put the employee at ease by saying this is an important communication skill. Be honest about the fact that younger workers often are unfamiliar with some terms and you want to avoid this problem. Taking a little more time to communicate clearly with a young worker can save a great deal of time later by avoiding mistakes or problem situations that you have to correct.

Couple the issues connected with generational value differences with the fact that you are likely to have employees from different cultures, ex-offenders, minorities, disabled, and economically disadvantaged. The values differences from one group to the next become even more important in recognizing the need to communicate effectively with all employees. Sounds challenging, doesn't it? It is, but you can do it and do it well. As we discuss different methods of dealing with people, remember the table on today's worker and how you can make the chart work for you.

Fundamentals of Communication

Communication is the transfer of information from one person to another person(s). It is a way that one can reach others by transmitting ideas, facts, and feelings. When communication is effective, it provides a bridge of meaning between two or more people. No matter what type of organization one is a member of, effective communication is important for the organization to survive. Organizations are unable to exist without effective communication. When communications are not effective, the members of organizations do not know what is going on or what they need to be doing.

For you as a supervisor, communicating effectively is extremely important because the majority of your time will be spent communicating with other people. Studies show that supervisors spend anywhere from 60 to 90 percent of their time communicating with other people and their success depends largely on their ability to get the message across in a convincing manner. Several studies have revealed that as much as 70 percent of attempts to communicate in business settings fail to achieve the intended objectives.

Since you are responsible for getting the job done through other people, you will not be able to delegate a task without communicating with an employee. However, communicating effectively is not a skill that comes automatically once you have been appointed to a supervisory position. It is a skill that only comes with practice on a daily basis, and you should know that there is more than one way to communicate. The primary ways to communicate in modern organizations are face-to-face communication, written communication, and electronic communication. We'll examine all three methods and provide you with ideas on how to become a better communicator.

Face-to-Face Communication

Effective communication is an extremely important aspect of a supervisor's job. You will meet one-on-one with employees, give talks to your department, engage in problem solving processes with employees, and meet with your manager. In all, communication comprises over 65 percent of a supervisor's activities. Face-to-face communication has some inherent key advantages. It is fast and involves a nonverbal component, which enhances the message being delivered.

To be a leader of people, you must be able to communicate with them in a manner they will understand. Communicating is the process of transmitting a message from a sender to a receiver. To have communication, the message must be fully understood by both parties. Communicating has three goals:

- To inform
- To influence
- To express specific feelings

The Eight-Step Two-Way Communication Process

Researchers have developed many models to help supervisors understand how to communicate more effectively. This model is appropriate to all forms of communication but since the first method discussed is oral communication, it appears at this point in the chapter. The model contains eight key steps that ensure good communication when carefully followed. First look over the model, then read the descriptions for each step in the model.

Older workers—Age differences between the supervisor and older workers increase the potential disparity in values and beliefs. Values and beliefs affect basic assumptions that we make in communicating with each other. Distortion in communication can occur because of these differences. For example, older workers tend to place a higher value on loyalty and have difficulty understanding a supervisor that doesn't value this characteristic in a worker. Older workers may send messages designed to convey their loyalty. A supervisor that doesn't place a high value on loyalty fails to interpret these messages correctly and doesn't respond appropriately. These communication problems can be overcome by identifying key values in older workers and using this information to interpret their messages.

Supervisors should take time to talk with older workers about their values and beliefs about work. Share your views about these values and beliefs. Do this in a way that doesn't demean their values but rather demonstrates that there is room for different points of view. Clarifying differences in values and beliefs often reduces the potential for communication breakdowns.

Sender						*Receiver*
Develop	Encode	Transmit	Receive	Decode	Accept	Use
↑		→	→	→		↓
↑						↓
	←	Feedback			←	

1. **Develop an idea.** The sender must develop an idea to transmit. This is a key step, because unless there is a worthwhile message, it renders all of the other steps relatively useless. Sometimes we fail to think before we speak. Take time before talking with an employee so that you know what you want to say before you send the message.

2. **Encode the message.** The message must be converted into suitable words or recognizable symbols for transmission to the receiver. Consider the vocabulary that you use with workers. Do they understand the meaning of words you are using? If not, use simpler words and concepts. Be careful about using jargon or acronyms. New workers or those unfamiliar with terms that are commonly used in your organization are only confused when you use these terms.

3. **Transmit the message.** Once the message is fully developed, the sender must transmit the message to the receiver by a chosen method—oral, written, or electronic. The more personal or emotion-laden a message is, the more appropriate it is to use oral communication. Written communication is best used to communicate to large numbers of workers or to ensure that there is a record of the communication. The use of electronic communication methods can combine the advantages of both oral and written communication.

4. **Receive the message.** The transmission allows another person to receive a message. If the receiver is not functioning, the message will be lost. It is important that you verify that the person you are talking to is listening. The more distractions that exist in the workplace, the more important it is to make sure that the employee is paying attention to the message you are sending. Persons with hearing problems often need you to face them directly so that they can see your lips at the same time you're speaking.

5. **Decode the message.** The receiver must decode the message so it can be understood exactly the way it was meant to be understood. Employees need to be trained well for messages to be understood. Most communications in an organization relate to the facilities, equipment, other workers, customers, procedures, policies, and work practices. The more that employees know about all of these, the better they can decode messages that you send. Also, keep in mind that immigrant workers may have some difficulties decoding messages because of language issues. They may not be able to respond as quickly to a message as workers who have English as their first language.

6. **Accept the message.** Once the receiver has decoded the message, the receiver then has the opportunity to either accept or reject it, or to possibly accept part of the message. Send messages in a way that encourages acceptance. Some ways to do this are to explain the reason for the message and describe benefits that the receiver gets from responding positively to the message.

7. **Use the information.** The receiver may use the information in some manner, such as reacting to the message immediately, store the information for future reference or do something else. The receiver has full control over the message at this point. Your choice of the method for sending the message impacts how the employee is likely to use the information. For example, sending an oral message about how to process a customer's order may create some problems in the way employees use the information. They may not remember all of the

instructions. They may use the information once, then forget it when processing future orders from the same customer. A written memo communicating this information provides a record for future reference that might prevent these negative actions. Consider how you want employees to use information and aid them by communicating it in a manner that helps them use the information correctly.

8. **Feedback.** When the receiver acknowledges the message and responds to the sender, feedback has occurred. This completes the communication loop—the message flow from sender to receiver and back to the sender. Take time to let employees process a message and communicate their understanding. Verify their understanding by asking them how they are going to use the information. You can also ask them to communicate at some specific future date what the outcomes of their actions are when implementing a message. For example, you might instruct your employees to improve customer relations by also thanking the customer after a sale. Two weeks after giving this instruction, ask the employees to give you examples about customers' reactions and their impressions about how it affects customers' attitudes. Employees who give specific examples have probably been following your instruction. Those that can't give specific examples probably haven't been following your instruction.

Remember, communicating is not what the sender says, but what the receiver understands! Following the ideas about the eight-step model of communication should help employees better understand your message.

Welfare-to-work employees—Welfare-to-work employees have lower than average education and work skills than the general labor force. Some have never held a job. The lack of experience and skills creates a need for them to learn to ask questions whenever necessary. Teach them some simple steps for asking questions.

1. Tell them who they should ask when they have a problem. Make yourself available when they are first starting a new job.

2. Make it clear that there are no stupid questions. Don't treat questions in a manner that conveys they are stupid or bothersome, or workers will stop asking questions.

3. When possible, they should request that someone demonstrate how to do the task they're unclear about.

4. After they receive an answer, have them state what they understand the answer to be.

5. They should ask any other questions that are necessary for them to fully understand how to solve their problem.

Asking questions is not an easy communication task for many people. That is why coaching workers in this simple five-step process can teach them an important skill.

Communicating by Listening

Employees are frequently going to come to you with a message. Instead of being the sender, you become the listener. A helpful tool in this form of communication is **active listening**. Active or effective listening is more than just hearing the person who is talking. Active listening requires the use of ears, and more importantly, the use of the mind. Active listening helps the receiver get the factual idea of the message and the emotional message that is being sent. An active listener not only hears what the person is saying but they also get the feelings and emotions that the sender is intending—more about body language later. The active listener sends the message that they really care about the person and their feelings. As a supervisor, it is critical that you let employees know that you care about them and their feelings.

Many people are not skilled at active listening, but with practice, they can improve. Active listening is like any skill: The more you practice, the better you become. The following list provides some simple guidelines to help you become a better active listener:

■ **Stop talking.** You cannot listen while you are talking. Moreover, don't think about what you want to say while the speaker is still talking. Concentrate on the employee and the message being sent.

■ **Make the employee feel at ease.** Help the employee feel comfortable by creating a rapport. You can often do this with some small talk before the important part of the conversation takes place. Also, place yourself in such a way that there aren't objects between you an the employee. Specifically, don't sit behind your desk but join the employee in a chair near the person. The same advice applies to a counter, large equipment, and so on.

■ **Show the person you want to listen.** Nonverbal responses such as eye contact are some of the best ways to show people you are interested in what they have to say. If you have ever been listening to a child about two or three years old and you turn your head away from them and break eye contact, they will grab your chin and pull your head back to make eye contact. They know that if you are not making eye contact, you are not listening.

■ **Remove any distractions that might interfere.** If it is noisy, close the door or take the person somewhere quiet. Don't doodle, tap your fingers, or do something else that might be a distraction. Unless there is an extremely important matter or pending emergency, don't allow interruptions. For example, turn off your phone's ringer and put a sign on your door that says not to interrupt you.

■ **Empathize with the person talking.** Try to see things from that individual's point of view. Many times we are only interested in our point of view and do not try to see the other person's perspective.

■ **Be patient.** Allow plenty of time for the conversation. If you don't have time, tell the person and schedule time for the conversation at a later time. Don't try to listen fast and finish sentences for the person. Once the person does start talking, don't interrupt.

■ **Hold your temper.** If the person says something you don't like or you disagree with, don't respond in an angry manner. Also, if you get angry, you may misinterpret the message being sent.

■ **Don't argue or criticize the person talking.** This usually puts a person on the defensive and may create an angry response. If this happens, you have two angry people trying to communicate, and this is usually an impossible situation for messages to be accurately sent and received.

■ **Ask relevant questions.** Don't interrupt people. Wait for a pause and then ask a question. If you can't find an appropriate pause to ask the question, wait until the person is finished to ask the question or questions. Asking relevant questions can also show the person you are listening.

■ **Stop talking.** This is the first and the last guideline. You cannot be an active listener while you are talking.

Barriers to Effective Communication

There are many barriers to communicating with other people. It is necessary for you to know what the barriers are so you can try to keep them from interfering when communicating with employees. Even when the receiver receives the message, a number of factors can interfere with and limit the meaning of a message.

Filtering

The person receiving the message will hear only what he or she wants to hear (sometimes called selective listening). This can be caused by a difference in the values, attitudes, needs, and expectations of the sender and receiver. As in the incident described at the beginning of the chapter, Shawna may have heard only what she expected to hear. However, the sender can use some methods to overcome the receiver hearing only what they want to hear. Be sure to:

- Have the full attention of the receiver.

- Use uncomplicated words and gestures.

- Get feedback from the receiver to be sure the message has been understood.

- Repeat the message if necessary.

Distortion

Distortion is when the receiver gives an incorrect interpretation to the words or symbols that have been communicated to them. This can happen when the message goes through several people before it reaches the intended receiver. It may happen when there is a distance between the sender and receiver. The distance may be a psychological distance or a physical distance. A psychological distance might occur because the employee is at a lower level in the organization than the supervisor. The employee may feel that the supervisor talks down to him or her. Also, distortion might occur when the sender and receiver have different backgrounds. The sender and receiver may be from different parts of the country, or in some cases, from different countries. These cultural differences present a challenge in communicating because of the difference in meaning of words (**semantics**) from one culture to another.

Inconsistency and/or Credibility of the Sender

Consistency between what the sender says and what the sender does is very important. If the sender delivers a message that says something will be done, then the sender must do what the message says. If the sender does not do what he or she has indicated, this may cause the receiver to not trust the sender. If the receiver does not trust the sender, then any future message may not be trusted. For example, suppose Jesse tells Samuel he can have next weekend off but then schedules him for work on Saturday. This creates a situation where Samuel is no longer sure that any message Jesse conveys can be trusted. For a message to be understood correctly, the receiver must trust the sender. Many times supervisors are criticized for not telling the truth to subordinates and intentionally lying to them.

Management often has this credibility problem when they tell employees what they are going to do but they never follow through. This happens in cases where management tends to be "faddish" by embracing new management ideas and practices but never following through with any of those processes. Employees get tired of hearing what is going to happen when it never does. As a result, they hear ideas about the latest system or practice and believe if they just ignore it for a while, it will go away.

Emotions

Our emotions act as perceptual filters in communications. We sometimes hear or see what we are emotionally "tuned" to hear or see. The emotional state of either the sender or receiver may enhance the opportunity for a message to misinterpreted. If Shawna had been in an angry emotional state on Monday morning, she may have misinterpreted what Herman had to say to her.

Cognitive dissonance—the internal conflict or anxiety that is caused when people receive messages and information that is incompatible with their value systems, prior decisions, or other information they may have received—is directly connected to emotions.

It is often possible to identify a person's emotional state as you begin to communicate a message. It is important to first deal with the emotion before you send the message. For example, if you approach an employee and judge the person to be frustrated, take time to find out why the employee is frustrated. You may discover that the computer just crashed and the employee lost information she had been working on in the last hour. Allowing her to talk about the frustration and making sure the problem can be solved clears the way for better communication.

Immigrant workers—At times, several different languages may be spoken by workers at one organization. At the Washington, D.C. Hilton, workers speak 36 different languages. This makes it difficult for workers to communicate with one another. Supervisors can't possibly learn all the languages that workers speak. It becomes necessary to find workers with the best English-speaking skills so they can act as interpreters for the supervisor. It also becomes more important than ever for supervisors to demonstrate tasks they expect workers to perform. As you demonstrate tasks, teach the workers some basic English terms.

Not Hearing the Message

People can listen much faster than a person can talk. In fact, the average person speaks at the rate of about 100 to 125 words per minute. The average person can listen three to four times that rate. This gives people a lot of time for their mind to wander during a conversation. They may start to think of the answer they are going to give to what the other person is saying, and they may think of what they did last night or what they are going to do tonight after work. In any case, they may not get your full message because their minds wander.

This problem can be overcome by working to engage the person in communication. A supervisor can do this in a number of ways.

- Ask the employee questions during the conversation.

- Periodically pause and ask the employee to cite examples of what you're talking about.

- Use concrete items—such as a document, picture, equipment, or product—to illustrate a point.

- Request that the person give his or her opinion about the message you're sending.

Nonverbal Communication

Nonverbal communication, or body language as it is sometimes known, affects oral communication in a very important way. Some communication experts estimate that as much as 70 percent of face-to-face communication is done through body language. Body language lets other people know how you are feeling before you ever say a word. In fact, some experts claim that the most important part of a message is delivered by nonverbal communications. Nonverbal communication takes different forms:

Types of Nonverbal Behavior	Examples
Voice	Tone, pitch of the voice, the rate of the words being spoken
Gestures	Finger pointing, moving hands, moving the head
Facial expressions	Frowning, smiling, glaring
Body posture	Slouching, standing, sitting straight
Paralanguage	Loudness, pitch, rate of speech
Oculesics	Eye contact or lack of eye contact
Touch	Shaking hands, pat on the back, putting an arm around a person's shoulder

Types of Nonverbal Behavior	*Examples*
Physical objects	Desk, chair, physical possessions
Dress/physical appearance	Types of clothes, hair, height
Physical space	Use of space including territorial space:
	1 to 1/2 feet is the intimate zone
	1/2 to 4 feet is the personal distance zone
	4 to 12 feet is the social (business) zone
	12 feet outward is the public distance zone
Time	Arriving late or early for an appointment

A clear example about the impact of body language in oral communication can be found in the simple message "hello." We all know that the word "hello" is a greeting. However, the tone of voice, facial expression, touch, and eye contact with the other person can convey many different meanings through this one word. "Hello, I'm glad to see you." "Hello, I'm very busy, now leave me alone." "Hello, I'm glad to meet you." "Hello, I'm not sure what to think about you." "Hello, I really would rather not be here." By now you should begin to understand what we mean about the way body language affects a message.

Be aware of your body language when you communicate with other people. You can judge the message your body language is sending by how the receiver responds to your message. When you have doubts about what your body language is saying, ask the receiver for his or her impressions about your message.

Written Communication

Oral communication is fast and is preferred by most people when delivering a message. It may, however, be the most unreliable if the receiver forgets the original message. If the receiver forgets the message and returns to the sender to hear the message again, the receiver will never get the exact same message. Oral communication only takes place the same way once and that is the first time the message is delivered.

Written communication is an important method for communicating policies and procedures. Employees can refer to the same message and usually interpret it in the same way. It also has an impact that can be more powerful than oral communication. Employees often think that if you put it in writing then it must be important.

One major drawback with written communication is that you don't have an opportunity to observe that two important steps in the eight-step communication process have occurred. First, you don't know if the person has received your messages. Written messages get lost, misplaced, or just plain aren't read. Second, you usually receive much less feedback than occurs in oral communication. You don't know how employees are responding to the message, if it has been interpreted correctly, or if they are acting in accordance with the message.

Communication by writing takes more time than oral communication, but the sender can typically find more precise and correct words to convey a message. Also, a copy can be retained so if the message is lost or forgotten, the receiver can get another copy of the exact message. When writing a message, the following guidelines should be kept in mind:

- Write so the reader will understand by using the appropriate vocabulary for the reader. The reader should not have to use a dictionary to interpret the message.

- Keep sentences short for clarity.

- Use simple words and avoid jargon—a thesaurus is useful for this purpose.

- Use correct spelling and punctuation—the spelling and grammar checks in word processors can help with this.

- Use illustrations, examples, or charts to help with clarity. Many easy-to-use business graphic software programs make it possible even for people without a great deal of artistic ability.

Word processing has made writing better and more efficient, although some would debate this point. It certainly makes it easier to edit and make corrections. Use this to your advantage by asking one or two coworkers to read what you've written. Incorporate their suggestions when it helps improve the clarity of your message.

Electronic Communications

Computers, microchips, and digitalization are changing a supervisor's communication options. Today, a supervisor can rely on a number of sophisticated electronic media to communicate a message. Just 25 years ago the only practical electronic communication medium was the telephone. Now we have e-mail, fax, and videoconferencing. Face-to-face communication has the advantage of high information content—the receiver is provided with both a verbal message and nonverbal message conveyed by the sender's body language. Electronic communication has the advantage of allowing the sender to overcome problems of time and distance.

Electronic communication has also allowed organizations to restructure themselves in some interesting ways. It makes it possible for a supervisor to be responsible for employees who work in widely dispersed geographic areas. A sales manager can have employees working in several different cities or states and communicate with them electronically.

Telephone

Telephones allow us to communicate with people who aren't located in the same building, city, state, or country. Cellular phones furnish the capability to communicate with employees from locations outside the workplace, such as a car, airport, or even the health club. Verbal communications that are transmitted over telephone lines or by cellular phone are high in information content, but a telephone conversation does not provide the receiver with nonverbal messages, except for tone, loudness, pitch, and rate of speech. The receiver can hear the message, interpret the tone of voice of the sender, hear which parts of the message their tone of voice emphasizes, and get a sense of the sender's general attitude about the conversation while they are communicating. A telephone conversation can also allow for instant feedback to the sender and if there is a problem or disagreement it can be cleared up quickly.

Avoid using the telephone for communication when you want to have a conversation with someone in the same building. Note, however, that this doesn't include simple fact gathering or to set up an appointment with a person. It is a less personal form of communication and doesn't have the high content of face-to-face communications. The person you want to talk with may interpret the use of the phone as a way to avoid true communication.

Another method of telephone communications is **voice mail**. Voice mail is a communication method that allows the sender to leave an audio message for a receiver. The receiver can retrieve this message even though he or she may not be in their office. Voice mail does allow the receiver to gather some nonverbal information about the sender's message from their tone of voice and the emphasis the caller places on specific parts of the message. When using voice mail, try to avoid the use of anger, sarcasm, or other negative impressions. The receiver can't process these in a constructive manner without personally talking with you. If you think that your message requires some of those negative impressions, just let the person know you need to talk with them and that they should call.

It should be noted that pagers are not really communication devices; instead, they allow for one-way conveyance of a message. They can be important to supervisors who need to be notified about critical events. However, be careful not to allow pagers to become a crutch for employees that allows them to avoid personal responsibility and acceptance of delegated tasks. Also, some people report a feeling of stress that comes with the use of pagers and cell phones because they are never entirely free of responsibility for what is happening at work.

Electronic Mail

E-mail allows people to communicate with one another through their personal computers and other digital devices. Senders transmit their messages to receivers by typing the message on their computer and addressing it to the receiver's electronic address. Messages can also be sent to several people at one time using e-mail. Many organizations have internal systems for sending e-mail. It is possible to send e-mail to people at other locations all over the world through the Internet.

This is a very popular method of delivering messages instantaneously. The primary advantages of e-mail are the dramatic speed with which a message can be delivered and the convenience in distributing a message to a large number of people at one time. The major disadvantage is the loss of face-to-face contact with people and the difficulty of accurately conveying and interpreting body language. It is a good method for conveying facts. For example, sending messages about meetings, reporting the latest sales figures, announcing a new benefit, or congratulating everyone on reaching a company-wide goal.

E-mail is a very sterile form of communication, and you should keep in mind some cautions when you use it.

- Many organizations have e-mail policies. Find out what these are and follow them. For example, some consider all e-mail to be company property, and any messages may be read by other supervisors and managers.

- Avoid sending e-mail messages on important matters when your message could result in a negative emotional reaction. For example, sending critical e-mail may anger the recipient much more than a direct conversation would. A personal conversation lets you observe the person's reactions. It also lets you make clear anything that could be misinterpreted.

- Carefully consider whether other people should receive copies of a message you send to someone. Generally, any message you send can be forwarded to other people. A message that may be considered as criticism should be kept private.

■ Avoid "flaming." This is a common occurrence with e-mail and involves sending a series of messages that become increasingly negative. For example, someone may make a suggestion and your response is negative. The person returns a negative e-mail to you. You send another e-mail that is even more negative, and the process continues until someone has the good sense to stop. When it appears that flaming is happening, talk with the person either face-to-face or over the telephone to avoid more conflict.

Facsimile (Fax) Machine

The fax machine allows the transmission of documents containing both text and graphics over the telephone lines. In sending a fax, the machine scans and digitizes the document and a receiving fax machine reads the scanned information and reproduces it in hard copy form. Most of the comments important in written communication apply to the use of the fax. Keep these points in mind when using a fax machine:

■ Avoid reading faxes sent to another person. Reading someone else's fax is an invasion of privacy—just like opening someone's mail.

■ Call someone before sending a fax, so they know it's on the way. Include a cover page so others at the receiving end know who the fax is for.

■ Know where the fax is going and who will have access to it before the recipient gets it. Unless it goes directly to a location where only the recipient has access to the machine, don't send private or confidential information.

Disabled workers—Persons that have a disability require special consideration during the communication process. Here are some simple suggestions to keep in mind when communicating with people who have different disabilities.

Speech impairment—Listen carefully to what the person says to you. Ask the person to repeat what he or she has said when you don't understand. Sometimes you might want to use questions that require only a yes or no answer.

Deafness and inability to speak—Some individuals are unable to speak and need some aid. This aid might take the form of sign language, a writing pad, or gestures. Supervisors may not have the time to learn sign language but can pick up simple phrases. When conversing with a person who has an aid or interpreter, talk directly to the person. Look directly at a person who is deaf so they can read your lips. Writing notes to one another takes time but may be the best method for facilitating communication. It may take extra effort from a supervisor to communicate, but it is worth it because of the skills that disabled workers bring to their jobs.

Wheelchairs—Sit when talking with employees who use a wheelchair. This puts you at eye level so neither of you have to strain your neck to see each other. Refrain from leaning or hanging onto a wheelchair because it is an extension of the individual's personal space.

Blind—Individuals with visual impairments should be verbally informed when you enter and leave a room. It is best to remain seated or not move around a room. It is distracting to the visually impaired person, who is trying to focus their attention on you, and partially relies on the direction your voice is coming from to determine your position in a room. Provisions need to be made for written communications to be read to the person or some other reasonable accommodation made.

Mental disability—People with a mental disability may have trouble with concentration and memory. It may be necessary to repeat conversations that you have with a mentally disabled person. Be patient because it might require several repetitions.

Learning disability—Many persons with learning disabilities have difficulty reading. Written communication is not an ideal method to use with workers who have learning disabilities that impede their reading skills. Read the written communications to workers with learning disabilities or make some other reasonable accommodation.

Teleconferencing and Videoconferencing

Teleconferencing and videoconferencing are communication methods that allow a group of people to confer simultaneously using telephone, microwave, or satellite transmissions. Meetings are sometimes held with employees in other buildings or with customers using one of these methods. Teleconferencing—like a telephone call—limits communication because it conveys only oral messages and limits nonverbal messages.

Since teleconferencing is not personal contact, you cannot interpret body language but you can interpret tone or the pitch of the voice and hear the rate of the words being spoken. If the participants of the meeting can see one another, this is known as videoconferencing; many organizations are now using this form of communication. It allows for each party to see the other participants on a television or video screen and it is almost as good as seeing one another in person. It allows for the reading of body language, as long as the camera is pointed to the person doing the talking.

Intranets

Intranets are communication systems that use Internet technology, but they are accessible only by the employees of the organization. The Intranet can be used for directories, product manuals, product specifications, delivery information, or to post minutes from meetings. It is also an effective way for people to share information in organizations and a convenient way for employees to elaborate on documents or projects from different locations in order to get their jobs done.

Communication Flow in Organizations

It is useful to understand communication flow in organizations. The direction of the flow affects communication dynamics and in turn, this affects communication strategies. This section explains the four directions of communication flow.

- **Downward communication.** The most common flow of communication in organizations is downward. It usually starts at or near the top of the organization and filters down through subsequent levels until it reaches its ultimate destination. Downward communication is powerful because it carries the weight of authority in the organization. The major purpose of downward communication is to inform, describe, and direct the flow of work by using policies, procedures, rules, and instructions.

  A common purpose of downward communication is to direct employee performance. Information from the top tends to be general in nature, but as it flows down the organization, it tends to gain more detail. Downward communication is essential and most of the time it is efficient, but it does have some drawbacks. Most of the time, there is no contact between employees at the top and the bottom of the organization. This causes employees at lower levels in the organization to feel isolated from the top. They sometimes feel that their perspective, ideas, and feelings are unimportant because the communication is in one direction. There is some information that can be handled only in downward flow, but it should not be relied upon as the only channel of communication.

- **Upward communication.** Communication flows upward to provide top managers in the organization with information related to attitudes, morale, and the state of mind of employees. It can also generate ideas, suggestions, and general information from lower levels. Upward flow of communication is vital for managers. It provides an accurate view of the organization's operations and performance. Without the upward flow of communication, managers tend to make decisions that are unrealistic and misguided. In order to encourage upward communication, managers and supervisors should create an organizational climate that allows and encourages upward communication. In unhealthy organizations, upward communication is usually stifled and no communication takes place. If this happens, employees will not even try to communicate with upper management—even when serious problems exist.

■ **Horizontal communication.** Communication in a horizontal direction occurs when employees who are on the same level in an organization— but in different units or departments—communicate with one another. In larger organizations, managers sometimes establish procedures to control this flow. However, if functional units within an organization are to achieve their maximum productivity, they must be able to communicate with a minimum of restrictions. The absence of horizontal communication can result in many problems such as:

◆ A lack of cooperation between departments

◆ A feeling of isolation in departments

◆ A development of tunnel vision in departments

◆ An inability to see the total organizational picture

■ **Diagonal communication.** Information that cuts across different levels and different units of the organization is referred to as diagonal communication. This type of communication typically occurs when advice and information is provided by specialists in one department that is vital to managers in another department. For example, managers at almost every level need advice and information from specialists in accounting, finance, and human resources. Improving the flow of diagonal communication dramatically improves organizational performance.

Contingent workers—Communicating with part-time workers is complicated by the schedule the employee works. A supervisor encounters a problem that requires a discussion with an employee, only to discover the employee isn't scheduled to be at work that day.

Part-time employees resent being called at home—this tends to diminish the flexibility that part-time work offers. So what can a supervisor do? Assuming the problem isn't an emergency and can wait for the next time the employee is at work, here are some simple tips:

- Don't rely on your memory; you may forget to talk with the employee until the problem occurs again.

- Send a short e-mail message to the employee requesting that he or she talk with you about the problem.

- Voice mail systems provide another good method for reminding a worker to talk with you.

- Place a sticky note at the employee's work station.

- Some workplaces—retailers, restaurants, and so on—don't have assigned work stations for employees. Supervisors should set up a system for getting messages to employees, like individual mail boxes or one box that employees are to check for envelopes addressed to them.

- Set up a personal computer in a work or break area that has individual file folders for each employee to scan for messages.

Informal Communication

All organizations have an informal communication system called the "grapevine." It coexists with management's formal system of communication. The term applies to all informal communications in an organization.

Although grapevine information is usually sent orally, with the advent of e-mail, an electronic grapevine now exists. The electronic grapevine will probably never totally replace the face-to-face grapevine because many people in organizations do not have access to a computer.

The grapevine works on the principle that everyone has at least one confidant. If a person gets information, they will pass it on to at least one person (sometimes more than one). It does not take long for information to run quickly through an organization. The grapevine also is a method for social interaction among employees and most employees are a part of the grapevine at one time or another. The only employees who do not take part are usually those who are disinterested in their work. The grapevine might involve information such as who was recently promoted, fired, or any layoffs that might be planned.

The grapevine can also be very helpful to supervisors and managers in the form of feedback. Sometimes, management may use the grapevine to run what is known as a "trial balloon." For example, the grapevine might be given information on a policy that management wants to implement but they want to know how employees will react to before it is put into place. Whether or not the policy is implemented might depend on the type of feedback that the grapevine gives them. Sometimes, the grapevine can help translate management's formal orders to the employees. It can actually help make up for management's inability to communicate with employees. However, one of the problems with the grapevine is that it can actually penetrate an organization's security. In some instances, confidential information is released through the grapevine.

The grapevine is a very influential communication method in organizations, both from a positive and negative standpoint. It cannot be done away with and management needs to learn how to deal effectively with it. You as the supervisor need to learn more about the grapevine in your organization—its key participants, how it operates, and what information is transmitted through it. The objective is to reduce the negative effects of the grapevine and the misunderstandings that it creates among employees.

The information contained in the grapevine may not always be complete or accurate. When people hear something, they might change it by adding what they would like to hear or what they think others might want to hear. One of the major problems with the grapevine is **rumor**. Rumors are communicated through the grapevine but may not be complete or accurate because they contain information that is ambiguous and unverified.

Generally, rumors are not accurate and may have undesirable consequences for the organization. The actions taken because of rumors may cause devastating problems. That is why it is desirable for the organization to eliminate them as soon as they are discovered. Rumors should be dealt with firmly and consistently and the best way to do this is to refute rumors with facts.

Here is an example of rumors creating negative consequences: Employees of the XYZ Company heard a rumor that the company was planning to move two of its assembly lines to Mexico. This was partially true, but not entirely accurate. In fact, management planned to move one line to its plant in Mexico, Indiana, to make room for a new product. This type of rumor may have caused valuable employees to leave because they thought think their jobs were not secure. When management related all facts to the employees, they were obviously relieved that their jobs weren't be relocated to Mexico—the country.

Some Ways of Improving Communication Effectiveness

The models for good communication provide the supervisor with some basic guidelines that will improve their communication skills. The following techniques draw from these models and are designed to offer some specific help.

- Think before you speak or write. Ask yourself what you want to convey. Then decide how it can be organized and presented to achieve the best outcome.

- Don't try to communicate when you or the receiver is emotional. Wait until emotions have subsided in either or both parties before you attempt to communicate.

- Listen. Practice active listening skills all the time.

- Be sure your language fits the receiver. Choose words and structure that you are sure the receiver can understand.

- Be sure your actions match the message you delivered. Actions do speak louder than words.

- Get feedback. If necessary ask the receiver what they heard you say or look for nonverbal feedback to make sure the receiver has understood the message.

Ex-offenders—Many ex-offenders have acquired slang and other terms during their time in prison life that can cause communication problems. In addition, prison culture tolerates the use of swearing that isn't acceptable in many workplaces. The use of sexist and racist terms are offensive and need to be eliminated when they are on the job. Cursing and swearing are unpleasant for many workers and should be avoided. Slang that isn't commonly used by other workers distorts the communication process.

Ex-offenders often aren't aware of the communication barriers that their use of language can create. Supervisors need to explain the problems to the ex-offender. Your discussion is likely to be better understood when it is presented as a distortion to communication. Avoid painting it as a moral issue. Describe specific instances where communication has been disrupted. Provide workers with examples about how to improve their communication. Finally, get their agreement to change and work at improving communication.

101

Women and Men Communicating

Dr. Deborah Tannen has done considerable research on the ways in which women and men communicate and the patterns they display when communicating. She makes the point that women and men often approach communication differently. The following list gives examples of communications characteristics of men and women:

- Men emphasize power, status, and independence; women stress rapport, connection, and intimacy.

- Men are more likely than women to take credit for their accomplishments.

- Men frequently complain that women talk on and on about their problems.

- Men criticize women for seeming to apologize all of the time. Men tend to see the phrase "I'm sorry" as a weakness and they perceive a women who uses it as accepting blame—even though she is not to blame.

- Women use the phrase "I'm sorry" to express regret and the fact that they feel bad about a situation.

- Women criticize men for not listening.

- Women ask questions to learn; men fear asking questions because it makes them look ignorant.

- Women tend to speak indirectly; men usually speak more directly.

Dr. Tannen has come to these conclusions on the ways women and men communicate:

- We must recognize that everyone lives in a different communication "world"; women and men simply value different patterns.

- Accept that the way you communicate is only one of many possible ways.

- Learn than people (male or female) will expect, value, and reward communication styles like their own.

- People need to read signals in their interactions with others and adjust their communication styles accordingly.

- People should allow a person with something to contribute to be heard, regardless of their own style preferences.

Effective communication between women and men is important in all organizations. Keeping gender differences from becoming a problem or barrier in organizations requires acceptance and understanding. Further, it requires a commitment from everyone in the organization to communicate adaptively, recognize the differences in styles of communicating, and realize that one style isn't better or worse than another.

By understanding your communication style, you will know yourself better and this will enable you to have a better relationship with others. Once you understand the communication style of your employees, you can communicate with them much more effectively.

Summary

Communication is the transfer of information and understanding from one person to one or more other people. Communication can take several forms, including oral, written, nonverbal, and listening. Listening might be the most difficult method for the supervisor to master. To be effective, organizations must have effective communication in all directions in the organization. An effective two-way communication process involves eight steps: the sender develops an idea, encodes it, and transmits it to a receiver; the receiver receives the idea, decodes it, accepts or rejects it, uses it, and then gives feedback to the sender. You as a supervisor must also pay close attention to the barriers that can affect the communication. There are also new electronic methods of communicating, such as e-mail, fax, voice mail, intranets, and teleconferencing that supervisors can use to be more effective. There are also informal methods that are used in organizations that can help or hurt an organization. You must be aware of the informal communication methods and work to use them in a constructive manner.

Chapter 6

Employee Socialization

Remember your first days at a new job? There is usually a great deal of excitement balanced by apprehension. If you're like many people, you had several thoughts: What is it really going to be like here? Am I going to be able to do this job? Are other workers going to like me? Will I get along with my supervisor? How can I best demonstrate my potential? Added to these questions are more minor but important concerns like: Where do I park? Where do I hang up my coat? When is lunch? Will I have to eat by myself? Where are the restrooms? Where do I get a drink of water? The list could go on for a long time. In fact, it probably brought to mind many other concerns you've had when you first started at a new job.

The more work experience people have, the less concerned they are about these things. Experience shows that everything gets worked out and eventually you find answers to all the questions you have when you start a new job. However, employees with little or no work experience come to work the first day with some fear and concern. Likewise, workers who have been out of the workforce for several years have some apprehensions. The first few days on the job can have a major impact on an employee's perception about an organization. Most people have seen employees start a job and leave within the first few days or weeks. This often happens because their concerns and fears are not addressed.

Evidence shows that employees make a decision within their first week on the job about their long-term employment with an organization. The process of helping a person become and feel like a part of the organization—moving from being an outsider to an insider—is termed **organizational socialization**. An effective socialization process increases employee retention. The supervisor is critical to the success of this process.

This chapter explains how supervisors can positively impact the socialization process. The socialization process has three stages: anticipatory, accommodation, and role management. We'll examine each stage and discuss how the supervisor can assist employees in successfully adapting.

Anticipatory Socialization

Anticipatory socialization begins before the employee starts a job. It shapes the employee's expectations about the organization and the job the employee will do. A new employee gets this information in a variety of ways. Often, it comes through friends, relatives, or acquaintances who work for the organization. Also, newspaper and magazine articles, brochures, catalogs, annual reports, and Internet sites about the organization are typical sources of information.

All contacts the employee has with the organization's managers and supervisors before starting the job are important sources of anticipatory socialization. This contact begins during the recruitment process and continues through the job offer and subsequent contacts.

The Interview Process

Strong evidence suggests that employees are going to be more satisfied with an organization when the interview process uses an approach known as **realistic job previews** (RJP). RJP provides the recruit with a realistic appraisal of the organization and the job. This includes telling the person about the positives and negatives. Doing so establishes a set of realistic expectations. Thus, the new employee isn't as likely to be disappointed or disillusioned when starting a new job.

Supervisors play an important role in the RJP process. You have the most realistic understanding of the new job because you are closer to the day-to-day activities than other managers in the organization. During job interviews, balance the questions you ask the recruit with information about the job. It is tempting to oversell the job to a recruit who appears to be a good prospect. However, a disgruntled employee who lacks motivation is difficult to deal with. Also, it wastes your time to recruit a new employee only to have them quit in a few days, weeks, or months—forcing you to repeat the recruitment process.

Following are a few helpful suggestions to keep in mind when using the RJP approach:

■ You shouldn't be pessimistic or negative in an RJP—just be factual. If recruits expect to be working with the most up-to-date computer equipment, they aren't going to be happy to start a job and find that this isn't the case. However, computer equipment that is only a year old shouldn't be pictured as obsolete.

- Don't overload recruits with information about the job. Discussing specific facts about a product or customers is likely to be distracting and result in the person losing interest in what you're saying. Highlight the most critical parts of the job, particularly the parts that seem to be most important to a recruit. A person who appears highly social should be told about opportunities to work as a team.

- There are some things that can't be fully explained or understood until the person starts the job, such as a difficult coworker or customer that the person must work with.

Younger workers—Beloit College developed and distributed a "Mindset List" to its faculty at the beginning of the 1999 school year. Some of the facts about students starting college include the following list of what has occurred in their lifetime:

- There has always been a woman on the Supreme Court, and women have always been traveling in space.

- They have never had to worry about the packaging of Tylenol.

- Strikes by highly paid athletes have been a routine part of professional athletics.

- They don't think there is anything terribly futuristic about 2001 and were never concerned about 1984.

- They were born and grew up with Microsoft, IBM PCs, in-line skates, fax machines, and film on disks.

- John Lennon and John Belushi have always been dead.

- They have spent half their lives watching Bart Simpson.

These facts provide an interesting insight for supervisors. Young people have a very different perspective about life than many adults have. Their interests are different, their assumptions are different, and they don't always understand the perspective of adults who find the preceding list of facts intriguing. Supervisors should encourage other employees to get to know younger workers and understand that they approach life from a different mindset. This difference shouldn't be perceived as a barrier to helping young people become part of the organization. Rather, it should be perceived as a challenge and approached as an opportunity to gain another viewpoint about life.

Preparation for the Job

A supervisor has additional opportunities to continue the anticipatory process. Once a job offer has been made and accepted, the supervisor can contact the employee and welcome the person to the organization. Another means to help socialize employees is to call them a few days before they start a job. Provide them with information to help prepare them for the first day on the job.

- **Start time**—Let the person know what date they are to start the job. In some cases, this date may have been negotiated with the human resources (HR) department or another manager. In this case, simply confirm the information. You should also set a time for the person to come to work.

- **Meeting place**—Inform the employee where to meet you. Even if the person is to report to the HR department, plan to meet the person so you can provide a personal welcome. This action sends a message that you are interested in the employee.

- **Dress**—It's embarrassing to show up for work dressed the wrong way. You stand out like a sore thumb and people remember you for weeks (or even months) because of how you looked that first day. Brief the person about dress standards. In some cases, the employee may be required to wear a uniform, and arrangements should be made for them to get one prior to their start date. In some jobs, the person may need to wear safety equipment and advance preparations must be made— prescription safety glasses are one example.

- **Parking**—Inform employees about parking locations if they plan to drive a car to work. This may include parking regulations and hours that the parking lot opens and closes.

- **Lunch**—A friendly gesture is to invite the person to lunch the first day. This is one more step in making the person feel a part of the group. It can help break the ice with experienced workers if you invite a few of them to lunch at the same time as the new person.

- **First day plans**—Provide a general description of the first day's agenda. This helps employees mentally prepare for the day's activities. For example, spending the first day in training has a different focus than actually working.

- **General questions**—Make sure that employees have an opportunity to ask any other questions they might have. Follow through and find answers to any questions that you can't immediately answer.

Employees are often forced to start a job with none of the previous information provided. The only contact they usually have with the organization is the phone call confirming a job offer. These employees begin work with doubts, concerns, and apprehensions about many small things. This results in their feeling like outsiders. Taking time to talk and prepare employees for work before they start the job begins the process of making them feel like insiders.

Accommodation Process

The accommodation process is the stage of socialization where employees become active participants and develop basic job competence. It may last a few days or a few weeks. More organizations focus on this process than on the anticipatory stage of socialization. It begins with the supervisor making plans for the employee to start the job.

Preparation

Everything should be ready for employees to begin working the first day they start the job. This makes them feel wanted, needed, and cared about. It makes the process of becoming an insider much easier. This means that the supervisor should carefully plan an employee's job start and consider it as important as any other primary duty.

- **Parking**—Employees that drive cars face the problem of parking before they can begin work. This is particularly important in an organization that has controlled parking—guards, keyed automatic gates, or assigned spaces.

- **Prepared work area**—The preparation of the work area varies greatly from one organization to the next. In an office environment, it means having a desk and chair ready for the employee. Also, phones, computers, and supplies should be at the desk and ready for the employee to begin work. In a non-office environment, it may mean that a locker is made ready for the person to store his or her belongings.

- **Identification badge**—Order the badge so that employees have a badge on the date they start. A personalized badge sends a strong signal that the person is now an insider. Waiting until the employee starts the job before ordering a badge delays the accommodation process.

- **Safety apparel, tools, and equipment**—The most important aspect to consider when employees begin a job is that they are protected from potential injuries. All safety apparel should be ready for them to wear the minute they enter the workplace. Likewise, having the proper tools and equipment demonstrates that you expect them to immediately contribute to the organization.

■ **Access codes and keys**—Technology has improved security and access to property and information. As a result, employees often need access codes to computers (like network and e-mail passwords), telephones, copy machines, postage meters, doors, and so on. In many cases, doors are still accessed with metal keys, so copies need to be made for the employee.

You may need to do other things to prepare for a new employee to start work. It is important to recognize that the better prepared you are, the more likely a new employee is going to feel like an insider.

Older workers—Many older workers change careers when they enter retirement. Often they choose to work at a lower paying job that provides them flexibility and less responsibility than they had before retiring. For example, a retired teacher might choose to work as a library aide. A new career results in a change in status. The status held by older workers in previous careers are typically derived from their skills and experience—which isn't as pertinent to their new job. The respect and deference that they once received from fellow employees is not provided by their new coworkers. This is frequently a difficult adjustment for older workers to make.

Supervisors can help older workers fit in better by helping them to understand the natural change in status that occurs when people change careers. Discuss their feelings about the change. Encourage them to understand why other workers view them differently and not to interpret this as disrespect. Other workers should be made aware that older employees have skills and experience that are not always present with new employees. They should be urged to take advantage of this experience when possible. For example, the teacher-turned-library aide could be consulted about issues and problems related to services that the library provides to educators.

Orientation

The first day of work for employees should involve an orientation by the supervisor. An orientation should provide employees with basic information about the workplace, facilities, and people they are going to work with. The focus should be on helping the employee feel like a part of the organization. It should be designed in such a way that employees' concerns and apprehensions about the new job are greatly diminished. You can do many simple things to help this happen.

- **Welcome and agenda.** Meet the employee as soon as he or she gets to work. Take them somewhere private and welcome them to the organization. Describe the day's agenda so there are no doubts about what the person is expected to do the first day, and encourage the person to take notes. It is also helpful to have checklists and guides that list the information that is going to be covered during the day.

- **Workplace information.** Show the person the assigned work area, desk, and so on. Provide access codes, keys, parking passes, and other basic items that should have been prepared in advance.

- **Tour of the facility.** Take the employee on a tour of the facility. Keep in mind that this should help the person know how to satisfy basic needs common to all work facilities. For example, this includes water fountains, restrooms, coat racks, lockers, break areas, drink dispensers, and supplies.

- **Introductions.** Introduce new employees to people they will be working with. However, keep in mind that a multitude of faces and names becomes difficult to remember. It helps to make these introductions gradually. The first day should focus mainly on presenting the employee to coworkers in the same department. Useful tools that can help employees remember names, positions, and responsibilities are organization charts and employee rosters.

- **Rules and regulations.** Review standard procedures—it is helpful to have a checklist for this. Certain jobs require special safety clothing. Working with chemicals demands a variety of clothing, depending on how toxic the chemicals are. Hard hats and steel-toed safety shoes are required on some jobs to avoid injury. Working near machinery may require you to avoid wearing jewelry or loose clothing that could get caught in mechanical parts. Discuss safety policies and procedures so that new employees recognize how important these are.

- **Work schedule.** Review the days and times that the employee is expected to work. In cases where work schedules change weekly, explain how these changes are made. For example, seniority and class schedules for students still in school must be given priority in setting the work schedule.

- **Breaks.** Different companies have different policies for taking breaks. In one, you might be able to take your breaks whenever you want to,

111

as long as you're responsible about it. In another, you might have to take your breaks only at specified times. In a factory, an entire line might take breaks together. Many organizations prohibit smoking on the job or restrict it to a smoking room. Let new employees know about the relevant policies for your organization.

- **Phone system.** Office phone systems can be incredibly complex and intimidating, with rows of buttons and lights, dozens of features, and as much wiring as a small computer. Explain the basic features employees need in order to answer, place, and transfer calls, and to access voice mail. Brief the employee on how to greet callers. Also, explain company policy on the use of the phone system for personal calls.

- **Basic equipment.** Equipment, such as copy machines and postage meters, is basic to many work sites. Demonstrate how this equipment is used. Inform employees about policies related to the use of the equipment—like entering a department code. Tell them who they contact if there are problems or they need additional instruction.

- **Computer system.** Many organizations have personal computers for all employees. This often includes e-mail, group collaboration software, and intranet access. Prep workers on the basics of these systems and describe further training that they will receive.

- **Job review.** The most important function of an orientation is to give employees a basic understanding of their job. This frequently begins with a review of the employee's job description. Then you begin the process of on-the-job training. More details about this process appear in chapter 7. Make new employees aware of goals and objectives and how their new job supports these.

- **Follow through.** During the first few days on the job, keep in close contact with new employees. Because of time constraints, it is tempting to limit the time spent with new employees. However, an investment of time at this point in the employee's socialization process can pay off with a happier and more productive employee in the long term.

Welfare-to-work employees—Basic details about getting to the workplace that most supervisors take for granted are not common knowledge among most welfare recipients. Administrators of welfare-to-work programs around the country cite the need to help welfare-to-work participants solve very basic problems. Only 6 percent of welfare recipients have automobiles. Child-care needs are cited as another major issue. Even the basic matters of dress codes, work ethic, and punctuality are often unfamiliar to these inexperienced workers.

Many organizations find that a solution to this problem is for supervisors to take an active role in helping workers deal with transportation and child care. Another effective method has been to develop mentoring programs. Identify some experienced and reliable workers that would be willing to mentor new employees. Orient them to problems that welfare-to-work employees are likely to face. Make it clear to these mentors that their role isn't to supervise but rather assist by coaching the new workers on basic job skills.

Role Management

Role management is the third stage in the socialization process, and it involves the employee resolving **role conflicts**. These issues may arise because home and work lives conflict with each other. For students, it can be complicated further by trying to balance school, home, and work. Role management also requires employees to balance conflicts between their roles and the roles of coworkers. In addition, they must balance the roles between their workgroup and other groups in the organization.

Supervisors often need to address some common issues during the role management stage, and some of these issues appear in the following sections. Because these are sensitive areas, some supervisors try to ignore them. However, the issues should be discussed with employees to prevent the problems from erupting into a more serious situation where the employee leaves or needs to be terminated. Some of the matters that we cover may seem quite basic or what some people might call "common sense." Just keep in mind that common sense isn't always so common. Surprisingly, many people are raised with little or no instruction about dress and grooming issues. At times, it becomes necessary for the supervisor to provide some practical instruction on these matters.

Dress

Dress for work has changed dramatically in the last decade, becoming decidedly more casual. Almost three-fourths of all organizations have at least one casual dress day a week. But even if dress is more casual, it's important to remember that clothes influence the way people view your employees. These perceptions affect how well an employee is accepted by coworkers and customers. A supervisor must sometimes step in and provide direction to employees about their dress. Following are some general guidelines to consider when talking with employees about their dressing habits.

- **Dress codes.** Many organizations have official and unofficial dress codes. An official dress code is one that should be followed by all employees without failure. Call a dress code violation to an employee's attention as soon as it occurs. Ignoring the problem won't make it go away and may in fact send a signal to employees that they can continue to dress in an unacceptable manner. Unofficial dress codes can affect work assignments, pay raises, and promotions because of the perceptions that managers and coworkers develop about an employee. Tell workers about informal dress codes and problems that might result from violating them. For example, a casual dress code may not prohibit wearing T-shirts with phrases on them but the phrases may offend other people.

- **Appropriate dress.** There are some very nice clothes that are not appropriate for the workplace. Clothes a person would wear for a night on the town probably aren't appropriate for the workplace. Neither are tight-fitting clothes, low-cut dresses, unbuttoned shirts, short skirts, and neon-hued outfits. It is sometimes embarrassing for a supervisor to approach a worker about these problems, but the employee needs to know when their style of dress isn't appropriate. In some cases, you might find it difficult to talk with an employee of the opposite sex about inappropriate clothing. When this happens, it might be good to have a colleague who is the same gender as the employee to sit in on the discussion.

- **Neatness.** Even casual dress must be appropriate. Clothes should be in good shape, with no tears or stains. They should be clean and neatly pressed. One problem with casual dress is that employees can become lax about these things. It is the supervisor's responsibility to call these problems to the employee's attention and request that they dress more neatly.

- **Uniforms.** Some businesses require employees to wear uniforms at work. This typically occurs in situations where employees have frequent contact with the public and the uniform projects a positive image for the organization. Company standards usually specify how the uniform is to be worn, whether uniforms may change from one day to the next, and that uniforms must be clean and neat. Supervisors need to enforce the guidelines on uniforms because they often affect customer's perceptions about employees.

Immigrant workers—The importance that American society places on timeliness is not common to many cultures. It may be necessary for a supervisor to teach the employee the basic skills needed to be timely. Explain the importance of timeliness in our culture. Describe your expectations and make it clear the employee must follow a time schedule. Assess the employees' abilities to tell time and train them to do this if they don't have this skill. Teach them how to use a calendar, if necessary, and provide them with an inexpensive one.

Cultural mores are difficult to change immediately and it may be necessary to exercise more patience. Always discuss the reason an immigrant worker is late or tardy each time it occurs. Determine the exact reason for the problem, coach them how to overcome the problem, and once again explain why they need to follow their work schedule. Timeliness is such a basic element of our culture that supervisors commonly respond by firing the employee who repeatedly has this problem. However, persistence on the part of a supervisor can help the worker overcome this cultural difference and become a reliable employee.

Grooming and Hygiene

Grooming habits and hygiene are subjects that some supervisors prefer to avoid. This is because the subjects are rather personal and can seem intrusive. However, they can have a major effect on the impressions that other workers and customers have about employees. In some cases—like body odor—it is very offensive to work around a fellow employee. Following are some common hygiene issues and tips that you might use in handling this type of problem.

- **Body odor.** It's not pleasant to work with someone who has body odor. It is even less so when you are a customer being served by an employee with body odor. Supervisors may get complaints from other workers about an employee with body odor—sometimes you smell it yourself. You need to act on this quickly. Explain to the employee that there have been complaints and action needs to be taken. Talk bluntly about the need to bathe or shower daily and the use of deodorant.

- **Bad breath.** Another odor problem is bad breath. Employees and customers are going to avoid a worker with bad breath. Talk with the worker about how frequently they brush their teeth. They should do so at least once a day, and when possible after each meal. You could also suggest that they gargle with mouthwash.

■ **Shaving.** Facial hair can be a distraction in the work setting. A court decision determined that a policy against facial hair may be unconstitutional. However, at many jobs you're expected to remain clean-shaven—in some cases this may be an informal policy. Talk with employees about beard stubble, mustaches, and beards, and let them know what the formal or informal policy may be. In food preparation or serving jobs, employees may be required to wear hair nets to cover beards. Make sure this policy is enforced. Sometimes it is necessary to remind employees that wear a beard or mustache to groom them and keep them neatly trimmed.

■ **Hair.** A variety of problems may arise related to a worker's hair. Extremely long hair on either sex may be considered unconventional in some organizations. Long hair worn loose may be a safety problem in certain jobs. It's also a hygienic problem in jobs such as food preparation and serving, for which employees may be expected to wear a hair net. An employer's control over hair length is limited when health and safety issues aren't involved. However, it may be important to remind employees that hair that is neatly trimmed, washed, and styled adds to a pleasant appearance.

■ **Fingernails.** Long or unclean fingernails can present problems in some organizations. Long fingernails may interfere in the operation of equipment and in some cases, they can endanger an operator. Clean fingernails are critical in organizations dealing with food and health services. Discuss standards related to fingernails with an employee who isn't following them and suggest practical ways, like using a brush or trimmers, that might help them.

■ **Makeup.** Makeup can improve a person's looks. Natural colors that compliment skin tone are appropriate. Bold colors, such as hot pinks and bright blues, are rarely appropriate in the workplace. Many department and drug stores have cosmetic counters where consultants help customers learn to use makeup in a flattering manner. You might want to suggest to an employee that they use this service.

■ **Body piercing.** Pierced earrings for women are almost the norm these days; and even for men, they have become more acceptable. Other types of piercing—lips, eyebrows, and noses, for example—are less acceptable. Body piercing may be considered inappropriate in some workplaces, but reasonable in others. Advise employees about what is proper in your organization. Exceptions to organizational policies are reasonable if piercing represents an employee's cultural or religious beliefs.

■ **Colognes and perfumes.** The smell from colognes and perfumes can be pleasant, but too much of either is offensive to many people. Overpowering odor is not appropriate in the workplace, no matter what the source. Some people have allergies to colognes and perfumes. When this becomes a problem for other workers or customers, the supervisor needs to take action. Explain the problem to the worker and ask that cologne or perfume not be used when the person is at work.

Special Hygiene Concerns

In some jobs, employees' own health, as well as that of customers or patients, depends on good hygienic practices. For example, health care organizations and food preparation facilities are required by law to enforce certain sanitary practices. Following is a list of the most commonly required hygienic practices.

■ Hair nets are sometimes required for jobs in food service or preparation.

■ Washing hands with soap and water after using the restroom is a requirement for food servers and preparers. This helps protect you from disease or from spreading germs and is particularly important in jobs where you prepare or serve food. Employees should be instructed to use soap and lather their hands for 10 to 15 seconds. Regulations require workers in health occupations to wash their hands each time they work with a patient.

■ Gloves help control exposure to germs in food preparation and health occupations.

■ Aprons may be required in food preparation jobs to prevent germs, dirt, or other foreign particles on your clothes from getting into the food.

Many occupations require additional precautions. You should become familiar with the hygiene practices required for your job. In some cases (such as food preparation jobs), there will be state and local laws that govern hygiene.

Absenteeism and Tardiness

An organization can't operate without dependable workers. A supervisor must be able to rely on employees coming to work every day on time. When a worker is late or absent, it causes many problems. In fact, employers list absenteeism as one of the major reasons for firing employees.

Consider this example: George supervises the morning shift in a fast food restaurant. The phone rings at 6 A.M. "George, this is Lee. My car won't start so I won't be at work today."

117

Meanwhile the breakfast crowd has started to arrive in the dining room. Several cars are lined up at the drive-through window. Lee has created a variety of problems by not coming to work that are typical, regardless of the organization.

Absenteeism reduces productivity. Fewer workers on the job means the organization produces fewer goods or cannot serve as many customers. In some instances the amount of goods and services remains the same but the quality is lowered. In addition, customer service suffers. Customers aren't served as well as they should be when not enough workers are present. For instance, if a worker in a production job is absent, a customer's shipment may not be made on time because there isn't enough help.

Absenteeism also creates problems for supervisors. Worker absence means supervisors must rearrange work schedules and plans. Another worker may have to fill in. Problems created by one absence usually continue throughout the day. Supervisors pick up the slack, which may make them angry. How the supervisor reacts depends largely on the reason and frequency of the absence.

In addition, absence and tardiness create problems for coworkers. Everyone must work harder when another worker is absent. A person who had the day off may be called into work. Someone who just finished a shift may be asked to stay and work a double shift. They, too, may be angry at the absent employee.

Workers who are tardy find that the problems they cause impede their socialization. The group begins to resent them and exclude them from group activities. Because absence and tardiness cause so many problems, it is one of the most common reasons for employees being terminated. The most common reasons for missing work are illness, dealing with family issues, taking care of personal business, and escaping stress. Supervisors can help employees overcome these and other problems through proper coaching. Often the problem can be resolved by talking with the employee and warning him or her about the consequences. When this fails, you can discuss some other practical solutions with the employee.

Disabled workers—Supervisors and coworkers can use some simple techniques to assist a blind employee. Use a normal tone of voice and identify yourself by name so the employee can locate you. Tell the person when you are leaving. Offer a blind person your arm to guide him or her to a location in the workplace—tell the employee which arm you're offering because it helps the person become oriented. When you are walking with a blind person, do so at a normal pace and alert the person to obstructions in the way.

Help the employee find a seat by placing his hand on the back of a chair and allowing him to seat himself. Most importantly, don't pity the employee; treat her with the same respect you would any person. Treating them like other employees, whenever possible, helps them feel a part of the organization.

Lifestyle

A lifestyle is made up of the habits and activities people engage in during their day-to-day living, and it includes what they eat, when and how long they sleep, and how they spend their time. Doctors and scientists know that a person's lifestyle can affect the amount of stress in the individual's daily life. Many of the reasons people miss work are directly related to their lifestyles. You have to be careful about not dictating an employee's lifestyle. Instead, talk with them about issues that can cause absence and tardiness.

- **Get a good night's sleep.** Most people need six to eight hours of sleep each night. In fact, some psychologists believe that people may need as many as nine to ten hours of sleep each night and that not getting enough sleep reduces work effectiveness as much as going to work drunk. People rest better when they sleep on a regular schedule. Many young people make the mistake of partying on work nights, which means they get less sleep, then skip work or arrive late the next morning.

- **Eat well.** People should eat well-balanced meals on a regular schedule and avoid too much junk food. They need to consume plenty of fruits and vegetables. Individuals who follow this advice are less likely to be ill.

- **Exercise regularly.** Most jobs in the United States are service- and information-related and don't require much exercise. Regular exercise keeps people in top physical and mental condition, and helps release job-related stress.

- **Smoking.** A great deal of medical evidence says that smoking is hazardous to both smokers and nonsmokers. Many organizations offer incentives and help for employees who want to quit smoking.

- **Drinking.** Alcohol can cause health problems. The more alcohol you drink, the more you may damage your body. Drinking to excess reduces a person's performance on the job the next day. Drinking during or before work is often cause for dismissal.

- **Drugs.** Illegal drugs are harmful to the body and mind. People should not take any drugs unless they are specifically prescribed by a physician.

119

Policies on illegal drug use vary among organizations. If your employees test positive for certain drugs, some organizations give them a choice of entering a rehabilitation program or being fired. Other employers simply fire them outright. Drug use increases health problems and makes functioning on a daily basis difficult or impossible.

■ **Keep good company.** Personal relationships affect a person's work. For instance, if friends don't work, they may want your employee to adapt to their schedule, which may leave the person too tired for work the next day. Employees should establish a priority for work and social activities. At an extreme, associating with the wrong people may get a person into trouble with the law. Employers *do not* appreciate workers who miss work because they are in jail.

■ **Socialize with coworkers.** We all need time to socialize with friends and acquaintances. Coworkers often become our best friends because we spend so much time with them. Relationships that are developed with coworkers typically can be positive. People want to come to work so they can see their friends. They definitely don't want to let them down by not being at work when they should.

These ideas can help employees when offered in a good-natured manner. Make it clear that the absenteeism or tardiness isn't acceptable. However, the suggestions related to lifestyle are just suggestions and in no way an attempt to tell the employees how to live their life. Rather, it is designed to help them overcome the tardiness and absenteeism problems.

Common Sense Ideas

There are also many "common sense" reasons that employees are late and absent from work. Better planning can help them do a better job about being dependable. Talking with employees about these matters and exploring solutions may help them resolve their problems.

Reliable Transportation

Transportation problems can occur even if a person owns a new car. However, workers can take some basic steps to ensure they have reliable transportation.

■ A car can be kept in good operating condition through regular maintenance. When a person suspects car trouble, try starting the car a couple of hours before work. This will give you time to find another method of transportation if you need to. Cold or wet days can mean problems starting a car, so check the car out early.

■ Know public transportation schedules. Employees should be encouraged to keep a schedule of the public transportation available to them. This is also a good backup plan for use when a car doesn't work.

■ Arrange with a coworker for a ride. Help employees find coworkers who live near them and have a reliable car. An agreement can be made to share a ride if either worker has car trouble. They may want to carpool with other coworkers.

■ Carpools may be organized. Workers can check with friends or advertise in the classifieds for someone who can share a ride to work with them. Some human resource departments have agreements with other organizations to promote car pools and help identify people who work in nearby buildings.

■ Walk or bicycle. Some employees may want to consider finding housing near the workplace. Even if they live two to four miles from the job, they can still walk or ride a bike in good weather.

■ If all else fails, call a cab. A taxi is costly, but it usually won't cost as much as losing a day's pay. And it's certainly less costly than losing a job. Advise employees that they might want to consider this option when all else fails.

Contingent workers—Some temporary workers find it difficult to fit into an organization when they are assigned a desk containing the belongings of a permanent worker. These personal items are a constant reminder that the worker is just temporary. When you have an employee who takes a leave of absence lasting several weeks, you might ask them to store their personal belongings in a drawer. Invite a temporary worker who will be with the organization for several weeks to put personal items, like photos or plants, at his or her desk.

Family Care

The most common reason employees need someone to care for family members is when they have young children. However, they may be caring for an elderly parent or a disabled spouse. Many organizations have implemented family-friendly policies that aid employees in arranging their schedules to accommodate family care. Supervisors should use these policies to help improve an employee's dependability. You can give workers the following practical advice.

121

■ Plan for reliable dependent care. You can often do this by selecting a good primary provider. However, problems can arise with primary care and the employee should develop a contingency plan in case bad weather closes a daycare center or the dependent becomes ill.

■ Hire good aides. Encourage employees to choose a reliable babysitter or home health aide. Lists of these aides are another resource that some HR departments have. Also, some communities have social agencies that can recommend trained and certified aides. An aide's reliability can be checked by asking for the person's references. These should come from people who have employed the aide in their own homes.

■ Select a good care center. Ask for references. Learn about their policy for closing. What is their policy if a child, parent, or spouse is ill? Some centers will now care for children when they are ill. Employees may pay more for centers with this service, but in the long run they may pay for themselves because the employee gets paid and doesn't endanger his or her job by being absent.

■ Have an emergency plan. Encourage employees to find a friend or relative who is willing to care for their dependents for one or two days in case of emergency. The best plan is to have at least two people who are willing to do this.

Use Scheduling Aids

Employees should have a calendar and use it to keep track of their work schedule. Some organizations pay for inexpensive calendars so that employees can record their schedules. Employees may forget to write down their schedule from a posted schedule. A tool that helps overcome this problem is a written schedule with copies for all employees. Encourage employees to give you at least a one-week notice for any personal appointments—like doctor and dental appointments—that may conflict with work. Be cooperative in developing schedules that accommodate employee wishes and needs. This increases the likelihood that employees will show up to work when scheduled.

Getting to Work on Time

Late workers cause the same problems for an employer as absent workers. There are reasonable causes for being late; however, more than once a month or four or five times a year is considered excessive by some employers. When employees develop this type of pattern, you need to discuss it with them. Here are some suggestions to help them accomplish this.

■ Employees should be encouraged to use a reliable alarm clock. If you have an electric clock, make sure it has a backup power source or use a wind-up clock as well in case the electricity shuts off. You can get portable or travel alarms that are battery-powered for less than an hour's wage. You can't afford to lose a job because you don't get to work on time. Don't rely on someone else to get you up.

■ Get up earlier if their current wake-up time isn't working. They need to allow more time to get ready and get to work. In fact, advise them that arriving a few minutes early is beneficial because this cushion of time helps them mentally prepare for the day and reduce stress. Often, this problem is attributable to lifestyle and you may want to review these same issues with the frequently tardy employee.

■ Plan for special conditions. There will be days when employees need more time to get to work. For example, poor weather conditions usually slow traffic. Encourage them to plan an earlier wake-up time so they will still arrive on time.

Notifying the Supervisor

Even the best planning won't cover all possible problems that can keep employees from getting to work. Your work as a supervisor can proceed more smoothly the more quickly an employee informs you that he or she is going to be absent or late.

Most supervisors have a personal preference about how they want to be notified. Some want employees to call them as soon as they are aware that they'll be absent or late. It doesn't matter to them whether they are called at home or work. Other supervisors only want to be called at the workplace. Make sure every employee knows what you expect.

Inform employees about the consequence of their absence or tardiness. They should be aware that they are in danger of violating policies on the number of absences or times they are late. Most organizations have policies that require disciplinary action for frequent or unexcused absences, for absences that occur a day before or after a holiday, and for not calling in or taking off to do personal business. The discipline may range from a verbal warning for the first offense to immediate discharge—although the latter is extreme in a labor market where workers are scarce.

Supervisors recognize a pattern that develops among some employees. It's most common among younger workers. The syndrome becomes apparent when a worker frequently calls in sick on Fridays and Mondays. This worker is eager to start the weekend, and when Monday rolls around, is either too tired or needs time off to do personal business. At times, you may want to call this to the employee's attention and explain that it jeopardizes their relationship with you and other workers because you can't depend on them.

Reliable workers are essential to an effective operation. That's why good attendance and punctuality are important to employers. Many organizations encourage good attendance and punctuality through raises, bonuses, and promotions. Encourage your employees to use a little planning and self-discipline to help them become dependable and valuable workers.

Ex-offenders—These workers can sometimes have a difficult time making the transition from the structure of prison to independent living. They may have trouble with the self-discipline required to get to work each day and be on time. The first day the ex-offender begins work, a supervisor should meet and discuss the issues of attendance and punctuality. Discuss the worker's plans for transportation, child care, waking up in the morning, and planning their activities for the week. You may need to suggest that they buy an alarm clock or watch. Give them an inexpensive calendar and ask them to write down their work schedule each week.

Interpersonal Problems

Everyone likes to be respected for skills, knowledge, or other contributions to the organization. This is a process that each employee must work through in an attempt to establish their role in the group. Coaching by a supervisor can sometimes help employees who have trouble fitting in. The following list gives some simple advice that you can give employees to help them fit into the organization.

- **Become involved in social activities.** Take lunch breaks with your coworkers. Join employee recreational and social activities.

- **Don't try to change everything.** New employees are treated like "the new kids on the block" when they start a job. Employees will fit in better when they first understand the organization before suggesting changes.

- **Be direct.** Let coworkers know when they have done something that bothers you. Most people want to know when there is a problem.

- **Don't be a complainer or a whiner.** Make sure your problem is important before you discuss it with others.

■ **Avoid gossip.** Don't listen to other people gossiping about coworkers. More important, never gossip about others. When you gossip, people wonder what you say about them and often avoid you.

■ **Be positive and supportive.** Listen to the ideas of other people. When someone makes a mistake, don't criticize. It's irritating to have someone else point out a mistake. When you realize you've made a mistake, admit it and try to do better next time.

■ **Show appreciation.** Be sure you thank a coworker who does something to make your job easier. Let coworkers know you appreciate their contributions to the team. People like to be recognized and praised.

■ **Share credit when it's deserved.** Take credit for the work you do. When other coworkers assist you, make sure you credit them. People feel they have been taken advantage of if someone else takes credit for their work.

■ **Return favors.** A coworker may help you out by exchanging a day off with you. Return that favor. A sure way to make people dislike you is to only take and never give.

■ **Live in the present.** Avoid talking about the way things used to be. People don't want to hear about how great your old job was or how great former coworkers were.

■ **Ask for help and advice when you need it.** People like to feel needed. Your coworkers can be a great resource. When you aren't sure what to do, they can give you advice and assistance.

■ **Avoid battles.** Let coworkers in conflict work out their own differences. Don't take sides in their arguments. This is a sure way to develop problems with your coworkers. When you take sides, other people usually resent your interference.

■ **Follow group standards.** Every group has standards. For example, they may take a coffee break at 9:15. Stop work and go on break with them if you are able. These group standards help build a team. Most standards are not major and require little effort to follow.

■ **Take an interest in your coworker's jobs.** People like positive attention. Taking an interest in another worker's job gives that person positive attention. It also helps you better understand how your team works together.

Most relationships between employees develop without serious problems. However, supervisors sometimes must help resolve problems, or in some cases, issue warnings to employees. Take action before serious problems develop.

Summary

The socialization process is key to making employees feel like insiders in the organization. Employees are happier, more productive, and stay on the job longer when they feel like insiders. An effective supervisor needs to spend time and devote attention to new workers to help them feel like insiders. This personal investment in employees provides a long-term payoff in a well-functioning team that contributes to the organization's success.

Chapter 7

Training Employees

Knowing how to learn is probably the most critical skill for job success. People spend the early years of their lives learning in school, which provides a structured approach to learning. Sometimes people think they only learn when they go to school, but humans learn in a variety of ways. We watch other people doing something, and we learn. We ask other people how to do something, and we learn. We read books and magazines, and we learn. We can learn in a number of ways besides formal schooling. This chapter is designed to help supervisors better understand the learning process and how they can assist employees in developing the knowledge and skills to do their jobs successfully.

Learning Is the Key to Success

Lifelong learning is a key to success in the new labor market. Management experts today emphasize the learning organization, which is one that creates a climate that helps employees learn from their experiences, both individually and collectively. Supervisors are a key part of building a learning organization.

The Supervisor As Instructor

A supervisor often needs to teach employees a skill. You might call this role instructor, trainer, or coach. We'll use all of these terms interchangeably when talking about the supervisor in an instructional role. The following list gives several reasons why a supervisor might need to help employees master new knowledge and skills.

- **Orientation of new employees.** When new employees begin a job, they have to learn a great many things. In fact, this is such an important process that all of chapter 6 is devoted to this topic.

- **New task assignments.** Employees generally only need to perform a set of tasks common to a job, but occasionally, they get an assignment that requires learning new skills. For example, a cashier in a retail store may one night be required to close out the register in his or her area. This might entail processing a cash register report and taking the report to a manager.

- **Correct a deficiency.** There are times that an employee has been adequately trained for only certain parts of a job. Perhaps, though, the supervisor doing the training wasn't thorough enough. This means that employees must be trained to do those tasks that weren't included in the original training process. An example might be hotel housekeepers who were taught how to stock the bathroom, but who were never shown how to fold the toilet paper and tissues.

- **Change of jobs.** A change of jobs requires that employees be trained on the new tasks and activities required for successful performance. A stock clerk promoted to a cashier needs to learn the skills of operating a scanner and cash register, processing credit cards, and redeeming coupons.

- **Relay new information.** Organizations frequently change policies and procedures. The supervisor usually is responsible for instructing employees in new procedures or informing them about new policies. A drug store chain may decide to change the procedure for verifying a customer's age when buying alcohol, and as a result, supervisors are expected to train employees on the new procedure.

- **Introduce new programs.** Organizations sometimes introduce entirely new programs, systems, or products. These involve such immense changes that a large amount of new knowledge and skills must be taught to employees. A frozen yogurt chain that decides its stores should begin to sell sandwiches must train workers how to prepare, package, and sell the new products.

- **Meet government regulations.** When new laws are passed by local, state, or federal governments, businesses must often train employees how to comply with these laws. A plant producing gaskets responds to a federal law governing employees by having supervisors instruct employees on new safety procedures.

■ **Development of employees.** People are such a valuable resource that many organizations encourage supervisors to develop employee skills so that they are prepared in advance to engage in new projects or accept promotions to new jobs. A sausage producer encourages workers to learn skills for many jobs in the company and gives them a raise for each job they learn.

On-Site Versus Off-Site Training

A decision needs to be made about whether the training needs can most effectively be done through on-site or off-site training. On-site refers to the actual work area of the employees—for example, a desk, counter, bench, conveyor belt, or store aisle. Typical methods of on-site training are on-the-job training (OJT), job rotation, apprenticeship, and job coaching. Off-site refers to a location away from the work area that may or may not be in the same building as the work area, like a meeting room, training room, break area, conference center, or hotel room. Typical off-site training methods include classroom training, workshops, seminars, conferences, and simulators. Some methods of training can be used in either location, like computer assisted instruction and videoconferencing.

The decision to use on-site or off-site training is usually made by managers in cooperation with front-line supervisors. In some cases, the organization's human resource development (HRD) department takes the lead in identifying the most appropriate training method and works closely with supervisors to implement the training. You should consider several issues when making this decision.

■ **Potential damage.** Some training could potentially damage equipment, the workplace, or waste product. In this case, off-site training would be more appropriate. A nuclear plant operator trains for months in a simulated plant because radioactive damage from a mistake at an actual plant would be a major disaster.

■ **Possible injury.** Injury to employees, customers, or bystanders is an important consideration. Airline pilots are trained in flight simulators before actually flying an airplane because of the possibility of injury.

■ **Distractions.** Distractions at the work site may make on-site training difficult. This includes disruptions like customers wanting service, telephone calls, or noise from operations. When disruptions would impede the flow of training, it is often better to use an off-site training method.

■ **Integration of operation.** Tasks and skills are sometimes integrated in such a way that disrupting work activities would cause a major financial

129

loss or inconvenience customers. Also, it would be so costly to simulate operation that employees must be trained on-site. A package shipping company continues sorting packages even though a new delivery location is added to the operation. Employees are trained while packages for the new location come down the line.

■ **Subject expertise.** The subject matter being taught is sometimes unfamiliar to employees in the company and an off-site location is the best place to obtain needed skills. Training experts from a computer manufacturer are the best source of training for operators of a new computer system. Training costs for a organization are typically lower when they send workers to off-site training at a location provided by the computer manufacturer.

■ **Number of employees.** The number of employees to be trained affects the decision about the training method to select. An insurance company that decides to add a new investment program needs to train large numbers of employees about the program. Off-site training in a classroom would reduce the time and cost by enabling the company to train large numbers of employees at one time.

■ **Cost of training.** The cost of training needs to be calculated. Just a few costs that need to be considered are employees' salaries, travel costs, loss of business, cost of classroom space, and the salaries or fees of trainers' versus supervisors' pay.

Younger workers—Young people are usually accustomed to structured learning because they are still attending high school or college. The speed that they learn at is typically faster than that of more mature workers. These are some positive traits that help young people learn a new job or task. However, supervisors need to give younger workers special attention during the job training process. Their lack of work experience means that you need to explain even small details about a task that experienced workers usually understand immediately.

Another characteristic of younger workers is their reluctance to ask questions— even when they are unclear about a supervisor's instructions. Encourage them to ask questions whenever they don't understand something. Ask them questions as you are demonstrating a task or conveying information to check how well they understand the task you're teaching them. The listening skills of many young people are not as well developed as more mature workers. Take time to repeat instructions, and ask the worker to repeat the instructions and to make notes when appropriate.

How Adults Learn

As people mature and move beyond high school—this maturity even begins with high school students—some common attributes affect their motivation and ability to learn. Adults prefer to learn using methods based on **andragogy**—a theory of adult learning. The following list contains four important characteristics of adult learners.

■ Adults learn better when they assume responsibility and control over learning activities. This means they will learn more if they are given opportunities to be responsible for their learning. Supervisors can promote this by encouraging employees to identify skills they want to learn and then assist them in developing plans to acquire those skills.

■ Adults learn more effectively by applying what they learn. There are progressive steps to learning. People learn the least when someone tells them how to do a task. They learn more when someone demonstrates the task. They learn the most by doing the task ourselves. This principle is a key element of on-the-job training (OJT) methods.

■ As people mature, they develop a broader experience base to draw on. This experience base can be used to help improve their learning. Encourage workers to compare a new task they are trying to learn with past experiences. Linking new skills and knowledge to a past experience usually improves learning. For example, training a worker to use an electronic file system can be assisted by comparing computer software functions to physical filing activities.

■ Adults learn better when it is clear why learning a skill or acquiring knowledge is necessary. In school, students often learn something because they are going to be tested and graded on it. On the job, an employee's motivation to learn will be stronger when he or she understands the reasons for and benefits of learning a new skill. For example, the motivation to learn how to operate a cash register is increased when workers are informed that it is necessary for keeping their job, getting a promotion, or receiving a raise.

Supervisors who want to be good instructors also need to understand some common principles about learning. Some practices are basic in helping a person to learn regardless of age or maturity. These practices can be used to help you improve the training that you provide to employees.

■ The more time we spend on a learning task, the more learning takes place. A common saying illustrates this point: *Practice makes perfect.* Supervisors should provide employees time to practice a new skills.

131

■ When learning is broken into shorter time periods with breaks between, more effective learning will occur—this is sometimes referred to as **spaced practice**. Breaks in training allow employees to assimilate what they've learned. They can practice the newly learned task, consider questions that they want to ask an instructor, and identify practical issues that arise at the job site. The design of training programs should take spaced practice into consideration and avoid marathon instructional sessions whenever possible.

■ When a person's behavior is followed by a satisfying experience, the behavior will be repeated. If the behavior is followed by an unpleasant experience, the behavior will be avoided. For the supervisor, this means that both the social and physical learning environments that are created will be critical to the learning process. Reduce the amount of stress that employees may feel by training them in private or making it less apparent that they are undergoing training. This is particularly the case with customer service jobs.

■ Learning patterns differ, so don't expect one employee's speed and ability to master a skill to compare with that of other employees. One employee may excel at learning new tasks quickly. However, another employee may develop a higher level of skill over time. Supervisors should also be aware that as a worker learns new skills, performance on some days will be better than others. This is normal, since we don't usually experience a straight line of improvement in our learning patterns. Don't let the more common, uneven pattern of learning discourage you. Supervisors sometimes think employees "just aren't getting it" when they fail at a skill that just an hour or day before they seemed to have mastered. In such cases, a supervisor is just observing the ups and downs that naturally occur as a person learns.

■ New facts, ideas, concepts, and skills are more easily learned when they are associated with known information. Organizing a learning activity so that it builds on past knowledge can make a critical difference in educational outcomes. Supervisors should structure training so that it uses association. For example, employees can memorize codes by associating them with a special date on the calendar, telephone numbers, addresses, or such. Many people find that memorizing facts is easier when they associate the fact with a word and make the words rhyme.

■ When you need to teach an employee a more complex task, use the whole-part-whole method. This means first reviewing the task as whole, doing every part in one continuous process. Next, break it into small parts and concentrate on learning each individual part in a sequential pattern. Finally, demonstrate the entire task as a whole again.

■ Positive reinforcement of learning, such as praise and recognition, enhances learning. This is one of the most thoroughly researched learning concepts. To be effective, reinforcement of learning needs to occur frequently and should occur immediately after the employee successfully demonstrates the skill being learned. Supervisors need to use praise and other simple rewards when an employee displays the learning that you expect. Little things, like taking a break, treating them to a snack or soft drink, or pointing out their success to another employee are little reinforcers that become powerful aids in the employee's learning process.

■ People learn through the use of their senses, and learning is enhanced when all of the senses are engaged in the learning process. The more senses that the supervisor stimulates in the instructional process, the more powerful learning will be. For example, learning a task can be done by watching someone perform the task (seeing) but learning is enhanced when the task is described (hearing), and is even further improved by doing the task (touching). Consider how you can make boring tasks more interesting to learn about by stimulating as many senses as possible.

Practicing these ideas can help you become a more effective instructor. You don't have to use all of the principles when teaching a new task or skill. In fact, some will be more useful than others, depending on what you're trying to teach. Pick out the ideas you think will help employees learn a task quickly and easily.

Older workers—Many myths surround the learning ability of older workers. These might be summed up by the adage, "You can't teach an old dog new tricks." This attitude developed because of research done in the first half of this century that suggested the intelligence of adults declines over time. However, more recent studies show that there is little or no noticeable loss of intelligence until people are well into their 70s. An explanation for the difference in these studies has to do with time. Older adults do not perform well on timed tests. They also don't learn material as quickly when it has no apparent value or relevance. Both of these factors explain the difference in performance on intelligence tests between adults and teenagers.

Supervisors can benefit from this knowledge by structuring training programs so they better meet the needs of older workers. Before training begins, explain the relevance between the task they are expected to learn and their job. Provide time for older adults to assimilate learning by relating it to their experience. This may mean that they will take slightly more time to learn the task than younger workers. However, the retention of learning is often better. Reassure older adults that they can learn when the task involves new technology. They are often intimidated by new technology because it lies outside their experience base. If you plan to use tests to evaluate training, don't use a timed test (this should apply to all workers). Most importantly, have confidence in the learning ability of older workers. Their ability to learn is supported by research and the experience of many supervisors.

The Training Process

Planning for training is important because it reduces the time and cost of the training. More importantly it increases the potential for learning to take place. Well-organized training puts an employee at ease, applies learning principles, and follows a logical sequence. These factors combine for a powerful learning experience that instills the skills and knowledge employees need to perform well at their jobs. Many complex models describe the training process, but you should find that this simple five-step approach works well.

1. Defining Training Needs

Begin this process by considering the list of reasons for training that appears at the beginning of the chapter. Then identify the specific content of the training. The tasks must first be identified by using job descriptions, orientation lists, equipment guides, interviews with managers and workers, observations of someone doing the task, and program descriptions. Then complete a task analysis for each task in the training program. This is a simple three-step process.

■ List and describe all steps that must be performed in order to satisfactorily complete the task. This is sometimes more difficult than it appears. For example, write down a list of every step that is involved in preparing a peanut butter and jelly sandwich. Did you include the step for unscrewing the lid on the peanut butter jar? You might protest that the step is obvious. It is only obvious because of your prior experience in unscrewing jars. You need to consider whether someone would understand this step who wasn't familiar with the use of jars. Apply this example to the process of learning to operate a telephone system. You might easily overlook steps in this process because you use the system every day but omission of a step could easily mislead the employee that is being trained.

■ Place each step in the proper sequence. There are some steps that can be done in any order without interfering in completing the task. For example, when cleaning the interior of a car the sequence of cleaning the upholstery, windows, trim, floor mats, and emptying the ash trays doesn't affect the task. However, the successful completion of some tasks are critically affected by the sequence of steps. An example is copying a document where the sequence of placing the document in the feeder, setting the controls—like size, number, and darkness—and then pressing the start button do matter.

■ Developing a flowchart is useful because it provides a visual aid that helps an employee better understand the entire process.

2. Setting Measurable Training Objectives

It is important that you identify the training objectives that a worker should achieve upon completion of the training. The objective should be measurable because it provides the basis for judging whether the training is successful and whether the employees can perform the new task correctly. **Learning objectives** are one-sentence statements that have three basic parts.

■ **Performance.** This describes the behavior that an employee should be able to demonstrate upon completion of the training program.

■ **Criterion.** A description of how well the learner must be able to perform is often needed. This may be defined in terms of time, quality, or cost.

■ **Condition.** This describes the conditions under which the performance is to take place. The condition is not always applicable and may be omitted from an objective.

The following is an example of a learning objective: "Given a manual and the necessary tools, the worker will be able to correctly diagnose the trouble that is causing a copy machine to jam, within a 15-minute time period." In this example, you can see the three parts of an objective.

■ Performance—Students will be able to correctly diagnose the trouble that is causing a copy machine to jam.

■ Criterion—Within a 15-minute time period.

■ Condition—Given a manual and the necessary tools.

135

Note that a learning objective typically uses the phrase "will be able to." This is a positive statement that implies a successful outcome. As you develop instructional objectives, keep in mind the following questions:

- What is the main intent of the objective? Answering this question helps determine the content of the performance statement. Center on what the employee must really learn to master a task or skill. Concentrate on the skills that are critical to the employee doing the job successfully. It is reasonable to try and identify three to five objectives that, once achieved, ensure the individual can do an effective job. This number provides a focus that helps achieve the learning goal. Consider the example of training a carpenter's helper to install a door. You could write three objectives for the process of installing the door handle that deal with measuring, cutting, and installing the handle. A better alternative would be to write one objective for installing the door handle. You can then specify the three steps that must be completed to install the handle in the training content.

- What must be demonstrated to ensure the objective is met? Answering this question results keeps the focus on developing an observable outcome as you write the performance statement. One purpose of a learning objective is to provide an instructor with a tool that can measure whether learning has taken place. We can't measure something unless we can observe it. That is why objectives must be measurable. Consider these examples because they illustrate the importance of having a measurable objective.

  Non-measurable objective: The employee will be able to use a scanner.

  Measurable objective: Using an accurately calibrated scanner, the employee will be able to scan a product with one pass over the scanner 95 percent of the time.

  The problem with the non-measurable objective is that you aren't sure what behavior is defined by using it. This problem is solved by the phrase "scan a product with one pass over the scanner." This phrase defines the word "use" in such a way that it can be observed.

- What object will the learner have to carry out the objective *with* or *to?* This question helps you consider the object that is the center of action. In the previous example, the answer to this question is that the product is the item the employee must do something *to*, and the scanner is the item the employee must do it *with*.

▪ How will we know if the performance is good enough? An answer to this question provides the criterion that is used in an objective. In the example of the scanner, a supervisor would need to consider whether scanning the item regardless of the number of passes over the scanner is sufficient. Considering that most customers want to get through a check-out line quickly, the supervisor would conclude that there needs to be a level of performance that would accomplish this. That is the reason that the criterion "with one pass over the scanner 95 percent of the time" is needed to complete this objective. An important feature of this sample objective is that it can be measured. A supervisor could observe an employee completing this task and judge whether the person successfully accomplished this objective.

▪ What, if anything, will the learner need or have to do without? The answer to this question affects any condition that is a part of the objective. The example objective contains the term "Using an accurately calibrated scanner" as a condition. This condition isn't absolutely necessary because it could be a basic assumption that the scanner used to test an employee would be in good working order. However, it makes the point that accuracy in the scanning process could be affected by the scanner.

Welfare-to-work employees—Slightly more than 40 percent of all welfare recipients have less than a high school education. This indicates the possibility that many of these workers may lack reading, writing, and mathematics skills. In some cases, these skill deficiencies may make it difficult for the worker to master skills needed to advance in the workplace. Supervisors don't have either the time or the expertise to develop these basic learning skills. Most communities have a literacy council that coordinates literacy programs. Local high schools sometimes operate remedial education programs. Either of these sources could provide assistance to workers who need to improve their basic educational skills. Encourage workers to develop these skills and look for ways to help them practice their newly developed skills on the job.

3. Identify Resources for Training

Once a supervisor knows the objectives, it is possible to select the best resource for achieving those objectives. Keep in mind some of the issues that were raised in the first part of this chapter like potential damage, possible injury, distractions at the work site, disruptions to normal operations, subject expertise, number of employees to be trained, and the cost of training. Then decide which of the following resources are going to most effectively meet the learning objectives.

- **Supervisors.** First consider whether you can adequately train the employee. Most organizations consider the supervisor to be the primary instructional resource for employees. You must understand the tasks to be taught and have the time to do the training to be the best resource. This option is also one of the most expensive when you calculate the time and pay for a supervisor. However, it is a cost that an organization has already calculated in its budget and this might not be the case with other training resources.

- **Classroom training.** This refers to classroom instruction—provided by a human resources (HR) department—that involves training several employees at the same time. Many methods are used in classroom instruction, including lectures, videos, discussion, role playing, case studies, games, and learning exercises. Some organizations allocate a certain amount of dollars to a supervisor's budget and expect a transfer of these dollars to the HR department in return for training employees from your unit. Supervisors are usually expected to work with HR to schedule training programs for their workers.

- **Computer-assisted instruction (CAI).** The use of CAI instruction for employees is rapidly increasing. Employers can provide it at the work site, in a classroom, or even at an employee's home. It also has the advantage of being completed at a time convenient for the employee and the supervisor. CAI can be purchased and installed on the organization's computer systems, or it can be obtained over the Internet. Many colleges offer courses on the Internet. Private companies provide many courses on the Internet. The U.S. Department of Labor has created an Internet site called America's Learning Exchange (www.alx.org) that contains information about thousands of training programs. An important point to consider when using CAI is that it allows a supervisor to verify an employee has completed the training program.

- **Schools.** Frequently career schools, community colleges, and universities provide classes where employees can get the training they need. For example, employees who need to learn how to prepare documents using Microsoft Word can probably locate a course that provides these skills at a nearby school.

- **Conferences.** Professional and trade associations often have conferences led by experts in special areas. Reviewing conference descriptions provides some indication about the potential for employees to achieve learning objectives by attending.

138

■ **Workshops.** Private training companies offer workshops you can attend to learn new skills. Costs for these workshops can range from $100 or less per day to several thousand dollars for a three- to five-day workshop. The quality of these workshops varies greatly. Check with other supervisors and managers and the HR department to find out what they know about a workshop or the company that provides it. Ask the training company to supply references from people who have attended. You may want to call some of these people. Look for companies that provide a money-back guarantee—a feature that more companies are providing in order to remain competitive.

4. Implement Training

The supervisor's responsibility during the implementation phase of training depends on the resource that is selected. Obviously there is a large amount of work when the supervisor provides the instruction and very little work when instruction is provided by HR, a school, or private training firm. The supervisor's role in providing instruction will be discussed at another point in this chapter and later in chapter 10. The following implementation tasks assume that the instruction is given by someone other than the supervisor.

■ **Authorization.** The supervisor should request authorization for the employee to attend training. The basis for justifying this request can be bolstered by providing information compiled in completing the first three steps of the planning process. This request should specify the amount of money and time that is required for the training.

■ **Notification.** Once authorization is received, an employee should receive notification from the supervisor. This should include information about the location, time, length of the program, objectives, content, instructor, and how the training will be evaluated.

■ **Arrangements.** Make sure that an employee is registered for training and the fee is paid. You may want to delegate this task to employees. If travel is involved, transportation and lodging reservations are needed.

■ **Preparation.** Request advance information about the training that can be used to help prepare employees for the training. This might include reading material, programmed instruction, skills surveys, or agendas. Review this material with your employees and discuss expectations that you have about their training. Describe what you expect them to be able to achieve after completing the training program.

■ **Monitor progress.** This is particularly important for employees that are involved in training that takes place over a period of time.

Immigrant workers—Immigrant workers often have limited English-speaking abilities. Supervisors should try to locate English-as-a-Second-Language (ESL) programs. Many educational institutions and nonprofit agencies that operate remedial education programs also offer ESL classes. Contact the adult and continuing education directors at local high schools and colleges to ask about these programs. Identify the financial resources within the organization that can be used to pay for the worker's ESL classes—cost is often a reason that immigrant workers won't enroll in an ESL class. Once you've arranged for an ESL program that your workers could attend, sit down, and discuss the opportunity with them. Explain how the class would benefit their work and provide opportunities for advancement.

5. Evaluate Training

The final step in the training process is to evaluate the training. Organizations use a variety of methods to do this including questionnaires, tests, interviews, and group discussions. We'd like to suggest that supervisors use reality-based evaluations. This involves evaluating the actual work output of employees. There are two basic ways that a supervisor can do this.

■ **Observation.** A supervisor can observe employees doing a job to measure the effectiveness of training. Observation is more objective and thorough when you use an observation form. This form should contain a checklist of steps an employee must complete to perform the job successfully. The task analysis that was described earlier in step 1 can be used to develop the checklist. Some tasks are move easily observed than others. For example, helping a customer select the right paint product, baking biscuits, repairing a tire, and framing a picture can be easily evaluated through observation. Observation works more effectively when it is unobtrusive. Stay as far away from the employee as possible. Don't interrupt the activity. Observe at a time when the employee isn't likely to notice your presence.

■ **Work samples.** Some tasks are difficult to observe. Also, employee behavior can change when they know they are being observed. These are two reasons why a supervisor might want to use work samples to evaluate training outcomes. An employee who has gone through training on the use of Lotus 1-2-3 should be able to create a spreadsheet that calculates new results when data is modified in the worksheet. Observing an employee create a spreadsheet may take hours or days depending on its complexity. It also might distract the employee to have you continuously monitor this activity. A work sample would provide a better evaluation of the employee's work in this example. A supervisor could randomly select a sample of the employee's work during the past week. The spreadsheets could then be reviewed to determine how well it incorporates the techniques employees were expected to master in the workshop. A checklist based on a task analysis can help in the evaluation.

Two Approaches to Training— Classroom and On the Job

Supervisors are often expected to provide training needed by employees. In training employees, supervisors typically play three roles:

1. **Content expert.** A supervisor may possess knowledge about a task or skill that other supervisors or specialists don't have. At the same time, the most skilled trainer in the organization is in the HR department. Many organizations team the supervisor with the trainer to jointly design and deliver the training program. The role of content expert is used for both types of training discussed in this section—classroom and on the job.

2. **Classroom instructor.** Supervisors are sometimes expected to provide classroom instruction. When supervisors are expected to provide classroom instruction, organizations often arrange train-the-trainer workshops. These workshops help develop knowledge and skills to needed to conduct classroom training programs.

3. **On-the-job training (OJT) instructor.** This training is routinely performed by most supervisors. It is most frequently used when new employees begin a job or an employee is transferred to a new job. This training combines instruction, demonstration, and immediate application of a skill.

Disabled workers—Persons with severe disabilities are often placed in what is termed "supported" employment. Supported employment involves placing workers in jobs at businesses, government agencies, and non-profit agencies. These workers are supported by job coaches from rehabilitation programs that provide intensive training, coaching, and follow up. Job coaches usually work the same hours as the employee for the first few weeks or months on the job—helping the employee learn the job. This intensive support is provided and paid for by the rehabilitation program, not the employer.

Job coaches use special techniques that are adapted to training and coaching severely disabled workers. Supervisors should observe supported employment job coaches in action and learn more about the techniques they use. If supervisors spend some time with the job coach, they can develop the skills needed to train and coach workers with severe disabilities. Improving your supervisory skills enhances the potential for the severely disabled employee to become a long-term productive worker.

Classroom Presentation

Classroom training is challenging because it requires that you keep the interest of a group of people at one time. You can use many instructional methods in classroom training such as case studies, role plays, and structured experiences. The most frequently used method, however, is the lecture and discussion. The lecture is an oral presentation of knowledge and skills by an instructor. It is the easiest instruction method to understand and master.

Preparing the Lecture

Preparation is the key to successful use of the lecture. You will feel more confident when you are well prepared with the items in the following list. This confidence in turn is sensed by students in the classroom.

- **Objectives.** Refer to the learning objectives as you prepare a lecture. Objectives help you focus on the outcomes that employees should achieve when their training is successfully complete.

- **Information.** Research and collect information that employees will need to know in order to achieve each objective.

- **Notes.** Outline the information that needs to be included in the lecture. Include enough information in the notes to remind you about the important points that need to be made. However, don't write out in detail everything you want to say. This usually results in an instructor reading the lecture—a very boring prospect.

- **Visual aids.** Visual aids might consist of slides, a video presentation, posters, or items for demonstrations. Computer software—like Microsoft PowerPoint—makes developing slides quick and easy. Slides help your students remember important points. Slides can be projected using an overhead projector, slide projector, or with a computer and large-screen projector. Follow these simple guidelines when creating a slide.

◆ Present only one main idea on each slide.

◆ Follow the "6 by 6 Rule." This rule states that people will remember what they see on the slide when there are no more than six words per line and no more than six lines per slide.

◆ Use a font that is easy to read, such as Arial or CG Times. Fancy fonts, like script and serif styles, make slides difficult to read.

◆ Make the size easy to read. Using 20- to 24-point type is usually adequate.

◆ Select the most appropriate orientation for the majority of your slides. A horizontal orientation (portrait) is typically the best for lists. A vertical orientation (landscape) is usually best for diagrams.

◆ Combine upper- and lowercase letters. This is the way we've been taught to read; and using all uppercase lettering is more difficult to read.

◆ Clip art should enhance and reinforce the point you are making. Don't include pictures just because it's easy to do.

■ **Prepare handouts.** Handouts can be used to supplement the lecture. You can also use them to guide note taking by designing them so that they contain blank spaces to be filled in with points contained in visual aids.

Presenting the Lecture

A lecture can be a straightforward presentation of information orally delivered by the instructor. However, this can be rather dull, and the style is partially responsible for giving the lecture a bad name. Lectures can be improved and made more interesting by using a variety of techniques.

■ **Change topics frequently.** Make your lecture a series of mini-lectures. Typically, the longer you continue talking about one point, the more disinterested students become. At the conclusion of a mini-lecture, you can use one of the other techniques described in this section to increase student interest. Changing topics requires listeners to change their thought process and keeps them engaged in the lecture.

■ **Be enthusiastic.** The fact that the instructor is interested in the topics in a lecture positively affects the students. They are likely to be more interested.

■ **Create a relaxed environment.** Don't impose rules that remind students of grade school or high school. Allow drinks in class—in some cases snacks can be permitted. Students should be able to use restrooms without seeking your permission.

■ **Take breaks.** Space breaks over reasonable periods of time. Whenever possible, try to provide a 5- to 10-minute break every 60 to 80 minutes. Students typically return from breaks with an improved ability to focus on the training.

■ **Use humor.** People enjoy a laugh. Studies suggest that laughter physically stimulates our bodies. People are energized by humor. However, not everyone tells jokes well. It is also possible to be humorous by using cartoons that reinforce a point you make. Make up a slide with the cartoon on it and present it at the appropriate time.

■ **War stories.** Tell "war stories" about incidents in your experience that illustrate a point you are trying to make. Stories are sometimes called "word pictures" because people tend to remember stories.

■ **Use visual aids.** Research shows that visual aids increase the amount of information participants remember. Students perceive instructors that use visual aids as better prepared and more professional. In addition, students are more persuaded to a point of view when visual aids are used.

■ **Guide note taking.** Tell the students when a point is important and should be written in their notes. Visual aids and handouts help in the process of guiding note taking.

■ **Ask questions.** Questions break up the monotony of a lecture. It keeps participants alert when they know a question might be asked. Questions also involve students in the process and this increases the motivation to learn the material.

■ **Ask for examples.** Ask students to provide a personal example of encountering a problem, issue, task, or situation like the one you're describing. This personalizes the concept that you're trying to make. Students take more interest when they realize that another employee has had an experience like the one you're describing.

■ **Give informal tests.** Ask students to answer three to five questions based on information that you just gave. Questions can be written on a white board or a prepared slide. Have students write the answers on a sheet of paper. You don't have to have them hand in the questions; rather it is a personal accounting of what they've learned. Then survey the class to find out the different answers that were given. Once you've used this technique, students are likely to pay more attention to the lecture because they want to answer questions on future quizzes.

■ **Solve a problem.** Present a problem that illustrates a concept you are explaining. Make the problem relevant to your organization. Describe or demonstrate the process you would follow to solve the problem.

■ **Demonstration.** When you are describing how to do something concrete, use a demonstration. Actually show the class how to do the process. It is also possible to involve students by having them repeat the process you've demonstrated.

■ **Invite questions.** Provide students an opportunity to ask questions. The point in the lecture where students can ask questions should be controlled by the instructor. At times it is appropriate to allow questions throughout the lecture. However, this can make it difficult for instructors to concentrate on the topic.

■ **Reward students.** When a student answers questions, provides an example, asks a question, or participates some way in the lecture, reward the person. Usually, this can be done by praising the student. However, a technique that can be used in a humorous and playful manner is to provide a small reward. This might be candy, tickets, coupons, promotional items, or even a funny item like a big star that the employee wears throughout the training.

■ **Planned action.** Have students stand up and engage in a planned activity. For example, have students stand, turn to the person on their right, and provide an example that illustrates a point you just made. The activity re-energizes people and brings their attention back to the training program.

■ **Avoid disputes with students.** Students may disagree with something you've said. Arguing with them can create a negative atmosphere that impedes learning among other students. When they disagree with a fact, state that students should accept your fact as accurate but you'll check it out later and confirm which fact is correct.

■ **Mingle with students.** Mingle with students before the class, during breaks, and at the end of the class. This creates a more relaxed feeling among most students. They don't perceive you as distant, but rather involved with them.

145

■ **Focus on students' concerns.** Often students' facial expressions convey important information to the instructor. They alert you to confusion, anger, fear, apprehension, or interest. Questions and comments from students also provide insights into their reactions to the lecture. Respond to this feedback by telling students what your thoughts are. Ask for their response and clarify points or items that are not understood or accepted.

Contingent workers—Temporary workers often have the same training needs as they start on the job. A supervisor can help save some time by compiling a handout that contains frequently asked questions (FAQs). You can start by writing down the questions that new employees or temporary workers often ask you. Keep a copy of all these questions in a file and add to them as you encounter new questions. This is a simple job aid but one that can increase the confidence of temporary workers.

Handling Difficult Students

Students can sometimes cause problems that disrupt or interfere with the learning process. Following is a list of common problems, traits, and behaviors that can interrupt a lecture or create a negative learning atmosphere.

■ **Disruption.** Disruptive behavior includes actions by students that make it difficult for other students to concentrate on learning or makes it difficult to teach. Some examples are talking with other students during class, making noises, falling asleep, and reading.

■ **Talking.** Some students want to do all the talking. They attempt to talk whenever the instructor asks for responses from the class. This behavior sometimes interferes with other students' opportunities to participate in the class. Eventually this reduces other students' interest because they aren't able to become active participants in the learning process.

■ **Know-it-all attitude.** There are some students who have a know-it-all attitude. They dispute everything an instructor says or imply they know a better way to do things. Sometimes a student may truly know a subject as well or better than the instructor. However, the instructor knows how the organization wants the subject to be taught.

■ **Griping.** Students can sometimes complain or gripe during training. This is particularly true when an instructor is introducing subject matter that involves change. Employees frequently resist change and this resistance is manifested by complaining.

- **Irrelevant comments.** It is difficult to deal with students who make irrelevant comments or ask irrelevant questions. The difficulty arises because an instructor must direct students' attention back to the relevant material without embarrassing the student who made the irrelevant comment.

- **Silence.** The most effective learning occurs when all students become active participants in making comments and answering questions. However, many people are hesitant to speak in a larger group.

It is difficult for an instructor to handle these problems without creating a negative learning environment. Directly confronting a student can sometimes cause other students to get upset with the instructor. This reaction sometimes confuses inexperienced instructors when they observe that the disruptive student's behavior is obviously upsetting other members of the class. That is why an instructor should try other strategies to deal less directly with problem students.

- **State expectations.** Some problems can be avoided by stating your expectations at the beginning of a class. This doesn't need to be a long list—in fact, such a list could set a negative tone. Three simple guides are: 1) Students are expected to actively participate in the training; 2) Don't disrupt class activities by talking, sleeping, or other inappropriate behavior; and 3) Students should remain positive even they disagree with the instructor or other students.

- **Gently intervene.** It is sometimes possible to gently urge students to control their behavior. For example, direct a question to a student who is talking to another student. Respond to a talkative student by saying something like, "Let's give someone else a chance to answer the question."

- **Use peer pressure.** It is sometimes possible to use peer pressure to change a student's behavior. An example would be to respond to a student who frequently complains by asking other students to state how they feel about the idea being expressed.

- **Discuss privately.** Take an opportunity during breaks to talk privately with a student who is continuously creating a problem in class. Explain your concern and how the person could behave more appropriately.

- **Dismiss student.** This is an extreme response. It should be done only when you have talked in private with the student and asked the student to change his or her behavior, and when the student continues to display inappropriate behavior in class. This action is extreme because it might result in the employee's termination.

On-the-Job Training Method

Organizations invest a significant amount of money in on-the-job training (OJT). Estimates suggest this investment is over $200 billion a year—more than all money spent for elementary, secondary, and post-secondary education. Most of the money for OJT is spent on salaries and wages for the supervisors and for the time employees spend in training. Almost three times as many jobs require OJT than require a college degree. These facts demonstrate why OJT is such an important method for training employees.

Sometimes OJT is haphazard and done very inefficiently. However, when done in an appropriate manner, it is a very effective method of training. A variety of models for OJT exist, but the one presented here has been developed and used successfully by the authors.

Supervisor Preparation

OJT is an important activity for a supervisor. It is an investment of time that can pay high dividends once an employee is trained. The productivity and motivation of well-trained workers is much greater than those for employees who don't feel adequately prepared for a job. Take the time and effort needed to make OJT a fruitful process for your employees by following these guidelines.

- **Review training guide.** Some organizations prepare training guides for the supervisors to use when conducting OJT. If a guide doesn't exist, you can create an outline for the training using the learning objectives and task analysis.

- **Set timetable.** Determine the number of hours, days, and months that will be involved to train employees. A good strategy to avoid distractions and interruptions during the training is to schedule these training times in your appointment book.

- **Notify employee.** Tell the employee when the training is scheduled. When the training involves several sessions, give the employee a printed copy of the schedule.

- **Ready training site.** Identify and prepare a location where the training can be conducted. It should be somewhere that is relatively free from disruptions by employees and customers. Sometimes this is impossible when training workers on equipment that has to be used concurrently in the organization's operations, such as a coating machine, pizza oven, or forklift.

■ **Prepare equipment and material.** Gather all necessary supplies and materials so that they are at the training site. Check any equipment that will be used in the training to make sure it is in good working order so that functional problems don't confuse the worker.

Employee Preparation

It is easy to become so focused on the training content that you forget that the employees are an important part of the process. Their level of motivation and mindset affects how well they will learn. Taking the time to adequately prepare them for the training results in a more powerful learning experience.

■ **Put workers at ease.** Employees often approach training with a great deal of apprehension. The ultimate reward for learning the job is continued employment, while failure might result in termination. Assure the workers that most employees successfully complete the training. Express confidence in the worker's ability—after all, you wouldn't have hired the worker unless you were confident about the person's ability.

■ **Find out what they know.** Ask workers to describe previous experience they have had in performing the tasks. If you feel they actually understand the task, have them demonstrate the task to assess how well they can do the task. This information is basic in conducting the OJT process. Instructing workers to do something they already know results in bored and disinterested employees. In turn, this causes employees to miss important facts, points, and tasks that they don't know about.

■ **Arouse interest.** Training is more potent when employees are focused on the training. Arousing their interest accomplishes this result. This can be done by relating training outcomes to success on the job. Explain how the training can make their job easier, help them better serve customers, get along with other employees, avoid mistakes, and prevent injuries. In some organizations, workers receive a raise upon successful completion of their OJT program—this certainly arouses interest.

■ **Place worker correctly.** The position workers are placed in when they are shown how to operate equipment is very important. Typically the best position is next to you. A common mistake is to position a worker directly across from you because the employee sees everything in reverse. For example, when you move a switch to your right, it is to the employee's left. Pay attention to the handedness of workers. About 15 percent of the population is left-handed. You may need to demonstrate to left-handed workers how they can perform the task with their left hand. Left-handed supervisors need to make a similar adjustment when demonstrating a task to other workers.

Ex-offenders—Illiteracy is quite high among prison inmates. Ex-offenders may lack some basic reading and math skills that are needed for the job. Encourage them to participate in literacy or remedial education programs. Many ex-offenders have worked in prison industries and developed some work skills. Literacy councils and local high schools are a good place to find these types of educational programs.

A powerful reinforcement to their literacy program is a mentor that can help them apply their new reading and math skills to the job. This mentor should be another employee but could be a community volunteer. Have the mentor review words that are commonly used in your organization. Supervisors can assist in this effort by developing a word list containing both words, definitions, and example sentences that a person frequently encounters while performing tasks in jobs that you supervise.

Instruction

People remember almost 50 percent of what they hear and see—this compares with just 20 percent of what they hear. This learning characteristic makes OJT instruction one of the most effective training methods available today. The instruction you provide is very important in helping employees understand and retain the skills needed to perform a task. Speak clearly and loudly—accounting for noise in the workplace—so that employees hear all your instructions. Avoid rushing through the instructions.

- **Introduction.** Explain to employees the task you are going to demonstrate. Tell them what you are going to do in broad terms. Explain why the task is performed in a certain way. Sometimes describing problems that arise when a task isn't done correctly can help employees realize how important it is to do the task exactly as instructed.

- **Demonstrate the task.** Take time to do the task slowly. A supervisor who is skilled at a task can perform it so quickly that it is difficult for trainees to follow the process. Make sure that there are no obstructions that block an employee's view while you demonstrate a task.

■ **Task sequence.** Repeat the task by demonstrating the process step-by-step—this is where a task analysis is most useful. Show employees each step in the correct sequence and explain the importance of the step to successful completion of the task. Complete this process without interruption—explain that they can ask questions during the next step in the training program.

■ **Answer questions.** Provide employees an opportunity to ask questions. It is usually best to allow questions to be asked while you repeat the task so they can interrupt during a step they don't understand. Your communication style during questions is quite important. Be open, patient, and nonjudgmental. If employees sense that you have a critical or impatient attitude, they become reluctant to ask questions. This prevents employees from developing a clear understanding of the task. It can also reduce the level of confidence employees have about their ability to perform a job.

■ **Employee explanation.** Have the employee describe the task while you complete it. Do exactly what they tell you to do unless it could cause damage or injury. At such a point, explain what would happen and warn employees of the potential danger.

Employee Practice

The next step in the OJT process is to have employees perform the task. This is the most powerful learning aspect of the class. Retention of learning rises to almost 70 percent when people do what they are taught.

■ **Employee performs task.** Instruct employees to do the task just like it was demonstrated. They should go through one step at a time rather than in a smooth continuous process. Have employees explain each step to verify how well they understand the task.

■ **Correct errors.** Point out errors that employees make at the exact moment they make them. You don't want employees developing bad habits as they learn a task. Correcting errors immediately increases the potential that employees will retain the skill as taught and use it correctly on the job.

■ **Reinforce good performance.** Learning is stronger when a correct response is followed immediately by a reward. The best way to do this is to praise the employee for completing a task correctly.

■ **Reinstruct when needed.** There are times employees clearly don't understand a step in completing a task. When this happens, stop and repeat your instructions on how to do the task correctly.

151

Follow Up

Once employees appear to understand the task and can successfully demonstrate it, you can leave them on their own. You need to judge whether they should continue to practice the task or whether they are actually ready to perform the task on the job. Continued follow up is very important but is frequently overlooked. Impatient supervisors often want employees to immediately perform the task without any errors or problems. Unless a task is quite simple—be aware that many tasks seem simple to supervisors who can perform them well—it is unrealistic to expect employees to learn them so well that they make no errors implementing them on the job.

- **Check frequently.** The more frequently you check employees' performance, the more quickly you can identify a problem. The longer employees perform a task incorrectly, the harder it is to extinguish the bad behavior. Checking on employees frequently also gives them more confidence because they know you are there to correct any mistakes.

- **Encourage questions.** Take time to check whether employees have questions. Practicing a task on the job is usually somewhat different than it was during the instruction process. For this reason, questions can often arise. Respond to questions in a patient and positive manner; otherwise, workers can become discouraged and eventually won't ask questions. The questions that employees ask can often point out a gap in the instruction process and gives you a chance to correct that lapse.

- **Correct and reinforce.** Praise employees when you see them doing the task well. As you observe employees doing something wrong, correct the problems as appropriate. Don't intervene immediately but rather give the employee an opportunity to correct the error first. Unlike during the employee practice phase of OJT, your role here isn't to make immediate corrections. It is to help the employee first identify, then correct his or her behavior. It is important for supervisors to balance out praise with correction. Otherwise, employees can develop the "Gotcha Syndrome," where they worry the supervisor is just waiting to catch them making a mistake. This creates a stressful working environment that is entirely unnecessary.

- **Reinstruct when needed.** Employees sometimes appear to have mastered a task during the practice stage but are later confused about how to do it. This becomes apparent as employees practice the task on the job. Take time to reinstruct them when mistakes seem to be related to a lack of understanding.

- **Gradually reduce assistance.** Reduce the number of times you check on employees as they demonstrate an ability to complete the task successfully. This behavior provides employees with more confidence because they assume that you have confidence in them. Continuing frequent checks sends the opposite message and makes employees hesitant and unsure about performing their jobs.

Summary

Training and coaching is one of the most important functions of a supervisor. Employees are an important asset to an organization—this importance increases in a tight labor market. Investing in the development of employee skills is important. A supervisor needs to be familiar with the resources, both within and outside the organization, that can provide skills needed by employees. Supervisors are often expected to provide the training employees need. Sometimes this is done with classroom training—primarily using the lecture method. More frequently, supervisors practice on-the-job training. Experienced employees need continued coaching by a supervisor to maintain a high level of performance.

Chapter 8

Leadership

There are many ways to define leadership, and over the last 50 years there have been several new definitions offered. Research has yielded several different theories of leadership. Since leadership means different things to different people, defining it is sometimes difficult. Leadership involves influencing and supporting others to work enthusiastically toward achieving goals. Without leadership, organizations would have difficulty meeting goals or even functioning on a daily basis. Leadership involves influencing other people and attaining goals. Thus, one definition that seems suitable is that *leadership is the process where an individual influences others to achieve a common goal.*

The leadership process could even be compared to that of a magical process—no one is sure *why* it happens, but everyone is sure *when* it happens. This chapter explores how this process happens. As a supervisor, you are responsible for influencing the employees who report to you to achieve the goals of the organization—this is leadership. After reading this chapter, you'll be able to determine many things about yourself and the different types of people you supervise. What motivates them? What motivates you? Are your interests and the interests of your employees beneficial to the company? If not, how can you fix the situation? The different sections in the chapter address those questions and many more.

It is important to understand that there is a difference between managers and leaders. The primary function of a manager is to maintain the status quo and administer operations. Leaders are people who visualize what an organization could be or the direction it should take to be effective in the long term for its survival. In their book *Leaders: The Strategies for Taking Charge*, Warren Bennis and Burt Namus state that "Managers are people who do things right and leaders are people who do the right thing." They go on to say that "the difference may be summarized as activities of vision and judgment—*effectiveness* versus activities of mastering routines—*efficiency*." For example, managers do things such as planning, budgeting, organizing, problem solving and controlling—basic day-to-day activities that provide order and consistency in an organization. Leaders, on the other hand, build visions, do strategic planning, align people, create motivating environments, and inspire events or situations that produce change and movement in organizations. Leaders can and do exist at any level of an organization. The question you need to ask yourself is, "Which do I want to be, a leader or manager?"

The Trait Theory of Leadership

In the early 1900s, researchers studied the traits of people who were thought to be great leaders. It was believed that identifying traits would reveal what made them great leaders. The theories developed from these studies were called "great man" theories because they were focused on trying to identify the innate qualities and characteristics possessed by "great leaders." Researchers studied social, political, and military leaders to determine these specific traits. It was believed that these people were born with the traits that were necessary to be leaders and that only "great" people possessed them.

Younger workers—The power that leaders find most useful with younger workers is derived primarily through personal and expert power. This means that your relationship and skills have the most significant impact on your leadership of younger workers. Young people are not particularly impressed with legitimate power or connective power. Thus, your position and connections within the organization are not impressive to these workers. Moreover, they perceive coercive power as very negative and often leave organizations where supervisors use this method for exercising leadership.

Supervisors can use this knowledge to increase their influence in two ways. Develop positive relationships with younger workers. Spend time with them at breaks and over lunch. Take time to learn about their interests and look for common interests that can further the development of a relationship. Organize social activities that interest younger workers as well as "old timers" in your department. Another way to increase your influence over younger workers is to share your skills and knowledge with them. They respect supervisors who are open in sharing skills and don't perceive them as a threat to their jobs.

In the mid-1900s, the Trait Theory was called into question. Researchers charged that no consistent set of traits had been identified that differentiated leaders from nonleaders. A person with leadership traits might be a leader in one situation but in another situation might not be a leader. This line of thinking focused more on relationships between people in social situations rather than the personal traits of the leader. However, in recent years, the trait theory was reborn when researchers found that personality traits were strongly associated with people's perceptions of leaders. These studies have reached a certain degree of concurrence on traits that are characteristic of leaders. The following list shows some specific traits that people associate with leaders.

- **Intelligence.** Verbal, perceptual, and reasoning abilities appear to make one a better leader. However, the intelligence of leaders differs significantly from that of their followers; it may prove to be counterproductive. The difference in intelligence may affect the leader's ability to communicate effectively with followers. Poor communication impedes followers from accepting the leader's vision and often fails to motivate them.

- **Self-confidence.** Leaders need to feel self-assured and believe that their attempts to influence people will lead to action on the part of followers. Leaders understand their strengths and weaknesses and feel comfortable applying their skills in appropriate situations.

- **Determination.** Leaders have a strong desire to accomplish a goal or task. They are doers. Leaders with determination may be more willing to assert themselves, be more proactive, and be willing to persevere against all odds.

- **Integrity.** Leaders possess the qualities of honesty and trustworthiness. Leaders are willing to take responsibility for their actions. They have a strong set of principles that often inspire confidence in others.

- **Sociability.** Leaders enjoy being around people and interacting with them. They display a high amount of friendliness. Leaders who exhibit this trait are more outgoing, courteous, tactful, and diplomatic, which allows them to be sensitive to others' needs.

As you read this list of common traits identified with leaders, you probably found yourself agreeing with most items. This is because the Trait Theory allows you to examine leaders you know and compare their traits with this list. It is likely that leaders you know possess many or most of these traits. However, you may want to consider some strengths and weaknesses of this theory before agreeing with it.

Strengths of the Trait Theory:

- The theory fits clearly with many people's notion that leaders are clearly out front and leading the way in organizations. It is also consistent with the premise that leaders are different than the masses of people and this difference lies in the special traits they possess.

- No other leadership theory has as much research to back it up as the Trait Theory does. The data clearly supports the importance of various personality traits in leadership.

- The theory gives people some benchmarks they can point to if they want to be a leader. It is possible to assess your traits and compare them with those found in leaders. In turn, this can help you in making decisions about whether to move into or accept leadership roles.

- It is possible to identify people with leadership traits and prepare them for leadership positions.

Weaknesses of the Trait Theory:

- The list of traits that have emerged seems to be endless. While some traits emerge overwhelmingly from the research, it is still difficult to focus on those that truly distinguish a leader from other people.

- From the list of traits, the final lists are highly subjective and may not even be accurate.

- Even if a list of traits is accurate, it presents some difficulties. Traits seem to be relative, fixed psychological structures—an example is intelligence—and are difficult to teach. This in turn means that we can't develop leaders but only identify them.

- The theory does not take into account the various situations that happen in organizations. Traits that make a leader effective in one situation may not make them effective in another situation. There are many military examples of generals that are great leaders during times of war but struggle as leaders in peacetime.

One of the ways you as a supervisor can use the Trait Theory is by analyzing your own traits, which helps you gain an idea of your own strengths and weaknesses and get some feel for how other employees see you. If you see that you may be lacking in some areas, you can try to make changes. Some traits like sociability can be learned. It doesn't mean that it is easy to develop the trait, but it's not impossible, either.

Style Theory

The Style approach focuses on what leaders do and how they act. The Style approach is different from the Trait approach because it focuses on the behaviors of leaders rather than their personality characteristics. Researchers, at both Ohio State University and the University of Michigan, who have studied the Style approach have determined that leadership is essentially composed of two kinds of behaviors—*task behaviors* and *relationship behaviors*.

- Task behaviors are those acts that organize the work, give structure to the work context, define role responsibilities, and schedule work activities.

- Relationship behaviors are those acts that focus on building relationships, such as creating respect, trust, and friendship between leaders and followers.

Leaders are individuals who develop the necessary behaviors to complete tasks successfully and can supplement these behaviors with those who are needed to establish positive relationships with followers. Good leaders aren't those who have only high task behaviors or those who have only high relationship behaviors. Rather, a good leader must possess both high task and high relationship behaviors.

Strengths of the Style Theory:

- Style is based on behavior and we know that behavior can be taught and modified. This means that it is possible to teach leadership.

- The theory provides a broad conceptual map that you can use to understand the complexities of leadership.

- It is possible to assess leadership style on both the task and relationship dimensions. This assessment then provides an opportunity for development and change.

- The theory helps leaders understand that their actions toward others occur on both task and relationship levels.

Weaknesses of the Style Theory:

- The Style Theory has failed to identify a universal style of leadership that can be effective in every situation.

- Highly effective leaders are expected to be high in task and relationship behaviors, but this behavior style doesn't lead to success in all situations. Some complicated situations may require high task behavior, while some situations may need only high relationship behavior.

159

- The Style approach does not provide a neatly organized set of prescriptions for effective leadership behavior.

In some situations, leaders will need to be more task-oriented, and in others they will need to be more relationship-oriented. Some employees need a supervisor who provides a lot of direction and others will need a supervisor who will show them a great deal of nurture and support. The Style approach will help you to look at your behavior along these two dimensions.

Situational Leadership Theory

One of the most widely recognized leadership theories is the Situational Leadership Theory developed by Hersey and Blanchard. The basic premise of the Situational Leadership Theory is that different situations should be approached with different leadership styles. It suggests that employees' behavior on the job is affected by two factors—level of commitment and competence.

- The degree to which employees have the competence to accomplish the task affects their behavior. Employees at a high competence level will have mastered the skills to do a specific task. Employees could have a competence level ranging from very low to very high, or something in between.

- The commitment employees have to complete the task is another key behavior. Employees who are committed to doing a task will have a positive attitude. Employees could have a high commitment or low commitment, and anywhere in between.

Older workers—Older workers respond positively to legitimate power, connective power, and information power. Their work experience has taught them the importance of these power sources. They are less likely to respond to personal power and coercive power. Personal power is less effective because mature adults tend to respond less to charisma and more to what a supervisor can do—particularly what they can do for the worker. Coercive power works best—when it works at all—with people who are unsure of themselves. Older workers are more confident and likely to quickly leave a job where a supervisor uses coercive power.

Supervisors can effectively use information and connective power with older workers. Their work experience has shown them the importance of information and connections with key people to be important in accomplishing a goal. Supervisors can gain influence with older workers by giving them information to do their job. They also respond positively when a supervisor can refer them to people who can provide the resources needed for accomplishing a task.

Leadership behavior is composed of both directive and supportive dimensions that have to be applied appropriately in a given situation. Effective leaders understand whether the response to employees' behavior calls for directive or supportive behavior. This contrasts with Trait and Style leadership theories, which imply that the same behavior is appropriate regardless of a specific situation. The following lists describe contrast between a leader's directive and supportive behaviors.

- Directive behaviors are behaviors that:
    - Involve mainly one-way communication
    - Help establish goals
    - Show how goals are to be achieved
    - Assist employees in goal accomplishment through giving directions
    - Establish methods of evaluation
    - Set timelines
    - Define roles
- Supportive behaviors are behaviors that:
    - Involve two-way communication
    - Help employees feel comfortable about themselves and the situation
    - Ask for input
    - Involve problem solving
    - Involve listening

The Situational Leadership Theory is a very practical model that can be used to evaluate any situation a leader faces in an organization. The following table provides a tool that can be used in evaluating a leadership situation.

Development Level of Employees	Recommended Approach
1. Low ability/low willingness	Tell the employee what to do (high direction/high support)
2. Low ability/high willingness	Sell/coach the employee (high direction/low support)
3. High ability/low willingness	Let employee participate (high support/low direction)
4. High ability/high willingness	Delegate to employee (low direction/low support)

The strengths of the Situational approach are:

■ It is well known and widely used in training programs for leaders.

■ It is easy to understand, sensible, and can be easily applied in a variety of settings.

■ It emphasizes the concept of leader flexibility.

The weaknesses of the Situational approach are:

■ The model concentrates on four possible situations when in fact, an infinite number of combinations exist, because the competence and commitment levels can occur anywhere between the high and low extremes.

■ It concentrates on the group's level of commitment and competence. In fact, each individual falls at a different point on the continuum. The question is, "Who in a group should you, as the leader, match your style to?"

According to the Situational Leadership approach, to be an effective leader, you have to adapt your style to fit the demands of different situations. In order to determine which style to use, you must evaluate your employees and assess both their competencies and their commitments in performing tasks. After determining these factors, you must match your style to the competencies and commitments of your employees. Because employees do move back an forth along the continuum, it is imperative for you to be flexible in your behavior. Employees may move from one place on the continuum to another rather quickly and over a short period of time, depending on the task. For this reason, you cannot use the same style in all contexts.

Leader-Member Exchange Theory

The Leader-Member Exchange (LMX) Theory—like the Situational Leadership Theory—takes an approach to leadership that is centered on the interactions between leaders and followers. Prior to the LMX Theory, leadership was treated as group-oriented process—something leaders direct toward all of their followers. The LMX Theory, first described by Graen and Haga, and Graen and Cashman, pays attention to the differences that might exist between leaders and each of their followers.

In the LMX Theory, a leader's relationship to her or his work unit is viewed as a series of vertical or one-on-one relationships. In looking at these vertical dyads, two general types of relationships were found.

- Relationships based on expanded and negotiated role responsibilities or extra roles, which are called in-group relationships. For example, an usher at a baseball stadium may negotiate a role of cheerleader for the team that goes well beyond his normal job responsibilities.

- Relationships based on the formal employment contract or defined roles, are called the out-group. For example, a fast-food cook who refuses to assist at the counter with customers because it isn't in her job description.

Within organizations, employees become part of either the in-group or the out-group, depending on how well they work with the leader and how well the leader works with them. Becoming part of one group or the other depends on how employees involve themselves in expanding their role responsibilities with the leader. Employees who negotiate with their leader on what extra things they are willing to do for their group may become part of the in-group. If an employee is not willing or interested in taking on new or different job responsibilities, they will become part of the out-group.

Employees in the in-group receive more information, have greater influence on the leader, and receive more support and attention from the leader than the out-group. In addition, in-group members are more dependable, more involved in the work, and more communicative than out-group employees. In-group employees do extra things for the leader and the leader will do extra things for them. High-quality leader and member exchanges may also produce less turnover by employees, better job attitudes, and greater organizational commitment. On the other hand, out-group employees usually just come to work, do their job and go home. This limited attachment to the leader results in a very limited commitment to an organization.

The leader-employee relationship does not happen quickly, and entrance into the in-group may take some time. Research suggests that the relationship develops over time and in three phases:

- **The stranger phase** focuses on the one-on-one relationship and is bound by organizational rules and the employment contract. The leader and subordinate relate to one another based within prescribed organizational rules and roles. Most often the subordinate will comply with the formal leader because of hierarchical status of the leader.

- **The acquaintance phase** involves an offer by either the leader or subordinate for improved relations, including sharing more resources and personal or work-related information. This may be a testing period for both the leader and subordinate to find out whether the subordinate is interested in taking on more responsibilities and/or roles in the organization. Interactions shift from being strictly governed by defined rules and eventually move to different ways of relating. Greater trust by the leader and subordinate begin to develop and they focus less on self-interests and more on the goals of the group.

- **The mature partnership phase** is recognized by high-quality leader member exchanges. Leaders and subordinates experience a high degree of mutual trust and respect for one another. Leaders and subordinates depend on one another and they carry out a high degree of interchange between them since they have tested their relationship and found they can depend on each other. Their relationship evolves to something beyond the traditional hierarchically-defined work relationship. The relationship may produce positive outcomes for themselves and the organization.

Supervisors can use the LMX Theory in two practical ways. First, the theory recognizes that effective leaders need to identify the presence of in-groups and out-groups within an organization. Leaders working with an in-group can accomplish more than they can with an out-group because in-group members are willing to do more than is required in their job description. Leaders need to respond to an in-group member's performance by giving him or her more responsibility, opportunity for development, and a greater amount of time and support.

Second, out-groups, unlike in-groups, will act quite differently by doing what is required of them and no more. The leader should treat them fairly, abide by company policies and procedures, and follow job descriptions, but it is not beneficial for the leader to give them any special attention. Out-group members should receive no more than the standard benefits of the position. Supervisors have a limited amount of time and their focus on out-group members doesn't have the same benefits to the organization that derives from the time spent with in-group members.

Initially, the concept of an in-group sounds elitist. It implies that the leader should select only a few people to be a part of this group. However, this is not the intent of the LMX Theory. The LMX Theory is prescriptive; it suggests that leaders should create a special relationship with all of their subordinates, similar to the in-group, and not limit this relationship to just a few employees. A leader should offer each subordinate new opportunities and relationships and nurture a high-quality relationship with subordinates. The more employees that feel a part of the in-group, the more a supervisor becomes a true leader who can motivate employees to achieve organizational goals.

The strengths of the LMX Theory are

- It validates our suspicions and experience of how people in organizations actually relate to one another. Some contribute more and receive more; some contribute less and receive less.

- Effective leadership will occur when communications of both leaders and subordinates are characterized by mutual respect, trust, and commitment.

The weaknesses of the LMX Theory are

- It does run counter to the basic values of fairness. We have always been taught to treat everyone equally and it is wrong to form in-groups and out-groups, but in reality, this is the way all organizations function. The LMX does give the appearance of discrimination against out-groups and in many instances, this is exactly what happens. The deliberate formation of in-groups and out-groups may have undesirable effects on a group as a whole. However, this weakness can be balanced when it is clear everyone has the opportunity to become a part of the in-group.

- The LMX does not tell you as a supervisor how to develop the relationships necessary to not have in-groups and out-groups. It assumes that these skills or traits are present in a supervisor and simply need to be exercised.

Welfare-to-work employees—Employers hiring welfare recipients have noted that two major problems are that they lack skills and are unaware of workplace culture. Workplace culture includes the importance of attendance, getting along with the supervisor and other workers, taking breaks, and so on. In fact, one study of welfare-to-work employees found that they often become very frustrated when they can't find a supervisor or co-workers to help deal with unfamiliar situations. Supervisors need to respond by taking a directive leadership style during the first few weeks and months of employment. This style doesn't involve "bossing" people around. Rather it recognizes the need for more direction, instruction, monitoring, and encouragement than other leadership styles.

Transformational Leadership

Transformational Leadership, first given importance by James MacGregor Burns, is a process designed to change and transform employees in an organization. It is concerned with the development of values, ethics, and long-term goals. The process involves assessing employees' motives, satisfying their needs, and treating them as human beings. It can be considered as an encompassing approach used to describe a wide range of leadership styles. The approach can be applied in either one-to-one relationships or on very broad attempts at influencing an entire organizational culture.

Transformational Leadership motivates employees to do more than is expected of them by using the following methods:

- **Raising an employee's level of consciousness about the importance and value of specified goals.** This can be done by talking about the program with employees, campaigns to promote the goals, and linking goal achievement to a reward.

- **Getting employees to transcend their own self-interests for the interests of the organization.** This is most effectively done when employees see these interests as symbiotic. Organizations can accomplish this by linking the organization's fortune with those of the employees. For example, organizations can utilize bonus plans. Increased wealth for the organization results in increased wealth for the employee.

- **Motivating employees to address higher-level needs.** In other words, don't focus on a security need like the employee merely keeping his or her job. Rather, Transformational Leadership would motivate the employee by encouraging the need to belong. This can be done by implementing activities that develop friendships among and between supervisors and employees.

Transformational Leadership is concerned with the development of employees, as well as their performance. Supervisors who exhibit Transformational Leadership skills often have a strong set of internal values and ideals. They can create a motivating environment to get employees to act in ways that will support the greater good rather than focusing on their own self-interests. Supervisors can use the following factors to achieve this transformational environment:

- **Charisma.** Idealized influence, or charisma, exists when the leaders act as strong role models. Employees identify with this and want to emulate the leader. A charismatic leader such as this usually has high standards of moral and ethical conduct and can be counted on to do the right thing in most situations. Employees respect them and usually place a great deal of trust in them because they can provide employees with direction and a sense of mission. The charisma factor describes a person who is special and who makes others want to follow them. However, management guru Peter Drucker has indicated that we need to beware of charisma because it is a great delusion that creates a diversion and may cover up incompetence.

- **Inspiration.** Inspiration is a factor that is descriptive of a leader who communicates high expectations to employees. Inspirational leaders create the motivating environment that allows employees to become committed and to be a part of the shared vision of the organization. The leader may use symbols or emotional appeals to focus employees to achieve more.

- **Stimulation.** Intellectual stimulation allows employees to be creative and innovative and to challenge their own beliefs and values as well as those of the leader. The leader empowers employees to try new approaches to deal with situations and acts as an agent of change.

- **Individualization.** Individualized consideration supports a climate where the leader listens carefully to the individual needs of employees. The leader acts as a coach and advisor while helping employees to be all they can be. The leader may use delegation to help employees grow and become more competent in what they are doing.

Strengths of Transformational Leadership:

■ It has an intuitive appeal to employees and is consistent with what many people feel a leader is; in other words, it just makes sense to people. It describes how the leader is out in front, advocating change. It is appealing to employees because the leader is providing a vision for the future.

■ It treats leadership as a process that occurs between leaders and employees and it incorporates both the needs of the employee and the leader. The needs of others are central to the transformational leader and a strong emphasis is placed on them.

Weaknesses of Transformational Leadership:

■ It is really difficult to define the parameters of Transformational Leadership because it does cover a wide range of skills such as:

◆ Creating a vision

◆ Creating a motivating environment

◆ Being a change agent

◆ Building trust with others

◆ Nurturing others

◆ Empowering others

■ Some see this approach from a trait perspective and that the transformational leader is a "special" person who has "special" qualities to transform others. If this is true, then it suggests an elitist and anti-democratic approach to leadership.

■ It does have the potential to be abused because it can be used for destructive purposes. Hitler is an example of a transformational leader who used his coercive powers to evil ends. Whoever is being influenced by a transformational leader should be aware of how they are being influenced and in what direction they are being asked to go.

A Model of Transformational Leadership

Idealized influence and charisma   Inspiration   Intellectual stimulation   Individualistic consideration

Path-Goal Leadership Theory

The Path-Goal Leadership Model, formulated by R.J. House, describes how leaders motivate employees to accomplish specific goals. Goals play a central role in the Path-Goal process, with the underlying premise being that human behavior is goal-oriented. A leader's challenge is to use a leadership strategy that best meets the employee's motivational needs. The process is illustrated in the following figure.

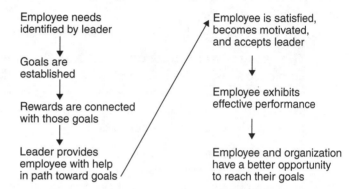

The Path-Goal Leadership Theory

Employee needs identified by leader
↓
Goals are established
↓
Rewards are connected with those goals
↓
Leader provides employee with help in path toward goals
→
Employee is satisfied, becomes motivated, and accepts leader
↓
Employee exhibits effective performance
↓
Employee and organization have a better opportunity to reach their goals

The Path-Goal Theory suggests that the leader's behavior has a direct impact on an employee by reinforcing a need. This makes the leader's choice of style in helping the employee fulfill their needs lead to differences in an employee's motivation. The Path-Goal Theory identifies four different style alternatives.

- **Directive leadership** focuses on clear task assignments, standards of successful performance, and work schedules. The leader seeks to fulfill an employee's needs in a deliberate and directive manner.

- **Supportive leadership** is friendly, approachable, demonstrates concern for employees' well-being, and attempts to create a pleasant work environment.

- **Achievement-oriented leadership** sets high expectations for employees, seeks continuous improvement, and models the desired behavior.

- **Participative leadership** invites employees to provide input in decisions and seriously attempts to integrate their suggestions into the decisions that are made.

Immigrant workers—The concept of power distance was developed by Geert Hofstede to describe how people in different cultures respond to inequalities in power. A country with a high power distance accepts a wide range of power between the leader and workers. Workers typically display a great deal of respect for anyone in authority and will unquestionably carry out instructions.

Countries with a high power distance are Arab countries, Ecuador, Guatemala, Hong Kong, India, Malaysia, Mexico, Panama, the Philippines, Singapore, and Venezuela. Supervisors are likely to find that workers from these countries are going to have difficulty adapting to a participative leadership style. It would be better to use a directive leadership style.

In the Path-Goal Theory, there are two major factors that must be looked at:

- **The general work environment.** A leader must identify whether an employee's task is appropriately designed, whether the organization's authority system is compatible with a directive or participative approach, and whether the present work group provides for the satisfaction of the employee's social and esteem needs.

- **The specific characteristics of the employee.** A leader must identify the needs and characteristics that govern the behavior of each employee. Four significant variables must be considered in this assessment:

  ◆ Identify whether the employee is motivated more by affiliation or by power. The theory predicts that employees who have strong affiliation needs prefer supportive leadership and those who are authoritarian and have to work in uncertain situations prefer a directive leader.

  ◆ Determine the extent of an employee's locus of control. This refers to whether a person believes his or her achievements are the product of personal efforts—an internal locus of control—or the result of an outside force—an external locus of control. The theory proposes that employees with an internal locus of control are more receptive to participative leadership, while those with an external locus of control are more receptive to a directive approach.

  ◆ Determine the employee's willingness to be influenced by others. An employee who is low in willingness is more likely to respond to a participative style of leadership. An employee that is high in willingness is more likely to respond to directive leadership.

  ◆ Assess the employee's perception of personal ability to complete a task. Employees who are confident in their ability to perform a task typically need a supportive form of leadership. Conversely, employees who are not confident in their ability to perform a task usually need an achievement-oriented form of leadership.

Strengths of the Path-Goal Theory:

■ The Path-Goal Theory attempts to integrate the motivational principles of the Expectancy Theory of Motivation into a theory of leadership.

■ It is the only leadership theory that deals with motivation in a direct way.

■ It provides a model that makes leaders aware of their responsibility to help remove the obstacles that keep an employee from reaching their desired goals.

Weaknesses of the Path-Goal Theory:

■ The theory is very complex and looks at so many different aspects of leadership that it is difficult to interpret.

■ It is broad and encompasses so many different interrelated sets of assumptions that it is difficult to utilize.

Contingency Model

An early model of leadership is the Contingency Model developed by Fred Fiedler and associates. The model builds on the previous distinctions between task and employee orientation, and it suggests that the most appropriate leadership style will depend on whether the overall situation is favorable or unfavorable or in an intermediate state of favor for the leader. As this situation changes, the requirements of the leader also change.

Fiedler indicates that a leader's effectiveness will be determined by the interaction of the employee's orientation with three additional variables:

■ **Leader-member relations** refers to the atmosphere and to the degree of confidence, loyalty, and attraction that employees feel for the leader. If the atmosphere is positive and employees trust, like, and get along with the leader, the leader-member relations are defined as good. On the other hand, if the atmosphere is unfriendly and abrasive, the leader-member relations are defined as poor.

■ **Task structure** refers to the degree to which the requirements of the task are clear and spelled out. The tasks that are very structured give more control to the leader. A task is considered structured when:

◆ The requirements of the task are clearly stated and are known by the employee required to perform them.

171

◆ The path to accomplishing the task has few alternatives.

◆ The completion of the task can be clearly demonstrated by the employee.

◆ Only a limited number of correct solutions to the task exist.

◆ Tasks that are unclear tend to lessen the control and influence of the leader.

■ **Position power** refers to the amount of authority the leader has to reward or punish the employee. It includes legitimate power that the leader acquires as a result of his or her position in the organization. The position of the leader is strong if the leader has the power to hire, fire, or give raises to employees. Conversely, the position power is weak if the leader does not have the right to do these things.

An effective leader moves to achieve a high level of achievement in all three areas. By creating positive relationships and tasks, the leader makes it easier for employees to function well in their jobs. At the same time a leader must clearly function from a position of power that limits employees from deviating from established standards in relationship and task areas.

Strengths of the Contingency Theory:

■ The Contingency Theory is predictive and it provides useful information regarding the type of leader that will be effective in certain contexts.

■ It also does not require the leader to be "all things to all people." The theory matches the leader and the situation but it does not require the leader to fit every situation.

Weaknesses of the Contingency Theory:

■ The theory does not explain why individuals with certain leadership styles are more effective in some situations than in others.

■ It also does not explain what organizations should do when there is a mismatch between the leader and the situation in the workplace. Situations are not always easily changed to match the leader's style.

Special Issues Related to Leadership

Three special topics are important in leadership today. One is the issue of women in leadership. Women are being given more opportunities for leadership than they have in the past. However, the continued lack of female leaders—and how this problem can be overcome—is an important matter to consider. Another

topic we want to consider is nonleadership. This is a phenomenon that sometimes occurs when a person is promoted to a leadership position but either
doesn't possess leadership skills or fails to use them. The third special issue
discussed in this section is the relationship between power and leadership.

Women and Leadership

Although women make up an increasing percentage of the workforce, in many
cases, they continue to be excluded from leadership positions in some organizations. Frequently, occupations that employ a high percentage of women still find
a higher percentage of men in leadership positions.

One of the most significant challenges that faces organizations in the coming
years is to find leaders who are adequately equipped to work in organizations
that emerge in the information economy. In some instances, men who follow the
traditional male role may find it difficult to adapt to new leadership requirements.
The modern organization requires leaders who are effective in building and
leading teams. A traditional male has been taught to emphasize individual
accomplishment and promote competition rather than collaboration. The
participatory, networking style frequently displayed by female leaders makes
them better candidates to lead teams. The traditional male leadership style may
be well suited for short-term organizational goals, but the typical female leadership style may be suited for long-term organizational effectiveness. In many
instances, leading means giving up power rather than accumulating it, and
women more often display this ability than do men. Some of the skills that
women have that make them effective in the workplace are

- Respect for feelings as an essential part of life

- The ability to recognize and express feelings

- Listening empathetically and effectively

- The ability to relate to people on a personal level

- The ability to touch and be close to both women and men
  without suggesting sexual connotations

- The ability to accept the emotional, spontaneous, and irrational
  parts of people

Although these strengths are frequently ones most needed in leadership for a
modern organization, they are sometimes held up as examples of weaknesses by
traditional males. This can hinder their ability to move ahead. Traditional males
often perceive either women or men who display these skills as weak, and hesi-
tate to promote them into positions of leadership. For women, it may be a

"catch-22," because their greatest strengths may be keeping them from positions they deserve because those strengths are perceived as weaknesses by traditional males who control their organizational destiny. In order to counteract this problem, women can develop some typical masculine strengths to help them:

- Have a more direct and visible impact on other people rather than just being behind the scenes.

- Build support systems with other men and women, and share competence with them rather than trying to compete with them.

- Turn anger outward and do not hold it in.

- Respond directly to others and use "I" statements.

- Learn to be more powerful and forthright.

- Behave more impersonally with others.

- Become more of a "risk taker."

- Calculate what might happen in situations and make trade-offs where necessary.

Disabled workers—Workers with disabilities provide a challenge to supervisors who want to use Situational Leadership principles. An important step in using Situational Leadership is to determine the degree to which employees have the competence to accomplish a task. The question for supervisors is how a worker's disabilities affect their competence to accomplish a task. However, there is a simple way to answer this question: Ask the worker. The disabled worker can describe any limitations that might prevent him or her from accomplishing a task. It is important for the supervisor to develop a good relationship and establish effective communication with the worker. Eventually you should develop the ability to accurately judge a worker's abilities or competence to accomplish a specific task.

Nonleadership

In some instances, individuals who are in leadership positions choose to use nonleadership, or "laissez-faire" (hands-off) leadership. This type of leadership is ineffective and really represents the absence of leadership. In these cases, a leader:

- Abdicates responsibility
- Delays decisions

■ Gives no feedback to employees

■ Makes little or no effort to help employees satisfy their needs

■ Exchanges nothing with employees to help them grow and become more effective

This nonleadership style depends on employees to establish their own goals and work out their own problems. Employees have to train themselves and provide their own motivating environment. Nonleadership can degenerate into chaos and is not effective in the long term for either organizations or employees. As a supervisor, it is not beneficial for you or the organization to practice nonleadership. Many supervisors in organizations fail because they do not provide the leadership that is needed for employees to become effective.

Power and Leadership

Power is not equivalent to leadership, but it is an essential ingredient of leadership. Power is the potential ability to influence employees. As a supervisor, you will use power (or at least the perception of power) to get things done through employees. It is difficult to influence people unless there is an ability to motivate them to action. It is often power that provides a supervisor with the tool needed to motivate employees. One of the most popular concepts on the use of power in leadership was devised by John French and Bertram Raven. They proposed that there are five sources or bases of power.

1. **Coercive power**—based on threats and punishment—can be used to influence employees to behave in a manner specified by the leader. Fear of reprimands, suspension, or dismissal can force employees to follow your directions. However, be careful with coercive power; it can sometimes lead to negative reactions from employees because fear has limits. A courageous employee can sometimes rally other workers to oppose—*en masse*—a coercive leader. Mass punishments are very difficult to administer because they may cause such a high degree of turnover that an organization is unable to operate.

2. **Reward power** is based on the ability to confer rewards on employees such as praise, recognition, pay raises, or promotions that ensure compliance. Using praise where it is deserved makes employees feel appreciated and confers power on the supervisor giving the praise. A supervisor can also control employees' performance through tools like performance appraisals that relate to raises and promotions. Two problems can arise from the use of reward powers. One problem is that the supervisor falls into the temptation of being liked by employees because of the rewards

175

that he or she gives and doesn't stop the rewards even when employee behavior is unacceptable. Another problem that reward power may create is an expectation on the part of employees for more rewards. They are never satisfied because they don't see their behavior being sufficiently or frequently rewarded.

3. **Legitimate power** is also known as position power and official power that comes from a higher authority within the organization. It is power delegated to you as a supervisor by the organization. Make sure your employees are aware of the power you possess and work at having people perceive that you do have power. Inexperienced workers are sometimes not aware of the power a supervisor has. It is appropriate for you to make them aware of this power and all that it entitles you to do.

4. **Personal power** is also known as referent power, charismatic power, or power of personality and comes from each person individually. It is the ability for you to develop followers among employees based on the strength of your personality. To increase your personal power, get to know your employees well, develop a good relationship with them, and show interest in them. Also, develop good personal relationships with others in the organization. This type of power is sometimes equated with the development of loyalty by employees. Some practical ways to increase loyalty include crediting employees—to management—for accomplishments and ideas, appropriately intervening on their behalf when inequities occur, and returning favors that employees do for you.

5. **Expert power** is also known as the authority of knowledge and comes from specialized learning. It is the power that will arise from your special skills, education, or experience you have, and that employees recognize. To increase your expert power, take all of the training and educational programs your organization provides or go to a local college or university to gain more expertise.

Other management experts have identified two additional sources of power.

■ **Connective power** is based on relationships you have with influential people. It relies on contacts and friends, who can influence the people you are dealing with. To increase your connective power, try to expand your network of contacts with important managers who have power. Try to get in with the "in crowd," make sure they are aware of your accomplishments, and when you need something, identify the people who can help you get it. Many people who aren't managers or supervisors have connective power. They have control over things that can help you or your employees. For example, administrative assistants often control access to executives, so developing a good relationship with the assistant helps you more easily gain access to an executive when you need to do so.

■ **Information power** is based on information you have that is desired by others. To increase your information power, know what is going on in the organization and have as much information as possible flow through you. You can gain power by serving on task forces or committees where you gain access to more information. The opportunity to gain this type of power has been diminished with the increasing application and availability of computers. Computers enable the organization to broaden access to information rather than narrow it among a few individuals.

Popular Approaches to Leadership

We have discussed several theories of leadership that originated among theorists and researchers. However, several popular concepts of leadership tend to define leadership in a more practical and applicable manner. Most of these concepts have a pragmatic approach to leadership—they focus on what should occur to make leadership effective:

■ **Servant-leadership** is an approach that focuses on the idea that leaders have the obligation to first pursue and satisfy the needs of their followers. In doing so, employees are enabled to achieve a high level of performance, but at the same time, be fulfilled individuals. Robert K. Greenleaf was one of the first proponents of this concept. A former management expert with AT&T, he wrote a small essay in 1970 called *The Servant As Leader*, which introduced the term "servant-leadership." If leaders have as their main concern their own professional advancement, they will fail to meet the requirements of servant leadership. To be effective servant-leaders, they must shift the focus of attention from their own needs and interests to those of employees. Effective servant-leaders are motivated from what their role as a leader can allow them to give to others—not what they can get from their positions.

■ Many popular writers pursue a **spiritual-ethical** theme when describing leadership, rather than focusing on leadership from a managerial perspective. In their writings, they pay less attention to the bottom line and more attention to issues of honesty, trust, integrity, and character. In his book

The Seven Habits of Highly Effective People, Stephen Covey describes the principles on which leadership should be based, including trustworthiness, character, competence, maturity, self-discipline, and integrity. He also emphasized the seven habits as:

♦ Being proactive

♦ Beginning with the end in mind

♦ Putting first things first

♦ Thinking win-win

♦ Seeking first to understand, then to be understood

♦ Using synergy (combining forces to work together)

♦ Engaging in continuous improvement

▓ **Empowerment of followers** is a popular approach to leadership that Peter Block has written about extensively. Empowerment emphasizes the importance of a leader's relationship with employees. It focuses on leaders building credibility when they allow authority to be shared with employees. It shifts the attention from the decision-making behaviors of the leader and allows the decision-making process to be given to employees who have the ability to make sound decisions. It also embraces a team approach to leadership and gives employees the opportunity to change their perspective, adjust their values, and develop a new way of behaving.

Most of these popular approaches of leadership focus on the employee as a human being with needs and concerns that need to be taken into consideration when decisions are being made. They imply that what is good for the employee is ultimately good for the organization. They are also easy to understand, they make sense, and they fit into what is currently accepted leadership principles—specifically, Total Quality Management. They make an important contribution to our understanding of leadership.

However, most of these "pop" approaches to leadership have not been tested through research and they may be quite difficult to apply in everyday real-life settings. They often are popular because they espouse idealistic concepts. However, the ideals may be difficult to implement because some organizations don't support their use. Many organizations are looking for simple solutions to complex problems and they often tend to oversimplify human behavior. In many organizations, they are only giving lip service to these concepts because they sound good. Some organizations tend to be "faddish"—they want to adopt whatever new fad is being written about, but only do it superficially.

Quick Tip

Contingent workers—It is difficult to practice Situational Leadership with contingent workers because a supervisor is familiar with neither their competence nor their motivation. It is important to interview temporary workers about their skills. Carefully observe their work to determine their motivation. Initially assume that a directive approach is best until you determine otherwise.

Practical Strategies for Leaders

When all the theories and popular models are considered, some common and significant ideas emerge. It is possible to be more effective as a leader when you recognize that your ultimate responsibility is the accomplishment of goals that the organization establishes. However, many people are distracted from true leadership by becoming entranced by the goal and failing to recognize that it is people who achieve goals. A leader can't function without followers. Here are some ways that you develop the kind of employees who will work with you to achieve the organization's goals.

- **Respect employees.** Human life is valuable and should be respected. Every person brings positive attributes to a job that are valuable. It is tempting to look at a person with a handicap and see only her disability and not her ability. Some supervisors look for the "handicap" in everyone. However, people respond in a positive way when we look for the best in them and advocate them to use this best in performing their job.

- **Provide meaning.** Victor Frankl was a psychotherapist who developed Logotherapy. The basic thought behind this approach is the idea that the most important need a person has is to find a meaning or purpose in life. Frankl developed this concept based on his personal observations when held captive in a Nazi extermination camp. He saw cold and starving people who gave their food and clothing to others. He saw prisoners who were willing to suffer death to save others from it. This led him to the conclusion that the need to find a meaning in life motivated them more than any other needs. Leaders seek to help their followers find a meaning in life.

- **Treat employees courteously.** Courtesy has sometimes been forgotten in as our society has adopted fewer formalities. For instance, the use of the "sir" and "ma'am" are used much less frequently—even in very formal restaurants where this behavior was once common. However, there are still simple things we can do and say that are courtesies. Particularly important are the use of "please" when requesting an employee to

179

do something and "thank you" when the action is complete. Ask an employee how they prefer to be addressed, and don't just assume this. For example, Timothy may not like to be addressed as Tim or perhaps Pat doesn't want to be called Patty. Also, be willing to show some considerate behavior, such as getting an employee a cup of coffee when you go to get one for yourself.

- **Treat employees like adults.** Outside of work employees may be parents, leaders in a scout troop, members of a church board, volunteers for social service organizations, and many other roles with a high degree of responsibility. They are respected and looked up to by others. Treating employees in a paternalistic or maternalistic manner is very demeaning. Such treatment stands in stark contrast to the roles they fulfill outside work and often develops a feeling of resentment toward the supervisor.

- **Use employee skills.** Provide people with an opportunity to use the skills they have. Employees often develop a feeling of being underused and not recognized when skills they have go unnoticed and unused. Conduct a skill survey of your employees. Ask employees to write down a list of all skills they use on a daily, weekly, and monthly basis. Ask them to list all skills that they have but don't use on the job. This provides you with information that you may not have compiled from resumes or job applications. For example, one of the authors knows a situation when a company struggled to have a document translated from French. After spending a great deal of time and money, it was discovered that one of the organization's employees translated books from French to English as a hobby. There was no reason that managers should have known about this skill because there had never been a need for the employee to use it. A skill survey would have identified this resource.

- **Assist in employability development.** Organizations can assist employees in the development of new skills. This increases the value of employees and thus their employability. This makes employees feel that a leader perceives them as valuable because they are willing to make an investment in the employee. Delegating new tasks to an employee, providing training opportunities, paying for college courses, and promoting employees are all strategies that develop employability. Some organizations view employability development as a replacement for job security. It is difficult because of competitive factors to guarantee a person employment, but you can provide them with employability so that if they must seek another job, they have a valuable set of skills to sell another employer.

- **Recognize employee achievements.** Leaders who take credit for ideas and achievements of their followers soon lose the respect of those followers. People need and value recognition for their contributions and a good leader doesn't rob them of this. Praising employees, making public announcements, distributing memos about employee achievements, awarding prizes, and publicizing accomplishments in newsletters are all ways of showing recognition.

- **Reward employees.** Most employees ultimately expect more substantial rewards for their accomplishments than just good treatment, trust, employability development, and recognition. Enthusiasm and support for a leader diminish when the leader fails to provide concrete rewards. That is why leaders should advocate salary and wage increases and promotions for their workers. Supervisors can sometimes control minor rewards like office space and location, special assignments, business trips, and distribution of obsolete equipment. Use this authority to also reward employees.

Good Followership

Scores of books have been written about leadership. People are encouraged to become leaders. A topic that hasn't received as much attention, but is also important, is followership. Leaders should teach their subordinates about followership because it improves the ability of followers to achieve organizational goals. It can also strengthen the relationship between leaders and followers. A good point to begin in the quest to understand followership is a two-dimensional model of leadership used by the United States Air Force.

The first dimension that must be examined is the degree of independence and critical thinking that exists among followers. In his book *An Invented Life: Reflections on Leadership and Change*, Warren Bennis writes "What makes a good follower? The single most important characteristic may well be a willingness to tell the truth. In a world of growing complexity, leaders are increasingly dependent on their subordinates for good information, whether the leaders want to hear it or not. Followers who tell the truth, and leaders who listen are an unbeatable combination." Good followers are able to think independently and critically so that they can provide honest responses to a leader about a situation, action, or idea.

A second dimension looks at how passive or active followers are in responding to situations. Good followers sometimes face problems that require a quick response. They must consider what a leader would do but move forward

181

without direction. In addition, some situations require initiative to take advantage of opportunities, and a good follower will do this. The following model illustrates how these dimensions are related and the type of followers who can be described using the model.

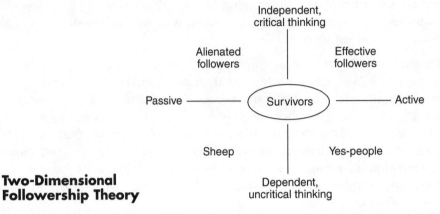

Two-Dimensional Followership Theory

Each of the possible follower types is described in this section, along with ideas that you as a leader can use when dealing with this type of follower.

- **Sheep.** This type of follower is a passive, dependent, uncritical person. They blindly go and do whatever the leader tells them to do but initiate no action. People often adopt this style when supervisors are quick to blame employees for their actions and aren't responsive to ideas that conflict with their own. Supervisors can and should encourage sheep by praising them for taking action—even when the results aren't what you expect. In addition, listen to their ideas and respond in a logical and unemotional manner.

- **Yes-people.** This type of follower is dependent, uncritical, but active. Yes-people say whatever they believe the leader wants to hear—thus preventing the leader from hearing some important facts. They are active because they think they can please the leader by initiating action in the same manner a leader would. Supervisors should encourage yes-people to be open and truthful about stating their own ideas and praise them for doing so.

- **Survivors.** This type of follower is always looking for the safest way to do things. They avoid being passive but don't want to be too active. They seldom express their own ideas. However, when they think that not stating an idea could hurt them at a later time, they'll speak up. The survivor style often develops in organizations where there is a great deal of turnover in supervisors or where the organization is given to faddish ideas. Their attitude often is "this too shall pass." An organization can function with survivors, but the ability to change and move forward is very difficult. The best thing a supervisor can do is display consistent behavior and persistence. Eventually, survivors begin to feel that a supervisor really is going to reach a goal and begin to actively support the leader.

■ **Alienated followers.** This type of follower is independent, a critical thinker, but passive. The style is usually adopted by talented and skilled people who find their actions to be frequently criticized by a leader. Alienated followers can sometimes display characteristics that are more destructive than any other type of follower. They undermine leaders' actions, criticize leaders behind their backs, and promote dissension among other followers. Some leaders criticize an action because it wasn't done the way they would do it. Good supervisors are flexible and praise employees' accomplishments even when things are not done exactly their way. Use the talents and abilities of your employees to overcome the problem of alienated followers.

■ **Effective followers.** This type of follower is independent, thinks critically, and is active. This style normally develops in organizations where leaders are honest, self-critical, and supportive.

Supervisors can give some practical suggestions to employees so that they can become effective followers. In turn, the supervisor must reward employees for these behaviors, not punish them for it.

■ **Support the leader.** Once a decision is made and action is taken by a leader, be supportive. There are times that a leader makes mistakes. Employees should support the leader during these times. Good leaders can develop this behavior by listening to employees' ideas and supporting them when they make mistakes.

■ **Be honest.** Tell the leader what you think. Provide facts that don't agree with the leader's point of view. Make sure that the leader has all the facts—even when these aren't pleasant to discuss.

■ **Protect the leader's time.** Take the initiative to perform tasks that don't need the leader's attention. Gather all the facts and be able to concisely present them before meeting with the leader.

■ **Ask questions.** When the leader is proposing an idea or action that isn't clear or understandable, ask questions. If you think that there is something unethical being proposed, raise the issue. However, ask questions in a respectful and thoughtful manner.

■ **Accept responsibility.** Be willing to take action on ideas you suggest and accept the consequences—both good and bad. Follow through with assignments that you are given. Report back to the leader about these assignments when it seems appropriate.

■ **State your expectations and explain how they can be fulfilled.** Good leaders develop good followers. Followership is like every other skill—it must be taught and developed. A leader can't sit passively by and expect it to develop naturally. It requires deliberate and thoughtful action on your part.

Summary

Leadership is the process of influencing and supporting others to work to achieve goals and objectives. It is a complex process. However, we're hopeful that after reading this chapter, you have many insights into the different theories and concepts about leadership. From these models you can gain some practical insights that will help you become more than a supervisor—a true leader. You can gain a great deal of satisfaction in being seen as a leader. In addition, you should better understand how to develop effective followers. You become a more effective supervisor when you are able to motivate workers to achieve their best for the organization.

Chapter 9

Teamwork—Reaching the Goal

Managing an organization today is a complicated business. Competition from other countries is increasing; technology continues to grow more complex; government regulations are sometimes difficult to understand and follow. Faced with these complexities, employers are looking for supervisors who are team leaders and problem solvers.

Managers in today's business world are relying on employees and work teams to help solve many problems. This management technique is sometimes referred to as **employee involvement** or **participatory management.** Teams may be expected to solve any problems that occur. For example, if the data your team or unit enters into a computer has a lot of mistakes, the team may be directed to solve the problem. There are several reasons for the growth of employee involvement, including these:

■ **Reduction of management.** In the last several years, businesses have made drastic cuts in the number of managers and supervisors they employ, thus saving a great deal of money. This means employees must assume some of the responsibilities previously performed by managers. Supervisors can have a larger number of employees reporting to them when employees accept more responsibility for problem solving.

185

- **Complexity.** Worldwide competition, high technology, government regulations, and a diverse workforce all make businesses more complex. An organization needs help from every employee to solve problems in these complex areas. It is extremely difficult for a supervisor to be an expert in all the knowledge and skills that are performed by employees on their team.

- **Motivation.** Employees are motivated to do a better job when they are involved in solving problems related to their work. Psychologists have discovered that people become emotionally invested in ideas that they propose or have a part in developing. Employees work harder to assure that their ideas succeed—much more so than when the idea was imposed by management.

- **Proximity.** Employees are closer to most problems than managers and supervisors. They often see solutions that escape managers. Employee involvement takes advantage of this perspective.

- **Change.** Modern organizations go through a great deal of change. If employers want their employees to be willing to change, they must involve them in problem-solving and decision-making processes.

The use of teams in organizations is a relatively recent development. This chapter will help you by discussing organizational concepts that have been popular and are still used by many organizations. From the variety of team models and examples presented here, you can identify ways to build and maintain effective teams in your organization.

Younger workers—Keep in mind that young people have grown up with the VCR, cable TV, remote controls, personal computers, and video games. They are able to process information quickly, including data coming from multiple sources, at one time. Younger workers feel more comfortable with technology than workers in the 30-plus age group. This gives them some insights in analyzing and solving technology-related problems—or problems that can be resolved using technology—that other workers may not possess. Young people also tend to bring an excitement and enthusiasm to the problem-solving process that can energize a team.

One of the biggest obstacles young people face in being part of a team is a lack of respect. Other workers often concentrate on the negative aspects of youth—inexperience, rash behavior, and audacity. It is important to coach other team members about the positive characteristics of young workers. They should be encouraged to treat younger workers and their ideas with the same regard they would any employee. They should also learn to encourage the enthusiasm of younger workers. Team members should learn to channel the eagerness of younger workers without discouraging them.

Classical Organizational Theory

The Classical Organization Theory of bureaucracy was that you start with the total amount of work to be done and then it was divided into divisions, departments, jobs, and assignments of responsibility for the people involved. Early management theorists believed bureaucracy creates organizational efficiency. Some of the principles of bureaucracy include the following:

■ **Specialization.** Each job should be structured so that an employee can exercise a special set of skills. For example, instead of having several accounting clerks who perform multiple tasks, it is better to have a billing clerk, accounts receivable clerk, credit authorization clerk, payroll clerk, and so on.

■ **Hierarchy** or **chain-of-command.** Every employee must report to a supervisor or manager, creating a layer of management. Management has several layers, ending with the top manager or head of the organization—usually called the executive director, president, or chief executive officer (CEO). Two key concepts related to organizing the chain-of-command rule are span of control and unity of command.

◆ **Span of control** describes how many employees one person can properly supervise. There is no established number that is considered ideal. Typically, it is considered reasonable to create a broad span of control—meaning a larger number of employees can report to a supervisor—when employees are highly specialized or have a high level of education. Proximity of employees, need to coordinate the work of employees, and other duties of the supervisor also affect the span of control.

◆ **Unity of command** is the philosophy that states an employee should report to one and only one supervisor. It is designed to help an employee focus on a task assigned by the supervisor. Otherwise, an employee faces a dilemma when he or she is assigned tasks by more than one supervisor. Which task should have priority? What should the employee do when instructions from supervisors conflict? Who is the employee accountable to for time and attendance? In other words, who approves the employee's pay? A lack of unity in command often causes confusion.

187

■ **Rules and regulations.** The organization functions primarily through policies and procedures developed by management. No actions are to be undertaken by an employee that run counter to policies or procedures. The assumption is that management knows more than employees and troubles arise when employees initiate action on their own.

■ **Rational decision making.** Decisions are made by following a logical thought process. It normally consists of the following steps:

1. Identification of a problem

2. Establishing alternative solutions

3. Selecting the best solution—usually the best results for the least cost

4. Implementing the decision

5. Evaluating the results of the decision and making appropriate adjustments

■ **Promotion based on technical competence.** The decision to promote an employee is based primarily on their technical competence and task performance.

All organizations still rely on these principles to some extent, which should be used as guidelines and not absolutes in organizations. However, although the concept of bureaucracy is associated with efficiency, a number of negative attributes still exist:

■ **Rigid application of rules, policies, and procedures.** Circumstances sometimes arise that are not covered by the policies or procedures. At other times, the rules prevent an employee from taking action that might be beneficial for the long-term health of the organization. For example, a mail delivery company clerk returns 500,000 dated advertisements to a retailer because the retailer lacked a few dollars in its account to pay for the shipping. The organization's rules state that a company must pay its account in full before any item is shipped. This action results in a loss of millions of dollars to the retailer. As a result, the retailer decides to distribute its advertisements by a newspaper, which ends up costing the delivery company a good customer and millions of dollars in future sales.

■ **A distinct lack of concern for the individual.** The focus of a bureaucracy is on creating a smooth functioning organization. The employee becomes a cog in the system that doesn't receive any attention unless it doesn't work properly. Likewise, customers often just become account numbers.

■ **Employee frustration.** In chapter 8, you read the quote by Warren Bennis that managers do things right, but leaders do the right thing. A bureaucracy creates a situation in which supervisors and employees are rewarded for doing things right. They often become frustrated when they aren't able to do the right thing—even when they are sure it is right.

■ **Inefficiency, red tape, and repetition of effort.** A bureaucracy has a tendency to develop more levels of hierarchy than are needed for efficient operation. The massive layoffs of managers during the 1990s was largely the result of organizations eliminating unnecessary layers of management. Rules and procedures usually are accompanied by the need for forms and reports. This creates red tape that slows an organization's ability to operate.

A bureaucracy can function well in a relatively stable environment, slow economic growth, and in circumstances where problems are easily identified and managed. Management theorists today advocate applying modified organizational theories to meet human needs within the bureaucratic structure. We are beginning to realize that the traditional bureaucracy has been pushed to its limits of effectiveness and something new must replace it.

Neoclassical Theory

During the 1960s, researchers proposed new concepts and theories concerning human resources within organizational structures. The major ideas were that individual and organizational goals should not be in conflict, but should complement one another. The Neoclassical theorists gave priority to the goals of the organization while recognizing the value of human resources—people—within the organization. They said there is a need for bureaucratic rules and procedures, but at times, they should be de-emphasized. Rules and procedures must exist to avoid chaos, but recognize that there is a need to be flexible in order to meet employee and customer needs. Neoclassical Theory proposes that when the proper balance between organizational and individual needs is achieved in the workplace, a healthy and well-adjusted organization results.

Contingency Organization Theory

The trend today is toward the application of the Contingency Organization Theory, which proposes that organizational design needs to be flexible. A key concept states that organizations need structures and processes to avoid chaos and confusion. In fact, some situations require a more bureaucratic approach for effectiveness. However, because of cultural, social, economic, and technological

189

changes, organizations must change over time. Organizational designs need to be flexible so they can fit these changing environments. This view requires a change in philosophy from the traditional ways of organizing that remain fixed over time. Two views of organizational form relate to the Contingency Theory:

■ **Mechanistic.** The mechanistic form of organizations fits with the traditional bureaucratic way of organizing. Employees are specialized, jobs are structured around common tasks, multiple levels of management direct these employees and tasks, and each higher level of management is assigned more power and influence. The work is carefully scheduled, tasks are certain, roles are strictly defined, and communication follows the chain of command.

■ **Organic.** The organic form is more flexible, open to change, and tasks and roles are not rigidly defined. This allows employees to adjust the organization's polices and procedures to fit the requirements of each situation. Communication is more multidirectional and consists of information and advice rather than instructions. Decision making is more decentralized. Employees are also given more authority and influence and are asked to solve problems. The organization is more open to its environment.

The Contingency Theory of organization suggests that in certain situations, a mechanistic form is desirable and in other situations, an organic form is more effective. An organic form is usually more effective for modern society, where the environment is dynamic and requires frequent change within the organization. Organic organizations are more likely to use teams to manage organizational activities and tasks.

Older workers—Older workers are valuable to a team because of their experience. Their experience often enables them to be proficient at problem solving. These are key resources they often bring to the team. However, a supervisor needs to be aware that these traits can sometimes be hampered because older workers often place a high value on individuality and stability. Baby Boomers and older generations gained much of their work experience in an era that stressed personal performance over team performance. This background can make it difficult for older workers to value teamwork.

Supervisors should discuss the value of teamwork with older workers. Get them to discuss their real feelings and thoughts about being part of a team. Respond to their concerns and explain the personal benefits that can be gained by working with a team. Encourage older workers to give the team concept an opportunity to work. Stress the importance of what the team can gain from the worker's experience. Inform other members of the team about the gains to be made from listening to the opinions of experienced workers—even when their experience with your organization is limited. A little extra coaching on your part can help develop a more cohesive team.

Teams in Organizations

We hear a lot about employee involvement, teamwork, and team building these days and teams are increasingly becoming the prime method around which work is designed. Teamwork recognizes that within an organization, small groups of employees can work closely and interdependently with one another. Though teams are popular, not all organizations have embraced them or have had success using them. Many organizations that try to implement teams fail because they do not realize the commitment that must be made to have effective teams. Failure also occurs because teams require a large investment in time and money—time for training, employee development, and management involvement, and money to support all of these activities. Some organizations also fail to effectively implement teams because they don't understand the concept. Others try to implement elements that they like and eliminate elements that they don't like, resulting in a fractured process that doesn't work well.

A difficult obstacle that many organizations face in implementing team management relates to employee involvement. Some managers have difficulty in relinquishing authority and responsibility to employees. However, it is possible to implement teams with limited employee involvement. Think of employee involvement in decision making as a continuum from very little involvement to almost total involvement. Teams can be implemented at any point along this continuum—although it is most effective as the level of employee involvement in decision making increases. The level of employee involvement selected by an organization is typically influenced by the organizational culture, management style, and employee preferences.

Stages in Team Development

Organizations typically go through several stages when developing teams. An awareness of these stages can help an organization anticipate difficulties in implementing teams and react appropriately to resolve them.

Planning stage

During this stage, the organization should appoint key managers and employees to a steering committee. The committee's primary task should be to conduct a study of the organization to determine whether teams could strengthen the organization and improve operations. This usually takes several weeks or months before the steering committee compiles the data needed to determine the appropriateness of teams for the organization. One of this book's authors—Tom Capozzoli—was part of the management startup team at General Motors' battery plant in Fitzgerald, Georgia. He thinks that the process of implementing teams at that plant could have been improved if an additional six months had been allocated to the planning process. The planning process also provides an opportunity for the committee to learn more about team management and employee involvement. Once the committee finishes its study, it can recommend whether the organization should implement teams in the organization.

Implementation stage

This usually takes one to three months. The organization needs to develop a mission statement that defines its concept of teams, affirms the organization's commitment to teams, and states the level of employee involvement that will result from the use of teams. The mission statement clearly informs employees of the organization's intent and level of commitment to teams. During the implementation stage, teams are formed and training starts to take place.

Training needs to be provided to all supervisors and managers so they understand their role in the development and implementation of teams. It is important that all levels of management are trained and that the training is sufficiently thorough. Managers and supervisors need more than just an understanding of the team concept. They need specific skills required for successful team implementation. Some organizations fail in the use of teams because managers and supervisors aren't properly trained in the implementation and development of teams.

Organizations sometimes choose to use teams on a limited basis. Not all employees are assigned to teams. This decision requires managers and supervisors to select employees that will be assigned to teams. In a **green-field startup**—a brand new organization—employees can be screened for their skills and abilities to work in a team. However, the employee selection task can be more difficult in an existing organization because everyone may not want to work in a team and may resist the change. The Fitzgerald, Georgia battery plant was a green-field plant, which made it easier to select team members. However, no matter what type of startup, it will be to the organization's advantage to use "natural" workgroups as teams. A natural workgroup is a group of employees who do similar work or have a common reason to work closely together.

Clarification stage

This stage can last for six to nine months. It is a time when roles, functions, responsibilities, and techniques are subject to confusion and need clarification. Supervisors and managers should be accessible to provide teams with coaching or training. Employees may need extensive training to help them understand and function in their new roles. The team's roles and responsibilities should be clarified and assistance should be provided to help teams focus on planning. Supervisors should reinforce the team's positive behavior and provide support for the teams. They should also create a motivating and positive environment.

This stage is critical because many managers and supervisors are uncomfortable with or misunderstand their role in helping teams develop. Managers and supervisors must be committed to the team concept. When this support is lacking, the likelihood of failure increases. If employees sense that supervisors and managers lack commitment, they often assume—correctly in most cases—that team building is being done for show and the use of teams is not really going to be practiced in the organization.

Emergence of leaders

This stage usually last 6 to 18 months. During this stage, team leaders emerge and teams become an integral part of the organization. Many organizations initially appoint team leaders during the implementation stage and wait for them to promote an environment where more leaders can develop. The organization should appoint leaders who are accepted by team members and have a strong commitment to the development of the team. At the Fitzgerald plant, team leaders were appointed by the management team to start with, but as soon as they were able, the teams were allowed to select their own leaders. Some of the teams chose to install new leaders, some chose to retain the leaders who were appointed. However, as new leaders emerged, all of the teams eventually replaced the initial team leader with one chosen by the team.

Collaboration and consolidation

At this stage members begin to work collaboratively and function as a tightly knit team. This stage encompasses about 3 to 12 months. At this stage, members receive information and are expected to solve problems and make decisions.

193

This is a delicate stage because some teams have difficulty solving problems and making appropriate decisions. Supervisors are very important at this point because they provide the guidance teams need in practicing problem-solving skills and making sound decisions. Teams may need to collect additional information, receive feedback on their performance on a daily basis, and learn to use self-assessment procedures.

Continuation stage

This is the stage where stasis is achieved in the organization and teams become integrated into the typical day-to-day operations of the organization. Teams are accepted by both managers and employees as an important and permanent part of the organization's structure. The continuation stage doesn't end unless the organization decides to terminate the use of the team management model. During this state teams need to be given ongoing training to help them learn new skills and refresh old ones. Management also needs ongoing training to help them work with teams. Team members, as well as management, will rotate and new people will fill their spots, creating the need for continued training and development.

Many organizations feel that when this stage is reached, the team-building process is complete and the organization can relax its efforts. However, for teams to be effective, they need continued support and development. Some organizations fail in their use of teams at this stage because they become stagnant.

Team Effectiveness

The effectiveness of each team and all the teams working together directly affects the results of an entire organization. Team building is designed to help groups of employees operate more effectively. Some basic concepts can help you better understand how teams function and provide ideas about how to improve team effectiveness.

Size of teams

The best teams tend to be small—six to nine employees. When a team has more than ten members, it becomes difficult for them to get things accomplished. They have trouble interacting constructively and agreeing on how to solve problems and what actions to take. Large numbers of employees tend to merely go through the motions rather than develop a common purpose or goal to accomplish.

Team life cycle

Teams also tend to go through a life cycle, or stages, as they learn to work together. Understanding these stages is useful because you aren't surprised and stressed about the group interactions.

The typical stages that a team goes through are

■ **Forming.** When a team holds its first meetings, it concentrates on sharing personal information, getting to know one another, and reviewing the team's tasks. During this stage, members usually tend to be courteous and interaction is cautious.

■ **Storming.** After the first few meetings, team members begin to compete for status within the team, jockey for positions of control, and argue about the directions the team should take. External pressures may interfere with the team and conflicts rise between employees as they assert themselves.

■ **Norming.** During this stage, the team begins to come together in a more cohesive fashion and members are more cooperative. A balance begins to occur between competing forces. Team norms emerge to guide behavior.

■ **Performing.** The team eventually matures and learns to handle complex challenges. Task assignments are efficiently accomplished.

■ **Adjourning.** Most teams—but not all—eventually adjourn. The adjournment stage is becoming more frequent with the advent of flexible organizations that feature temporary teams. Organizations that use self-directed teams try and keep the team together as long as possible with no adjournment in mind. However, when a team member leaves, the group often reverts to behavior found in the early stages of development. Moving through the stages may not take as long or be as difficult to go through as they were when the team was first formed.

Obstacles to teams

If teams are to succeed in organizations, they have to have the proper environment and be free from obstacles that prevent teams from performing. A supervisor should watch for and help eliminate several obstacles.

■ **A weak sense of direction.** A team must have some sense of its purpose or goals. If a team does not have focus, it becomes distracted and unproductive. A supervisor can coach group members to help them work through this and establish goals and objectives.

■ **Lack of trust.** Members must develop a trust and learn to believe and value the integrity, character, and abilities of one another. If this doesn't occur, a supervisor needs to talk with members to discover the reasons for the distrust. Sometimes it is difficult to overcome this problem—particularly when a member has violated the team's trust. It may be necessary to reassign a team member to another team or temporarily pull that person from team activities.

■ **Skill gaps.** The team members do not have the skills necessary to function together. The team needs to recognize the importance of identifying a skill gap and request training when it is needed. They often will come to you for assistance in identifying the training source.

■ **Lack of external support.** Since teams exist in a larger organization, they must have continued support from management and the necessary resources to accomplish their assigned tasks. If they do not have support and resources, they will not survive.

Welfare-to-work employees—Some studies of welfare-to-work employees have indicated that they feel alienated from their coworkers. Their lack of work experience and knowledge of the work culture probably contributes to this feeling. When someone steps outside the group's norms, they typically are embarrassed and feel singled out. Supervisors can help make welfare recipients feel more a part of the team by carving out a small part of the work that they can excel at. Talk with the worker and find out their greatest strengths—keeping in mind that they often lack many skills. Focus on the one or two skills that they can use and identify some tasks that fit them well. This takes some additional effort on your part but can make the difference between the employee's success or failure on the job.

Labor law and teams

The National Labor Relations Act of 1935 forbids employers from dominating or interfering with the formation of "any organization of any kind, or any employee representation committee which exists for the purpose of dealing with employers concerning grievances, wages, hours of employment, or conditions of work." It is important to recognize this provision and be careful about assigning tasks to teams that might violate this law. Supervisors—in a unionized organization—should avoid using teams in a way that could be interpreted as subverting the union. You may not set up a team to represent the employees of the company in matters of pay or working conditions, but they can focus on solving problems.

Types of teams

Teams can be classified on the basis of their objectives. The following list discusses the three most common types of teams found in organizations today:

- **Problem-solving teams** consist of employees from the same department. In problem-solving teams, employees usually share their ideas or offer suggestions on how work processes and methods can be improved. Although these teams may solve problems, they rarely are given the authority to implement their suggestions. They must learn to persuade management to implement their solutions.

- **Cross-functional teams** are composed of employees from the same hierarchical level but different work areas. In other words, first-line supervisors are teamed with first-line supervisors. These teams are usually created to accomplish a specific task. In most cases, all of the employees are from the same organization but there are some situations where a cross-functional team may include employees from different organizations. Task forces and committees are examples of cross-functional teams.

- **Self-directed work teams** are an extension of problem-solving teams that didn't go quite far enough. They are composed of employees who take on many of the responsibilities that management formerly had. They may control the pace of the work, determination of work assignments and breaks, hiring of team members, and in some cases, the discipline of team members.

Diversity in teams

On a team, the strengths of one worker can overcome the weaknesses of another. The balance created by such variety makes a team stronger. People differ from one another in three basic ways: in values, temperament, and individual diversity. Consider these factors when building a team and strive to create a mix of team members.

Values

Values are the importance we give to ideas, things, or people. The development of our values is influenced by our parents, friends, teachers, religious and political leaders, significant events in our lives, and our community. While our values may be quite different, organizational behavior expert Stephen Robbins suggests that people fall into one of three general categories.

1. **Traditionalist.** People in this category value

   ◆ Hard work

   ◆ Doing things the way they've always been done

   ◆ Loyalty to the organization

   ◆ The authority of leaders

2. **Humanist.** People in this category value

   ◆ Quality of life

   ◆ Autonomy (self-direction)

   ◆ Loyalty to self

   ◆ Leaders who are attentive to worker's needs

3. **Pragmatist.** People in this category value

   ◆ Success

   ◆ Achievement

   ◆ Loyalty to career

   ◆ Leaders who reward people for hard work

An effective work team is made up of people who have values in each category. At times the team needs the traditionalist to make sure it does what is best for the organization. At other times, the team needs the humanist, who stresses the need to balance life and work. There also are times that the team needs the pragmatist, who will strive to advance the team because it also advances personal achievement. Each person's values are important to the team.

Not everyone fits neatly into one of these categories. However, this model can help you better understand and appreciate values that differentiate one person from another. Helping team members recognize these differences and the benefits that derive from each may resolve some conflicts and increase tolerance—if not appreciation—among group members. Team members should be shown that they can't think in terms of right or wrong, good or bad, when they talk about value differences. Each set of values is sometimes positive and sometimes negative. Appreciate the differences and learn to be tolerant of people who hold a different set.

Temperaments

Your temperament is the distinctive way you think, feel, and react to the world. Everyone has their own individual temperament. Management specialists assess temperaments in many ways. One of the most famous is the *Myers-Briggs Type Indicator (MBTI)*. David Keirsey has adapted the Myers-Briggs in the form of the Keirsey Temperament Sorter—in fact, his model and one form of this instrument appear on the Internet at http://keirsey.com. Consider using the MBTI or Keirsey Temperament Sorter to help employees identify their type.

Compose membership in teams so that they contain employees representative of each type because the strengths and weaknesses of one temperament balance out those of other members. It is easier to understand differences in temperament by classifying people into four categories. The four types described in the following list are based on the MBTI and Keirsey instruments. Supervisors can use these type descriptions to assess how well they describe individual employees and make team assignments accordingly.

- **Optimist.** People with this temperament

    - Must be free and not tied down

    - Are impulsive

    - Enjoy the immediate

    - Enjoy action for action's sake

    - Like working with things

    - Like to try new things

    - Can survive major setbacks

    - Are generous

    - Are cheerful

- **Realist.** People with this temperament

    - Like to belong to groups

    - Feel obligations strongly

    - Have a strong work ethic

    - Need order

    - Are realistic

    - Find tradition important

    - Are willing to do a job when asked

    - Are serious

    - Are committed to society's standards

■ **Futurist.** People with this temperament

◆ Like to control things

◆ Want to be highly competent

◆ Are the most self-critical of all temperaments

◆ Strive for excellence

◆ Judge people on their merits

◆ Cause people to feel they don't measure up

◆ Live for their work

◆ Are highly creative

◆ Tend to focus on the future

■ **Idealist.** People with this temperament

◆ Are constantly in search of their "self"

◆ Want to know the meaning of things

◆ Value integrity

◆ Write fluently

◆ Are romantics

◆ Have difficulty placing limits on work

◆ Are highly personable

◆ Appreciate people

◆ Get along well with all temperaments

Individual diversity

In chapter 1, we saw that the workforce has become more diverse over the past 20 years. This trend will continue throughout the first half of the next century. Consider the impact that this workforce diversity will have in the next few years.

■ **Gender.** By the year 2005, women will make up 47.8 percent of the workforce.

■ **Ethnicity.** Blacks and Hispanics are expected to comprise 11.1 percent of the workforce by the year 2005. Asian and other ethnic groups will make up another 4.1 percent. This means that over a quarter of the workforce will be made up of ethnic minorities.

■ **Age.** The average age of workers will be 40.6 by the year 2005.

Individual diversity strengthens a team. Men and women often approach problems differently. Women often are more attentive to the needs of other people, while men tend to be more task-oriented. Team members can learn from one another and build these positive characteristics into the work group.

People from different cultural and ethnic backgrounds look at problems from different points of view. East-Asian cultures traditionally value cooperation, while Western cultures emphasize individualism. People from different cultures can help one another develop a better appreciation of their values.

A diversity of ages also can be positive. Younger workers typically bring enthusiasm and energy into a job. Older workers bring patience, maturity, and experience. These combined characteristics often make a team stronger.

No matter what the differences are, each person can contribute to the team. It's important for all members of a team to share their thoughts and ideas. Team members need to understand and respect that each individual adds valuable perspective to the team. The credibility of a team is increased when its composition reflects the organization's workforce.

Immigrant workers—There is a contrast between the way societies view individualism and collectivism. Cultures that emphasize individualism encourage people to look after their own interests and that of their immediate family members. Wealth and freedom are dominant in individualist cultures. Collectivist cultures encourage people to rely on organizations to protect their interests. Places where collectivism is high include most Central and South American countries, Arab countries, Mexico, Hong Kong, Greece, Jamaica, Japan, South Korea, Pakistan, and the Philippines. Workers from countries where collectivism is high tend to appreciate teamwork. They have a high degree of loyalty to groups and organizations that they belong to. These workers can help bring cohesion to a work team.

Conflict Management

Conflict management is one of the most important interpersonal skills a team member can have. Almost every working relationship produces some degree of conflict and working closely with a team can cause conflict to erupt on a frequent basis. Conflict can be either destructive or constructive, depending on the attitudes and skills of team members. Team members need to be familiar with the following conflict management strategies.

■ **Avoiding.** This is the physical or mental withdrawal from conflict. This reflects a low concern by either party to resolve the conflict and may often result in a lose-lose situation. The avoiding strategy is both unassertive and uncooperative and usually represents an attempt by one party to satisfy their needs by avoiding or postponing the conflict. Some employees will use the avoiding strategy out of fear that they can't handle the conflict and may only make the situation worse.

■ **Accommodating.** This strategy involves allowing other team members to gratify their own interests and needs in an effort to avoid conflict. The advantage of the accommodating strategy is that relationships within the team may be preserved. However, the danger is that the employee using the strategy may actually have a better solution to the conflict. If an employee "overuses" this strategy, other employees may begin to take advantage of him or her.

■ **Win-lose.** Some employees attempt to use power tactics to resolve a conflict. This strategy relies on both aggressiveness and dominance by one party to achieve their personal goals—usually at the expense of the other party. One party wins and the other party loses. The party attempting to win may use authority, threats, intimidation, or call for a vote, hoping to get a majority of the team to side with them. This style has been commonly used by supervisors over the years but doesn't work effectively in a team environment.

■ **Compromise.** Employees who use this approach are searching for a middle ground or are willing to give up something in exchange for gaining something else. The compromising strategy involves both assertiveness and cooperation in an attempt to keep relationships harmonious. Usually there is no clear-cut outcome to this type of resolution and the parties often feel they have not really resolved anything or that they have really reached a suboptimum decision. If this strategy is overused, it could result in game-playing among team members.

■ **Collaboration.** Facing conflict directly and working through to a mutually satisfactory resolution is collaboration. It is the only strategy that can be truly viewed as a resolution approach because it addresses the basic differences involved in the conflict. A problem-solving method is used to seek a solution that maximizes the goals of all parties in conflict. This results in a win-win outcome. Collaboration does take time and the parties must be willing to commit the time necessary to resolve the issues. This is the best method for teams to use but they must be well trained in the problem-solving process. Some guidelines to use in the collaboration strategy:

◆ Agree on the common goal.

◆ Do not commit yourself to a fixed position.

◆ Look at the strengths and weaknesses of all parties.

◆ Be candid and upfront with information.

◆ Avoid arguing. Don't get emotional.

◆ Try to look at the viewpoint of the other team members.

◆ Ask questions to understand the meanings of their positions.

◆ Make sure all team members have a vested interest in the outcome.

◆ Make sure all team members get credit for their input and work in resolving the conflict.

The Problem-Solving Process

Problem solving is one of the most important functions of teams. It is important that a common model for problem solving is adopted by the members of the team. This section examines the problem solving and describes a model that can be used to solve problems.

A person or team must accept some basic assumptions before they can effectively use a problem-solving model.

Problems can be solved. It's important to believe a problem can be solved. This belief motivated some of the greatest problem solvers of history, such as Thomas Edison, inventor of the light bulb; Henry Ford, the creator of modern manufacturing processes; and Jonas Salk, who discovered the polio vaccine. These people persisted despite many failures. Thomas Edison failed more than 900 times before he produced a lightbulb that worked.

There is a cause for everything that happens. Problems have causes. You must look for the causes to solve the problem. Often, it is possible to find only probable causes.

Problem solving is a continuous process. Any problem-solving system must be a continuous process. In other words, after finishing the last step in the process, we must return to the first step and begin the process again. This gives us the opportunity to evaluate whether the solution is working or if it can be improved.

The problem-solving process can develop in a number of ways, but the steps and order you follow are important. Leaving out any of the steps or doing them in a different order limits the probability of successfully solving a problem.

1. **Identify the problem.** The biggest mistake you can make in solving a problem is to work on the wrong problem. Take time to discover what the real problem is. Here is an example of the importance of this step. A bookstore manager notices that the store is frequently out of certain titles. She defines the problem this way: "Employees need to order books when they see that we have run out of a title." She then develops ideas on how she can get employee to reorder books. However, the real problem could be something else. The problem should be defined as, "How can inventory control be improved so that we keep titles in stock?" This expands the search for a solution beyond a narrow approach—"it must be the employees' fault"—to a broader approach that is more likely to identify the real problem.

2. **Gather and organize data about the problem.** You should gather as much data on the problem as possible. The best way to collect data is to observe what happens. Other good methods include talking with other people—employees, customers, vendors—examining records, and reading reports. Organize the data in a way that will help you arrive at a solution. This process is called **analysis**. Analysis requires some mathematical skills. There are three simple methods you can use to analyze data so that it reveals patterns—frequency tables, percentages, and graphs. If you are unfamiliar with these techniques, there are many easy-to-understand books on business statistics and problem solving that can provide more detailed information.

3. **Develop solutions to the problem.** After collecting data about the problem, you can begin to develop solutions. Develop as many solutions as possible. There are several things you can do to develop solutions.

   ◆ **Talk to other people.** Talk the problem over with coworkers who have previously encountered the problem and find out how they solved it in the past. One of the best ways to learn about something is to ask questions. Ask friends from other organizations if they have had a similar problem and how they solved it. (When talking to people outside your organization, do not reveal information that would be considered confidential.)

   ◆ **Hold a group discussion.** The two most popular types of group discussion are as follows:

❖ **Brainstorming.** A brainstorming session is a group process where employees try to generate as many ideas as possible in a short time period. There are some important rules to follow when brainstorming. First, don't criticize any ideas. You want to develop as many ideas as possible without being concerned about their quality. Second, stretch for ideas. When the group thinks it has exhausted all ideas, try again. Third, write all ideas on flip charts so that the entire group can see what's been suggested.

❖ **Nominal group technique.** This is a more controlled method than brainstorming. First, each person thinks of as many ideas as possible and writes them on a piece of paper. Second, the group shares these ideas, taking one idea from one person at a time in a round-robin manner. Third, the group discusses the ideas. Fourth, the group ranks or rates the ideas from best to worst.

◆ **Change places with other employees.** Spend four to eight hours in another department. See how other employees handle problems similar to ones in your department. A change in roles often provides a new viewpoint that can help you solve a problem. This method also allows employees in another department to ask you for ideas about their problems.

◆ **Visit other organizations with similar problems.** You can learn a lot by discovering how other organizations solve their problems. Many businesses are willing to let you visit if you don't work for a direct competitor. Look at their solutions and evaluate how they solved similar problems. Discover how well they think the solutions work. Decide if the solutions could apply to your organization.

◆ **Read about the problem.** Trade journals provide valuable information about how organizations like yours have solved problems. There are trade journals for computer dealers, retailers, publishers, fast food restaurateurs, and the list goes on and on. Since trade journals deal with businesses just like yours, they publish articles that give helpful ideas about problems. Other business magazines or books may also give you some good ideas.

4. **Evaluate possible solutions.** You should ask a number of questions when evaluating possible solutions:

◆ **Is the idea logical?** Look for a direct relationship between the problem and the solution. For example, giving dissatisfied customers a discount doesn't solve a poor customer service problem.

205

◆ **How much will it cost?** You may have a great idea, but if it isn't affordable, it doesn't do the organization any good. Some problems are not complicated, so the solutions are not costly. However, costs for solutions to more complex problems can vary greatly. For example, pizza delivery time might improve if a store bought a new truck, but it may not be able to afford one.

◆ **Does the organization have workers who know how to implement the solution?** Some solutions require specialized knowledge. Either employees must have the expertise, the organization must be willing to hire employees with the skills, or the organization must pay for a consultant. Without these resources, the solution won't work.

◆ **Is the solution timely?** Some problems need immediate solutions. Some ideas are good but take too long to implement. Sometimes you must choose two solutions: one that works immediately and another that will be a better solution for the future. For example, a new printing press will improve the quality of the company's printed documents, but delivery is three months away. The immediate solution might be to reduce press speed, re-ink more often, and have employees work overtime.

Even after applying these rules, it's sometimes difficult to select the right solution from a large number of ideas. Two methods that can help complete the evaluation process are rating and ranking.

◆ **Rating** is a process in which each idea is evaluated separately. You apply all four of the preceding questions to each idea. Then you rate it on a scale of 1 to 5, 1 being a great idea and 5 being a terrible idea. One drawback to this method is that you may end up with several ideas that are rated equal or almost equal.

◆ **Ranking** involves looking at all ideas, choosing the best solution, and ranking it number one. Then you compare the remaining ideas and select number two. Continue this process until all ideas have been ranked. A weakness of this method is that it's difficult to rank more than ten ideas at a time.

Probably the best way to select the number one idea is to use both rating and ranking. First, rate all ideas. Then rank the top ten. This uses the strengths of each method and omits its weaknesses.

5. **Select the best solution.** By the time you complete the analysis, you should be able to decide on the best solution. The best solution may not

always be the top idea, but it will usually be among the top three to five ideas. Keep these three things in mind when choosing a solution:

◆ **The best idea may not be affordable.** This means you should select an idea that will solve the problem without greatly increasing cost. If the top two or three ideas are basically equal, select the less costly one.

◆ **There's always risk involved in problem solving.** No solution will be foolproof. This often keeps people from making a decision. You can try to reduce the risk, but you can't eliminate it.

◆ **Don't worry about being wrong.** Mistakes can't be totally eliminated. Think about what to do if the solution fails. Contingency planning prepares you to quickly respond when a solution goes awry.

6. **Implement the solution.** A good idea can be ruined if you fail to implement it correctly. Here are some guidelines for implementing ideas:

◆ **Believe in the idea.** Never implement an idea if you don't think it solves a problem. Sometimes, if people believe an idea will be successful, it's easier to overcome difficulties that would otherwise jeopardize it.

◆ **Convince others to support the idea.** When a team solves the problem, you already have this step covered. It's critical for a team to get supervisor's or manager's support for the idea. A group consensus helps convince management to support a solution.

◆ **Don't let fear hold you back.** It's normal to be afraid of failure. Worries about losing your job or reputation if an idea fails need to be kept in check. People sometimes wait too long before implementing a solution. Remember, inaction can kill a good idea.

◆ **Follow through.** A solution shouldn't be immediately rejected because it doesn't work. It takes time for ideas to work. Continue trying the solution until you know why it isn't working before taking a new approach.

7. **Evaluate the solution.** Within a reasonable period of time, evaluate the effectiveness of the solution and decide whether it's working. One good way to evaluate is to repeat the analysis step. For example, go back and do another frequency table to find out whether customers are happier or whether production or quality is improved.

Disabled workers—Employees who work with people with disabilities should be informed about proper behavior and attitudes. Disabled workers don't want pity or to be treated in a demeaning manner. They basically expect to be given the same opportunities as other workers with reasonable accommodation for their disability. Words often convey a person's attitude, and workers should be informed about words that convey a negative meaning to disabled workers. Some of these terms include "handicap," "the handicapped," "crippled with," "victim of," "spastic," "invalid," "deaf and dumb," "incapacitated," and "deformed." Instead, workers should use terms like "physically disabled," "person with a disability," "person with cerebral palsy," "caused by," and "deaf person." Thoughtful consideration in the way we treat others is important in building a team. Supervisors play a key role in helping employees understand how to do this.

Creative Thinking

Teams need members that can think creatively. Here are some suggestions to help people think creatively. Many organizations realize they must be innovative to compete with other businesses. Creativity is the ability to think of new ideas. This may mean applying old ideas to new problems or coming up with entirely new ideas. Several techniques are useful in helping a person think more creatively:

■ **Don't let the problem limit your thinking.** Our thinking process sometimes limits the way we look at a problem. We often allow the problem to define the solution. Consider how a solution to the problem can be solved in a truly creative way. This is often illustrated using the "nine dot" exercise. Try to connect all nine dots shown in the following figure with four straight lines, and without lifting your pencil or pen off the paper.

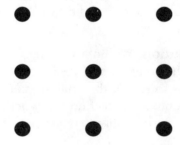

Hint: When most people try to solve this problem, they limit their thinking by viewing these nine dots as a box. They don't think outside the box. (See the end of the chapter for the solution.)

■ **Look at the problem from different viewpoints.** Here's a simple way to do this. List ridiculous solutions to the problem. Then turn those ideas around and ask how they might make sense. This process is illustrated in the following example. The team has been asked how to increase the number of customers who visit the shoe store where you work. Here are some ideas: give shoes away, yell at people to come into the store, carry every style of shoe made, and pay customers to take shoes. Consider these absurd ideas and use them to stimulate a realistic solution to the problem. The realistic counters to the previous ideas include discounting shoes as much as possible, getting people's attention through advertising, maintaining a wide variety of styles, and including a free pair of socks with each purchase.

■ **Use hazy thinking.** Other words for hazy are unclear or vague. Sometimes we're very specific and take things too literally in the problem-solving process. Maybe our thinking should be hazy and unclear. For example, looking at a picture of the forest, do you see the forest or the trees? Each perspective yields a different view of the picture. This is similar to the idea of hazy thinking.

■ **Joke about the problem.** Humor is a good way to find alternative solutions to a problem. Humor often relies on expectations. You are led to think one way, then are surprised after seeing another way. This old riddle is an example. Question: What is black and white and read all over? Answer: A newspaper. When this joke is spoken, "read" is usually interpreted as "red," because black and white lead a person to think about colors. Humor might allow you to view the problem in an entirely different way—an unexpected way.

■ **Give yourself time to think.** Take time to think about the problem and solutions. Relax and look at the ideas you've come up with. Don't allow anything to distract you. Get away from phones, customers, coworkers, radios, televisions, and anything else that might distract you. Write down your thoughts during this time, or better yet, record them on tape so you're not distracted by writing. Then get away from the problem. Do something entertaining. Get together with friends. Relax. Often, this relaxation frees your subconscious to come up with more possible solutions.

Contingent workers—It is sometimes necessary to assign an independent contractor to a project team. The contractor often brings an expertise to the project that other workers don't have. However, this expertise can also cause workers to be jealous and resent the independent contractor's presence. The contractor is viewed as an outsider and not knowing the other workers, it becomes difficult for the person to develop a strategy to develop effective relationships with other team members.

The supervisor can help facilitate the development of team cohesion in this type of situation. Talk to employees about the fact that they can learn new knowledge or skills from the independent contractor if they are open to this possibility. Make it clear to the contractor that being a trainer and coach is a part of their role on the team. It is good to remind contractors that while they have specialized knowledge and skills, they need other members of the team to help them understand how to apply the skills within your organization. Help employees and contractors see the mutual benefits that can be gained by working together.

Conducting Meetings

Organizations use meetings to impart and exchange information, involve all members, conduct problem solving, and coordinate projects. Supervisors and team leaders need to conduct meetings to accomplish these same purposes. This section provides information to help you facilitate meetings so that they are more productive and satisfying to participants.

Meetings typically fail due to a number of factors. The most frequent mistakes that are made include a lack of planning, poor structure, and improper goal, including the wrong people, taking too much time for the meeting, and producing poor results. The following guidelines should help you avoid these mistakes.

■ **Prepare an agenda for the meeting.** Developing an agenda is your preparation for a meeting. Take time to identify the objectives for the meeting. A good resource to use when beginning this process are minutes or notes from previous meetings of the group. Consult with other team members in determining the objectives of the meeting. Make sure you follow through with actions, requests, and questions from previous meetings. Decide the outcomes that should be achieved when the meeting concludes. Compile a list of topics that must be considered by the group in order to meet the objectives. Determine the schedule, including the amount of time that can be allotted to each topic. Prepare a written agenda and distribute it to all group members. The agenda should be distributed to all team members so they will have time to review it before the team meeting starts. Be sure your agenda includes the length of the meeting.

■ **Physically prepare for the meeting.** Reserve a room that offers privacy and provides a relaxing environment. Notify members of the time and location of the meeting. Sometimes a group expects drinks and refreshments, so these must be arranged. Make sure that equipment, supplies, and other materials needed for the meeting are ready.

■ **Prepare members for the meeting.** Start the meeting on time. This demonstrates respect for all of the members and it encourages them to be on time. Greet members and introduce guests or new members others may not know. State the meeting's purpose, review the agenda, and get an affirmation from the group that these are acceptable.

■ **Encourage the free expression of ideas.** Members should be allowed to freely state their opinions without the fear of personal attacks. Inform members that responses to ideas should avoid emotion-laden language. For example, using phrases like "if you had more experience...," "we've tried that idea before," "a well-informed person wouldn't propose this idea," and so on are likely to provoke negative reactions from a person. This critical behavior may result in members being reluctant to express ideas. When a member says something inappropriate, call it to his attention and note that this isn't in accord with group rules.

■ **Encourage participation by all team members.** Make sure each team member gets the opportunity to participate. You may have to monitor the meeting to make sure that one or two members don't dominate the meeting. When participants are interrupted, intervene and allow the member to finish her statement.

■ **Restate all of the key points.** If necessary, write them on a flip chart. Be as accurate as possible in making these statements and ask members if they concur.

■ **Follow the agenda.** Be sure the participants do not get off track and talk about unrelated subjects that waste time.

■ **Respond to all statements made by members.** The leader doesn't need to always make a response but you should ensure that every statement is acknowledged by someone in the group. A person can feel quite uncomfortable about participating in a meeting when a comment goes unacknowledged.

- **Avoid arguments between participants in the meeting.** When this occurs, state that the group understands the position of each person and other members should have an opportunity to make comments. Sometimes you need to state that the group agrees to disagree and needs to review the issue at the next meeting.

- **Encourage humor.** People are more willing to express ideas when humor, laughter, and joking are encouraged in the meeting. Meetings can be boring, and humor helps reduce this factor. Some participants feel they can hide behind humor; an idea that is received poorly can be passed off as humor, and the person that suggested it is often more willing to make comments in the future.

- **Encourage questions.** Ask questions about statements that are unclear. This creates a climate where other members feel more comfortable asking questions. This technique also reduces confusion and ensures that everyone understands statements that are made.

- **End the meeting on time.** People's time is important. Recognizing this fact imparts a certain amount of respect to members of the group. Ending on time is a reward and people are more likely to attend future meetings.

- **Prepare and distribute minutes of the meeting.** This provides a record that everyone can refer to when implementing actions agreed upon by the group.

- **Evaluate the meeting.** It is good for you and other members to evaluate meetings. Following is a list of questions that you should ask yourself. You may want to distribute them in the form of a questionnaire to other members. Such a list is particularly useful when team meetings are just beginning. The reason for distributing the evaluation at the beginning of the meeting is twofold. First, participants become aware of what factors are important for the meeting to be successful. Some of these factors are controlled by participants and can motivate them toward positive behavior during the meeting. Second, participants can more effectively evaluate a meeting when they know what to observe as the meeting progresses.

  - ◆ Did the meeting accomplish its objectives?

  - ◆ Were the right people in attendance?

  - ◆ Were the facilities adequate?

  - ◆ Was there adequate planning and preparation?

  - ◆ Do members feel well informed about meetings?

  - ◆ Did members feel comfortable in making comments?

◆ Did members feel comfortable asking questions?

◆ Was the length of the meeting appropriate?

◆ Did participants remain interested throughout the meeting?

◆ Did the meeting end on a high note?

■ **Follow up.** Review the minutes of a meeting and implement actions that were agreed upon by the group. Meet with people outside the group that made comments you think should be responded to in a personal manner. Be prepared to report back to the group and explain outcomes that have occurred since the last meeting.

Applying the techniques described here can help you conduct more effective meetings. In turn, this should increase interest and motivation among your team members. They are more likely to enjoy meeting together and this should improve team productivity.

Ex-offenders—Many times workers are reluctant to work with ex-offenders. They are afraid they might be assaulted or that the person will steal from them—even though the ex-offender may not have been convicted of these crimes. Supervisors may need to intercede in extreme cases. You may need to talk with workers and explain that they should give the person a chance to prove herself or himself. Discuss their feelings about ex-offenders and ask them to explore ways to ease their fears. Suggest that they observe the person and adjust their feelings in accordance with reality. Changing biases takes time, so continue to coach workers until they feel more comfortable working with ex-offenders.

Team Development

Supervisors should monitor the progress of teams under their supervision. Use the description of stages in team development to determine a team's status. A team may have difficulty progressing through a stage—a team's growth sometimes becomes stunted. At these junctures, supervisors need to consider the most appropriate method for intervening and helping a team move forward. In most cases, it takes several years for teams to achieve their full potential. This section describes some appropriate intervention strategies.

One of the most difficult tasks for a supervisor is to determine the appropriate level of involvement in a team's decision-making process. Sometimes it is appropriate to let a group struggle because the members are able to resolve issues related to roles, functions, responsibilities, and techniques. However, the supervisor should be sensitive to a team's inability to reach a consensus on these matters and intervene at the appropriate time. You can do this by talking with team members. When you sense that they are ready for your assistance, take action. Meet with the team and observe the dynamics and employee participation patterns. Make notes about how frequently each member talks, values and attitudes that drive the discussion, positive and negative behaviors among members, information that is available to the team, and problem-solving techniques. Analyze this information and identify the key problems that seem to impede team development. Reveal your observations to the team and ask them to respond. Provide them with an opportunity to resolve the difficulties.

Team members periodically need feedback on their progress even when there are no apparent problems. A supervisor can observe a team meeting and offer insights that often aren't self-evident to team members. Provide the team a choice about whether it wants feedback. Some things you must remember when giving team members feedback are

- **Focus on specific behaviors.** Feedback should be specific rather than general. Don't say, "you have a bad attitude"—that is too general. Instead point out specific behaviors that you think indicate a bad attitude, like the number of negative comments made about managers, policies, activities, goals, and other employees.

- **Keep the feedback impersonal.** Don't criticize an employee's personality. The feedback should describe behaviors, not the employees themselves. For example, saying that a person is stubborn may relate to a positive trait in the individual—persistence in accomplishing a goal or an unwillingness to compromise an important value. These can be positive traits but become negative traits when used to an extreme degree. If you point out that continued efforts to block a team's solution will result in a continuing problem, it will have a more beneficial effect on the employee and the person's subsequent interactions with the team.

- **Make the feedback well timed.** Give the employee feedback after the behavior occurs rather than waiting until later. If you wait two weeks to give feedback, the employee may have forgotten the situation and not consider the advice to be relevant.

- **Make sure the employee understands the feedback.** Provide feedback that is concise and complete enough that employees understand what you are telling them. Have employees rephrase what you say to make certain they understand you.

214

Summary

Organizational structure is important to performance and productivity. Organizations may use formal organizational structures like bureaucracy, or less formal structures like teams. The success of teams in producing highly positive outcomes in organizations has encouraged many businesses, nonprofit agencies, and governmental entities to adopt this structure. The effective application of the team concept is based on an understanding of core team concepts and techniques. Supervisors play an important role in building, teaching, and coaching teams. Conflict management, problem solving, creative thinking, and facilitating meetings are all important skills that supervisors should help develop in team members.

Solution to the "Nine Dot" Exercise

Most people see that the dots make a square, so they think they can't make their lines go outside the box. However, the instructions don't place this limit. You can't solve the problem unless you go outside the lines.

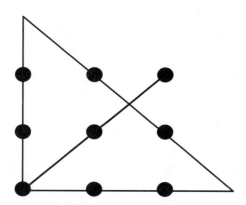

Chapter 10

Improving Employee Performance

Supervisors frequently must address the problem of employees that are not performing at the level or standards that are expected.

- **Employees who have problems:** These employees have some problem that is affecting their job performance; however, the problem may or may not be related to the job. Personal problems such as with a spouse or child may be affecting an employee to the point that it is affecting job performance. These employees are not overtly breaking company policies, but their work performance isn't as good as it should be.

- **Employees who cause problems:** These employees choose to break the rules or they are not willing to make an effort to meet the standards of the job on which they are working. The employees deliberately violate the law, company policies, or a supervisor's instructions.

Regardless of the type of employee problem that exists, you must be prepared to deal with these employees in a positive manner. The more knowledge you have about each individual employee, the better chance you have of interpreting the slightest change in an employee's behavior and heading off any major problems with the employee. As with any situation, you may be dealing with employees who are in different age groups and have different values, but this shouldn't keep you from taking direct and immediate action in solving the problem.

This chapter looks at the supervisor's role as coach, counselor, and disciplinarian. Employees are a valuable resource and it is important for supervisors to work hard at retaining employees. Too often supervisors concentrate on their role as a disciplinarian. The need to take disciplinary action with employees can be greatly reduced when effective coaching and counseling skills are used by the supervisor. Discipline should be the last resort, not the first response.

The Supervisor As Coach

The supervisor at times needs to function like a coach. A coach provides ongoing guidance and instruction. Coaching sometimes involves teaching people the basic skills. However, the coach spends most of their time on continued development and practice of skills that have been learned. The focus of coaching is improved performance. A good coach observes performance and encourages improvement through encouragement, demonstration, and instruction. A supervisor can many times prevent performance problems by using a proactive approach.

■ **Communicate standards.** Employees should never have doubts about what they are expected to do. Take time to present goals and objectives so that employees know where the organization is headed and why it wants to move in that direction. Discuss performance standards related to the quantity and quality of work that employees must produce to reach the objectives. Discuss policies and procedures with employees on a regular basis so they are aware of the need to follow organizational rules.

■ **Provide and encourage feedback.** Employees need to feel comfortable in a job to achieve a high level of productivity. Feedback from supervisors is important in helping an employee feel comfortable. Provide employees with feedback on all tasks. However, you should keep some simple rules in mind.

◆ Employees need more frequent feedback when performing unfamiliar tasks. These are tasks they have just learned or ones they perform infrequently. Instructing, coaching, and praising are all important during this phase of performance.

◆ Employees gradually become more experienced in completing a task. Supervisors should be sensitive to the fact that they need less instruction. However, coaching may still be important, and continued praise is needed. As a supervisor, a good strategy to use is to wait for employees to approach you with questions. Encourage employees to approach you with questions when they need answers. Focus your attention on employees when they come to ask a question. Otherwise they begin to feel that they are interrupting your work and won't approach you with questions in the future. Answer questions in an affirming manner. Demeaning employees or making them feel stupid certainly squelches future questions.

◆ Employees who are experienced in a job expect little or no instruction and coaching. A mistake that some supervisors make is thinking employees should perform a job in the exact same manner that the supervisor would do it. Deviations in work that don't affect other workers, customers, or productivity don't need to be corrected. Praise for performance that an employee considers to be routine can be either confusing or demeaning.

◆ The experience level of employees differs from task to task. Employees who have a high level of experience in a job may have little experience with a specific task. These employees usually need very little instruction, coaching, and praise. However, when employees face a new or unfamiliar task, supervisors need to increase the level of feedback.

■ **Maintain equity.** Employees do their best work when they feel that supervisors are treating everyone in an equitable manner. Keep in mind that equity doesn't always mean treating everyone in the exact same way, rather treating each of them in the most appropriate way. For example, one employee may need a flexible schedule because of childcare needs, while another employee wants to work through lunch to get off early and play in a softball league. Employees who feel supervisors are responsive to their personal needs are typically motivated to do their job well.

■ **Communicate discipline policies.** Employees should clearly understand what actions the organization expects supervisors to take when there are performance problems or violations of organization policies. These actions shouldn't come as a surprise to employees. Policy manuals, memos, and face-to-face communications from supervisors should keep workers informed about discipline policies. It isn't necessary to remind workers about disciplinary policies unless it is possible such action might be needed to correct their behavior.

219

Prevention is the best strategy to avoid performance problems. However, the best organizations and the most effective supervisors are going to encounter performance problems. When these occur, it is necessary to use a systematic approach to analyzing performance problems.

Sexual harassment—An American Management Association study found that 31 percent of human resource officials reported incidents where employees were sent sexually harassing e-mails. Employers have the right to monitor and read e-mail sent through their computer systems. Supervisors should inform all employees that their e-mail may be monitored and that appropriate action will be taken if they send any sexually offensive e-mail to other workers.

Analyzing Performance Problems

Good coaching includes the ability to analyze employee performance. A supervisor needs to measure performance and determine the cause of ineffective or inefficient work behavior. You can do this by asking a series of questions. These questions center around five basic decision points. Typically performance problems relate to skills, practice, motivation, organization, or personal factors.

Skill-related problems

Employees are expected to start work with the skills they need for a job or to acquire them through on-the-job training. However, an employee may sometimes appear to lack skills required for the job. Following are some questions to ask to determine how to remedy this problem:

- **What task(s) is the worker unable to perform?** Identify tasks that are not performed well. Review training programs to ensure that the tasks are sufficiently covered in a training program. It may be necessary to retrain workers that weren't sufficiently informed in initial training.

- **What specific skills does the worker lack?** Make sure the job descriptions specify that the particular skill is required for the job. Review recruitment procedures for deficiencies in finding workers with the basic skills needed to perform a task. For example, licensed practical nurses should have the skills needed to take a patient's blood pressure.

However, they are probably not going to have the skill to start an IV drip. Thus, an organization must sometimes develop skills that a worker didn't receive in a formal training program.

■ **Does the worker have the ability to learn the task?** Employees sometimes don't have the ability to develop the skills needed to perform a task. For example, a person with poor hand-eye coordination is unlikely to perform well in operating a lathe.

■ **What is the best way to train the worker to perform the task?** Identify the best method for training the employee and implement the instructional process.

■ **Has a new task been added to a job description?** Rapid changes in business often result in new task assignments. It may be that employees weren't adequately prepared to perform the new task.

Practice-related problems

Employees develop certain skills in order to perform a job but may have problems practicing the skill on the job. A very well understood learning principle is that the more we practice a behavior, the better we become at doing it. Ask the following questions to determine whether this is cause for an employee's performance problem.

■ **Is the worker provided with feedback about performance?** Employees may assume a lack of feedback about a task as an indication of its unimportance.

■ **Does the worker perform the task frequently enough to maintain the skills?** Some tasks are critical for job performance, but they are done infrequently. An obvious example is a police officer. Police officers need the skills to use a gun to defend themselves against criminals. However, officers actually use this skill few times on the job.

■ **What method can be developed to allow more practice opportunities?** In the case of police officers, they must practice using their weapons on a regular basis. Officers are usually expected to fire a specific number of rounds each month. In addition, they must achieve an acceptable accuracy rate.

Motivational problems

Employees may have the knowledge and skills to perform well at a task. When you are certain that employees possess the skills required for a task, a supervisor needs to consider motivational issues. It is sometimes difficult for supervisors to recognize this problem because they are often responsible for it. Many times people have blind spots and supervisors may not realize how their actions affect the motivation of employees. It is important that you be willing to take a critical look at yourself and how you have been responding to employees.

- **Is performance punishing to the worker?** A common example of this problem is giving a good worker additional work or responsibilities without increasing pay or privileges.

- **Is there a reward for performance?** Pay and fringe benefits are often not perceived as rewards for performance because they continue whether performance is good or bad. A supervisor can use praise, special considerations, minor privileges, and awards to provide regular rewards to employees.

- **Is non-performance rewarded?** This can happen when a supervisor reassigns an employee's unfinished work to other employees.

- **Are rewards appropriate and meaningful to the worker?** Get to know individual workers and discover what they value as important. This provides insights into how you can reward them. For example, workers with children are likely to appreciate a juggled schedule that allows them to attend school functions much more than they would appreciate a certificate recognizing their performance.

- **Are rewards made in a consistent manner?** Workers should all be rewarded for good performance. Not everyone needs to receive the same reward. They need to receive rewards that appeal to them as individuals yet appear equitable.

- **Are rewards provided frequently enough to continue reinforcement of performance?** This is something that puzzles organizations that give annual bonuses. They can't understand why performance is lower during the middle of the year but seems to increase as bonus time nears. Basing bonuses on a quarter's performance would result in higher work performance because the reward occurs more frequently.

Organizational problems

In some situations, the organization is responsible for poor performance—not the employees. It is sometimes difficult for managers and supervisors to acknowledge these problems because it involves recognizing a personal mistake. These issues may also be difficult for the supervisor to correct because they require a change in policy, allocation of more money, purchase of new equipment, or a variety of other factors that must be approved by managers or executives. However, the supervisor must be able to identify these problems and bring them to a manager's attention for further action. The persistence of a supervisor in pushing for change can make a significant difference in how an organization reacts to a performance problem. Consider the following questions when checking for the existence of this type of problem.

- **Is the organizational structure creating the performance problem?** An organization can be structured in a way that inhibits communication between employees that, in turn, results in poor performance.

- **Is the job properly designed?** Sometimes tasks are combined in one job that are difficult to obtain or develop in a single individual. Also, simple tasks can be mixed with complex tasks so you have employees who are bored at the simple tasks and unable to complete the more complex tasks.

- **Are duties and responsibilities clearly defined?** One reason for job descriptions is that they help clarify duties and responsibilities. However, they don't always cover all important tasks and may need to be incorporated into a description.

- **Does the worker have adequate resources to perform a task?** This includes tools, equipment, money, time, assistance from coworkers, and support from the supervisor. There is usually a tension in balancing resources because employees often would like them to be unlimited, but the organization wants to limit them as much as possible to maximize profit. A supervisor should be sensitive and make a correction when this balance tilts in one direction or the other.

- **Are environmental factors inhibiting performance?** This includes any facility-related issue like lighting, phone systems, properly designed work areas, or accessibility.

Younger workers—A poll of 15- to 17-year-olds was conducted by Drexel University in 1997. It asked young people about factors that were important to their future careers. Security was rated as highly important by 84 percent of the respondents. This was followed by creativity at 74 percent, individuality at 72 percent, and just over 50 percent indicated routine structure was highly important.

Supervisors can build on this information by providing a secure environment to younger workers. A supervisor that is fair but firm can provide this type of environment. Tell younger workers what your expectations are so that they aren't surprised when confronted about a problem. Take time to praise and compliment younger workers as a way to build their confidence and make them feel more secure.

If younger workers make a mistake or do something wrong, let them know about it in a firm but nonthreatening manner. Many young people assume that a reprimand is just a prelude to punishment—in their mind this often means being fired. This is one reason that young workers frequently take preemptive action and quit. Supervisors obviously don't want this to happen and there are some simple ways to approach a problem that can help avoid this behavior. When young workers make a mistake, be patient with them. Avoid raising your voice and calmly explain what they've done wrong. Inform them what they should do in the future and encourage them to get you or an experienced worker to help them with the task in the future if they are still not sure how to do it correctly. Assure them that making a simple mistake isn't going to affect their job status.

Personal problems

An old adage states that employees should leave their personal business at home. We are now aware that this isn't a realistic practice. It is very difficult to compartmentalize our lives so that everything personal is kept in one area and everything business-related is in another area. Many of the following questions affect job performance. A supervisor, of course, isn't able to function as a counselor, but it is possible to help the employee identify resources that can help. Some organizations have employee assistance programs to deal with these issues. A good supervisor should know what type of employee assistance is available.

■ **Are family-related issues diminishing performance?** Sometimes the supervisor can help with these problems by changing an employee's schedule or temporarily reducing their work load.

- **Does the employee have a drug or alcohol problem?** A supervisor needs to refer an employee with this type of problem to professional counseling. You should be aware that employees with these types of problems may be protected by the Americans with Disabilities Act.

- **Is an emotional or mental health problem affecting the employee?** This is another problem that needs to be referred to a professional.

- **Are economic problems affecting work performance?** This may be caused by employees spending more than they earn. It is even more common in low-paying or minimum wage jobs. Some organizations have programs that advance a worker money on their wages and this might solve the problem. A supervisor should be cautious about ever loaning money to workers with this problem.

- **Are health problems affecting performance?** In some circumstances, workers are reluctant to discuss medical problems with their supervisor. Keep in mind that some health problems are protected by the Americans with Disabilities Act.

Coaching Techniques

The first step in coaching is identifying the problem and this process has been described earlier in this chapter, in the section on analyzing performance. Once a performance problem has been identified, the supervisor should take action. Sometimes a supervisor must intervene with managers to correct the problem. This is usually true when the performance problems are organizational in nature. In some circumstances, the performance problem can be corrected by the supervisor modifying her or his behavior. This is the case with motivational problems. Other problems require that employees change their behavior. This section examines techniques that a supervisor can use to encourage improved performance in employees.

- **Respond quickly.** Once you notice a performance problem, act quickly to correct it. Delaying action can result in the problem getting worse. Also, when you do finally take action, employees can be confused or angry, wondering why you didn't let them know about the performance problem sooner.

- **Use examples.** Have specific examples of poor performance on the part of an employee. An order that was entered incorrectly, a cash drawer that doesn't balance, and a customer that registers a complaint are all concrete examples that can be used to discuss a problem with an employee.

225

A problem stated in generalities can just cause frustration. The employee doesn't know what specific behavior to change in order to improve performance and the supervisor can't provide specific suggestions.

■ **Ask for employee suggestions.** Tell the employee about the problem you've observed. Then take time to listen to what the person has to say about it. Incorporate his or her suggestions—when appropriate—into the solution. Employees are more likely to follow through with a solution when they've had an opportunity to develop the solution.

■ **Try other approaches.** Despite your analysis and the employee's suggestions about a problem, the first solution may not work. Just like the old saying goes, "When at first you don't succeed, try, try again." The second or third solution may resolve the problem. Employees are valuable to an organization. Don't give up too quickly and assume the best solution is to terminate their employment.

■ **Demonstrate the wrong approach.** It is difficult for some employees to visualize what you mean with just an oral description. A demonstration of the poor behavior can sometimes clarify the problem.

■ **Model the correct behavior.** This technique often goes hand-in-hand with demonstrating the wrong approach. Show the employee exactly how a task should be performed. Modeling is particularly useful in developing skills that are "soft" or not concrete. For example, pleasantly greeting a caller on the phone is a soft skill. You can make it more concrete by modeling this behavior.

■ **Reverse roles.** Sometimes an employee can see a supervisor's point more clearly when the employee is asked to reverse roles. Use the role play technique. Repeat the behavior that you have observed in the employee and ask the employee to respond in the way he or she thinks you would respond. This can often yield some interesting insights for both parties.

■ **Agreement on improved behavior.** Get an agreement from the employee that the person's behavior will change. Specify the performance that is considered satisfactory and how quickly this performance must take place. The agreement may be oral or a written one for more serious behavior issues.

A supervisor should use good human relations and communication skills when coaching employees. Be attentive, engage in active listening, ask questions, and make supportive responses to employee concerns. Always be assertive in arriving at an acceptable conclusion. Don't leave a meeting until both you and the employee have agreed on an acceptable change in the person's behavior. Provide employees with information they need to correct their performance. In situations where professional assistance is needed, provide the employee with referral information.

Older workers—Studies have shown that older workers miss fewer days and are more productive than younger workers. They have more highly developed basic work skills than other workers. This means that you often have fewer performance problems with older workers.

However, many managers report that older workers are sometimes reluctant to change—more so than other workers. Changes in policies, procedures, plans, technology, and jobs occur frequently in most organizations. The need to help older workers change is an important role for supervisors.

Supervisors can follow a three-step change process to help workers change. First, unfreeze workers from their current status quo position. Find out why they might resist change and provide an explanation that responds to concerns expressed by workers. Be firm and clear about the need to change and that you expect workers to implement the changes. Help them understand the consequences both organizationally and personally if change doesn't occur.

The second step is referred to as changing. This is when the supervisor implements the change. This should include training needed to implement the change. Keep an open line of communication so that workers understand everything that is taking place during this step in the process.

Third, refreezing must occur. During this step supervisors build support and acceptance for the change. Reward and praise workers who are implementing the change. When workers realize that performance appraisals and raises are affected by their adoption of the change, it begins to take the form of the status quo.

The Supervisor As Counselor

Some performance problems are related to personal issues that employees are trying to cope with in their lives. These are often referred to as personal problems. The section on analyzing performance problems suggested some questions you can ask to help identify this type of problem. You can follow some additional tips to help identify when this might be the cause of an employee's performance problem. In particular, unusual changes in behavior may alert supervisors that personal problems are causing performance problems. Following are some behaviors that can warn a supervisor about personal problems.

■ **Change in personality.** The employee does not seem to be the same person. If she was outgoing and happy but has changed to being withdrawn and moody, these may be symptoms of a problem.

■ **Change in quantity of work.** An employee who has been productive in the past is suddenly not able to meet the standards of his job.

■ **Change in quality of work.** Along with quantity of work, an employee may also start producing work that is of a lower quality than work produced in the past.

■ **Missing work.** An employee with a good attendance record starts to miss more work, or the employee who is always on time starts to be late frequently.

■ **Frequent breaks and long lunches.** The employee starts to take long lunches and is not at his work station when he should be.

■ **Alcohol and drug use.** Signs that the employee may be using alcohol or drugs include coming to work or returning from lunch with alcohol on her breath. Another sign is when an employee's appearance changes and he exhibits less regard for his personal appearance.

■ **Accidents or negligent acts.** One or two accidents or overlooked tasks can happen to anyone. However, a supervisor should become concerned when a pattern—multiple problems—begins to develop.

■ **Legal problems.** Legal problems may be indicators of personal problems that can affect work performance. For example, arrests for driving under the influence of alcohol or drugs should increase a supervisor's diligence in watching for similar problems at work. Also, employees arrested for spouse or child abuse may be acting out due to emotional problems that can also affect job performance.

Counseling a Problem Employee

Once you have determined that one of your employees does have some kind of problem, you can help by employing counseling techniques. You can use three types of counseling:

■ **Directive counseling** is the process of listening to an employee's problem and giving the employee advice on how to solve the problem. This type of counseling method may help the employee by reassuring him and giving him an emotional outlet for the problem. A drawback to this approach is that employees may not be motivated to take advice offered by the supervisor.

■ **Non-directive counseling** is the opposite of directive counseling; it is the process of listening to the employee and encouraging her to explain her problems, but determining appropriate responses is directly up to the employee. Non-directive methods are not easily learned and take a great deal of practice. They normally are used by professional counselors. It is also less appropriate in a work situation where a supervisor does expect certain improvements in job performance.

■ **Participative counseling** is a mutual relationship between the employee and supervisor; the supervisor listens to the employee, encourages him to talk and explain the problem, and then helps him solve the problem. This approach is probably the most appropriate in a work situation.

Counseling Techniques

Supervisors find some basic techniques useful when counseling employees. Many of these are natural extensions of good communication skills. The main difference is that the focus is on discovering an employee's problem and helping the person to resolve it. To help achieve this a supervisor should do the following:

■ **Pay attention.** Counsel an employee in an area free from disruptions. Eliminate distractions by putting a telephone on hold and closing the door to your office—if you don't have a private office, reserve a meeting room for the conversation. Concentrate your attention on the employee. The purpose is to make employees feel that you are focused on them.

■ **Be nonjudgmental.** Refrain from expressing a judgment—either verbally or nonverbally—about what employees tell you. When people feel that they are being judged, they often stop talking and it is difficult to get them to resume freely expressing themselves.

■ **Practice active listening.** Listen carefully to what an employee says. Ask questions, where appropriate, to clarify thoughts or facts you don't understand. Encourage employees to be honest and freely express what they perceive the actual problem to be.

■ **Interpret.** As employees pause in their conversations with you, describe what you understand them to be saying. This is referred to as interpretation because it provides an opportunity to confirm that you understand what they are saying. Sometimes employees indirectly express their thoughts and feelings, and interpretation allows you to express what you think they really mean. In turn, the employee can confirm that the interpretation is accurate or restate what he or she means.

■ **Empathize.** Try to relate to the employee's situation and his feelings. You may not be able to fully understand the situation if you haven't experienced it yourself. Even when you've had a similar experience, your reaction may be different. Empathy is an attempt to come as close as you can to putting yourself in someone else's position. Avoid using the term "I understand how you feel." Rather, use a statement like "I'm sure that feeling isn't unusual."

■ **Be assertive.** This technique distinguishes supervisory counseling from a professional counseling session. You need to assert how the personal problem is affecting the employee's job performance. They need to be aware of the impact the problem has had on their job performance so they understand the eventual consequences.

Welfare-to-work employees—Many family-based issues can interfere with the performance of welfare-to-work employees. Some common barriers to employment include unstable housing arrangements, family illness, being victims of physical abuse, and financial emergencies. These problems have such a significant impact on welfare-to-work employees that some organizations, like the Marriott Corporation, have hired full-time case-workers to assist these workers.

Some of these problems can be handled by Employee Assistance Programs (EAP). If your organization has one, refer the worker there. When this service doesn't exist, the supervisor must assume the role of a caseworker in helping the employee resolve the problem. Contact the United Way office in your area and find out whether there is a referral service in your community for social service agencies. Ask for their help in finding an agency that can help solve the worker's problem.

Participative Counseling

The participative counseling approach is typically used by supervisors to help employees resolve personal problems that are interfering with their work. The focus during participative counseling is on behavior. A supervisor isn't a therapist and can't deal with developmental and emotional causes of behavior. However, a supervisor has the right to expect certain behavior from employees during their time at the work site. The counseling session should be conducted so that employees recognize that your purpose is to resolve problems related to conduct at work and their job performance. The participative counseling process has seven steps.

1. **Describe to the employee the change in behavior you have observed.** Do this in a nonthreatening manner and do not make statements about the employee's attitude or motivation. You must remember to stick to the behaviors the employee has exhibited. Don't project motivations or problems you think may be causing these behaviors.

2. **Ask the employee to comment on your observations and allow the employee to explain their actions.** In rare cases you may simply have misunderstood what took place. The purpose of this step is to help you and the employee determine specifically the type of problem the employee is having or causing. Don't let employees avoid responsibility for what they are doing by accepting excuses for their behavior. Also, don't permit them to blame their behavior on someone or something else. The intent of this step is to have employees accept responsibility for the problem and acknowledge a need to change their behavior.

3. **Help the employee generate solutions to the problem.** Don't get caught in the trap of generating all of the solutions. The employee needs to take ownership of the solution. Once you have helped the employee generate solutions, guide him or her in deciding on the best solution to the problem. Again, don't get caught in the trap of selecting the solution. If it fails, you are the one who gets the blame. The outcome should be a specific change in behavior and criteria for judging this behavior that is acceptable to both the supervisor and employee.

4. **Make sure you agree on the solution and get a commitment from the employee to implement the solution you have agreed on.** Establish a time frame for implementation of the solution and specific outcomes. Most of the time changes in behavior need to take place immediately; make sure the employee understands this.

5. **Follow up to make sure the solution has solved the problem and there are no more performance problems.** It is very important the employee understands there will be a follow up because if there isn't, chances are their behavior will not change.

6. **Document the counseling sessions you have had with the employee.** These records are important should some form of disciplinary action be necessary. Also, a record helps protect you from complaints that may be made by the employee. Keep in mind that employees facing severe personal problems are not always stable. They may perceive you in a positive light during the counseling session and appreciate your assistance. However, they later might begin to resent your actions and try to retaliate by complaining to a manager about your actions.

7. **Be prepared to refer the employee elsewhere.** If you do not feel that you have sufficient expertise to help the employee in a situation, refer the employee to someone who can provide professional help. If your organization has an in-house employee assistance program (EAP), recommend that the person see the EAP representative. If not, recommend the employee see an outside counseling agency for help. Referral may be the final outcome that you and the employee agree is the solution to her or his problem, as is described in step 4.

The Supervisor As Disciplinarian

Discipline should be considered a last resort, except for cases of extreme behavior, like physically assaulting another employee, that call for immediate disciplinary action. Counseling or coaching should be used by the supervisor before taking disciplinary action. However, if an employee is unwilling or unable to change, you may have to use disciplinary measures to try and correct the behavior.

Discipline is the action taken to force a change in the employee's behavior when employees do not follow policies and rules or meet performance standards. As a supervisor, you are responsible for directly issuing discipline or providing the information to the person in the organization who is responsible for issuing discipline. In many organizations, there are specific procedures for disciplinary action—in a unionized organization this is usually part of the collective bargaining contract. Always review these procedures before taking disciplinary action. It is usually good to get the advice of the human resource (HR) department or your manager before proceeding with disciplinary action. There are some guidelines to consider as you move forward in taking disciplinary action.

Immigrant workers—A potential conflict can arise between immigrant workers and female workers. Some countries have a sharp division between the role of men and women. The more masculine-oriented societies emphasize assertiveness and acquisition while feminine societies emphasize quality of life and caring for others. Highly masculine societies typically confine women to caring relationships, such as taking care of children at home. The power, influence, and leadership of women is very limited. Countries where the role of women is quite limited include Japan, Iran, Saudi Arabia, and Iraq.

Workers from these countries sometimes have difficulty relating to women in the workplace. In particular, they find assertive, confident, and powerful women a curiosity. They simply have no experience in relating to women in the workplace. It is important for supervisors to recognize this problem. Spend time with the worker and discuss how Americans perceive the role of women in the workplace. You can also prevent potential problems by clarifying laws and policies related to discrimination based on sex and sexual harassment.

Types of Discipline

Douglas McGregor—the creator of Theory X and Theory Y—also developed the "hot stove" rule in discipline. A hot stove gives you a warning when it is about to be touched: "If you touch me, you will get burned immediately." Employees should be aware if they violate rules (touch the hot stove) they will get burned (disciplined). When an employee violates a rule, the results of the violation should be immediate. Employees who violate rules should receive the same consistency of discipline, but this does not mean they should receive the same measure. Everyone who touches a hot stove will get burned, but not necessarily to the same degree. If you hold your hand on the stove, you may get burned severely and if you only touch it lightly you will not get burned badly. If you touch the stove often, you will get burned often, if you touch it only once, you will get burned only once. A hot stove is also impersonal as to who it burns, and discipline should be impersonal as well. The discipline should be determined by the severity of an act, not your feelings about the employee.

Progressive discipline is a policy that imposes increasing degrees of penalty to repeated violations. For example, if an employee misses work and is unexcused, you may give him a written reprimand. If the same employee misses another day of work and is unexcused, you may give him a day off without pay. If the same employee misses still another unexcused day from work, you may give him one or two days off without pay. This type of progression can continue until the employee is terminated for missing work.

Nonpunitive discipline is a new approach to discipline. There is no penalty assessed in the discipline procedure. Consider the preceding example—the employee missing work. On the first offense, you would have a private meeting with the employee to discuss the situation and gain the employee's agreement on how to solve the problem. If the employee misses another day, you would again meet with the employee to review their failure to change their behavior.

233

A summary of this meeting would be written and placed on the employee's record. If the employee misses another unexcused day, the employee will be given a day off, with pay, to consider the behavior and decide whether he really wants to change the behavior or leave the employment of the organization. When the employee returns to work, you should meet with him to determine the decision he has reached. During this meeting, you should help the employee set specific goals and objectives he will meet and the time frame in which he will meet them. The employee must understand that if he does not make the changes, the next step will be termination.

Implementing Disciplinary Action

Most organizations select a specific type of discipline and expect all supervisors to use it when taking disciplinary action against an employee. There are several steps that you should follow when implementing disciplinary action:

- **Know your authority.** Determine your rights and responsibilities as a supervisor to take needed disciplinary action. Your authority is partially determined by how firmly management backs your action. That is why it is important to inform them and get their support before proceeding.

- **Know the rules of the organization.** Read the disciplinary procedure for your organization. Ask HR or managers to clarify points that are unclear to you. Confirm that your action is consistent with responses to the same behavior problem in other employees. The reaction from employees may be very negative if disciplinary action is taken to correct behavior that has been tolerated in the past or in other parts of the organization.

- **Be sure all of the rules and standards are communicated and employees understand what is expected of them.** It is your responsibility as a supervisor to be sure this happens—don't rely on someone else to do it. Employees are typically told about rules and expectations during orientation but you may have to refresh their memories to make sure they have not forgotten what they were told. When talking with employees about rules or policies, don't make negative comments about the policies.

- **Get all of the facts before you discipline an employee.** Never discipline an employee before all of the facts of the situation are known. If you've tried coaching or counseling the employee—which you should do before taking disciplinary action—then you already should be aware of the facts.

- **Determine the appropriate action in the process.** The typical disciplinary process involves four steps. The first step is to provide the employee a verbal warning and specify corrective action. The second step is to present the employee with a verbal warning. The third step is to suspend the employee—this may be with or without pay. The fourth step is to terminate the employee.

- **Discipline the employee in private.** It is embarrassing for an employee to be disciplined in front of other people. This embarrassment may cause the employee to become angry, resulting in a communication problem between the supervisor and employee.

- **Document all actions you take against an employee.** This includes all of the conversations and written actions you take. These records provide protection to the supervisor and organization during grievance or legal proceedings.

The supervisor's actions during the disciplinary process have a significant influence on an employee's response. Keep in mind that disciplinary action takes place after coaching and counseling have failed to change an employee's behavior. That is why the supervisor's approach should be somewhat different when implementing disciplinary action. Remembering the following rules will make the disciplinary process as smooth as possible.

- **Remain calm.** Employees often react emotionally—crying, yelling, and so on—when faced with disciplinary action. A supervisor should remain calm and not escalate emotional responses. Allow the emotional response to continue for a reasonable amount of time. This is a venting process that can help employees relieve stress. Once they have vented emotionally, they are better able to listen to what you have to say.

- **Be confident.** Supervisors are more likely to be confident when they have prepared for the disciplinary meeting. Be prepared with facts. Know the exact disciplinary action that is going to be taken. Present the facts to the employee and explain the action that is going to be taken.

- **Listen actively.** This remains an important communication tool. It is important to listen to what the employee has to say about the situation. However, if you've used active listening during the coaching and counseling stages, you probably aren't going to hear anything new.

- **Be firm.** Respond to what the employee says but remain firm about the disciplinary action. Explain that the employee has had an opportunity to change her or his behavior and because it continued, disciplinary action had to be taken.

235

■ **Be persistent and consistent.** Supervisors need to follow through with the disciplinary action. If an employee's undesirable behavior continues, point the fact out to her. Follow the next step in the disciplinary process. Continue step-by-step until her behavior changes. This persistent and consistent action by a supervisor sends a message that the problem is serious and the consequences are going to be unpleasant unless the employee changes her behavior.

Disabled workers—Supervisors can help workers with disabilities improve their performance by looking for ways that technology can be adapted to assist them. A simple way to improve the performance of workers with disabilities is to provide them with tape recorders, electronic organizers, digital watches, and voice synthesizers to process and organize information. Braille keyboards, screen magnifiers, voice synthesizers, and voice input devices can help workers with vision disabilities more effectively use computers.

Workers who need wheelchairs can be provided with motorized wheelchairs, obstacles in the workplace can be removed, and walkways kept clear of clutter to make it easier to move throughout the work site. These are just a few examples of steps supervisors can take to use technology to improve performance. You should take time to talk with workers who have disabilities to determine what can be done to assist them. In addition, you can research tools that are being developed to help workers with disabilities.

Termination

When all else fails, you may find it necessary to terminate an employee. If this happens, you should move cautiously to protect yourself and the organization. You should consider several matters when you terminate an employee.

Plan the termination

Consider three basic issues when planning an employee's termination—strategy, benefits, and legal protection:

■ **Strategy.** Decide when the employee will be told. Every organization has its own preference. There is some merit—when immediate action isn't required—to do it late in the day Friday. This avoids a turmoil in the office and the employee has the weekend to adjust to the news. Determine who is going to inform the employee. At the minimum, the supervisor should inform the employee, but some organizations prefer that a manager and/or HR representative be present to assure that everything is done correctly and there are witnesses to the fact.

Set a date when the termination becomes effective. It is sometimes best for the termination to take place immediately. In some cases, the organization may need the employee's assistance with work that needs to be passed along to other employees. An option to consider is allowing the employee to resign. This can sometimes reduce animosity and "save face" for the employee. In some situations this might not be appropriate, depending on the employee's actions that caused the termination. Determine what kind of reference the organization will provide when prospective employers inquire about the person's employment. It is usually better for the organization and employee to make the termination as pleasant as possible—keeping in mind that it is typically a stressful and unpleasant action. Other employees are affected by the termination of another employee. The better employees are treated when they are terminated, the less negative an effect it has on other employees.

■ **Benefits.** Determine the benefits and rights that the employee will have upon termination. You should request that HR or accounting provide information on the employee's pay, vacation time, retirement benefits, health benefits, and any other benefits that they are owed. Typically, health insurance benefits can be retained after termination—but the employee must pay for these benefits. A document must be signed by the employee acknowledging that they've been informed about this provision. Some retirement programs have provisions for the employee to transfer her benefits to another program and also require the employee to sign a document acknowledging she has been informed about these matters. Determine when the employee is expected to sign these documents.

■ **Legal protection.** Review all actions that you have taken in disciplining the employee and make sure that nothing has been done illegally or in violation of organization policies. Collect all documentation on actions that have been taken to correct an employee's behavior. Consult all the appropriate managers in the organization so that they are aware of the termination and agree with the supervisor's decision to terminate the employee.

237

Security precautions

You should take several security precautions whenever you terminate an employee.

- ■ **Secure information.** Computers make it easy for employees to either quickly copy or erase files in a computer. Passwords that give employees access to a computer system or network should be changed prior to meeting with the employee or arrange for them to be changed as the meeting is taking place. Personal computers with confidential or key information should be immediately taken from the employee's work site and locked in another office in the organization. Determine whether it is necessary to have locks or combination codes changed.

- ■ **Employee safety.** If there is a chance that the employee may act in a hostile manner, have security personnel present. There is no reason to risk other employees being injured if an employee might react violently. This action should be taken if the employee has reacted in an angry or violent manner in other situations or if he has threatened violence if he is terminated. In the past, managers and supervisors have often considered violent threats as just a natural occurrence. Given the violent acts that have occurred in the workplace, however, it is prudent to consider the personal safety of employees when a person is terminated from a job.

- ■ **Notify the employee.** The termination of an employee needs to be done in person. It should follow the strategy developed during the planning stage. In addition, here are some other considerations for employee notification.

  - ◆ **Respect privacy.** Terminating an employee should always be done in private. It increases the anger of an employee to terminate them in front of other employees or customers. Also, terminating an employee in public is demoralizing to other employees. They are not aware of all the steps that may have been taken to correct an employee's behavior and retain him as an employee. All they see is the employee being fired and it immediately causes them to be concerned about their own jobs. In addition, it is very inappropriate to terminate an employee in front of customers. Such behavior causes an adverse reaction to the organization because customers observe only the termination—a very negative event—and know nothing of the circumstances that caused the event.

  - ◆ **Maintain documentation.** Present the employee with written official notice of his or her termination. This has the psychological effect of making the termination appear more official. It often is a legal or organizational requirement.

◆ **Confiscate items if necessary.** Take possession of all items that the employee should return to the organization. The more common items are identification badges, keys, access cards, parking passes, uniforms, and equipment.

◆ **Take action.** Request that the employee immediately follow through with the action you specify. This may be leaving the office immediately, at the end of the day, or within a few days or weeks. Inform the employee that the reason for termination is going to be kept confidential and you prefer that he or she not talk to other employees about it.

Contingent workers—It is difficult to orient temporary workers and independent contractors on all policies and procedures for an organization. That is why they might unknowingly violate a policy. For example, they might eat a piece of pie that was left in the cafeteria line when the policy calls for all leftover food to be thrown away. Supervisors should immediately inform contingent workers when a policy is violated. However, they shouldn't be rebuked. This can sometimes cause problems with permanent employees because they would be reprimanded for the same action. It is important to explain to permanent employees why your reaction is fair and appropriate. Most employees will understand the reason for differential treatment. Watch the behavior of employees who don't understand because they may attempt to violate the same policy.

Special Problems

Supervisors often face four problems that deserve special attention: sexual harassment, racial harassment, dating among employees, and workplace violence. We present these four because they create some special problems for supervisors. Sexual and racial harassment by employees—or by the supervisor—create legal problems, demoralize the organization's workforce, and cause the organization to lose skilled employees. We examine dating because the workplace is now a common place for people to meet members of the opposite sex. Workplace violence has certainly dominated the news in the past few years. A new phrase in our language has been generated by the problem—"going postal." It is a problem supervisors need to know how to control.

Sexual Harassment

Sexual harassment is unwelcome verbal or physical conduct of a sexual nature. This can include such things as staring at another person, touching another person, telling sexual jokes, making sexual comments, commenting on a person's sexual characteristics, or displaying nude pictures or obscene cartoons. Warn employees about this type of behavior to try and avoid it from the start.

Employers are required by law to protect employees from sexual harassment. Supervisor should take immediate action when there is any appearance of sexual harassment. Employees should be warned—or in extreme situations, severely disciplined or fired—for sexual harassment.

Racial Harassment

Racial harassment is unwelcome verbal or physical conduct of a racial nature. This includes but isn't limited to telling racial jokes, using racial slurs, commenting on a person's racial characteristics, distributing racist materials, or excluding someone from company activities because of race.

This form of harassment often results from ignorance. It's sometimes tempting to participate in the bad behavior of other workers. However, when employees engage in racial harassment, point out the harm that can result. Supervisors should be as aggressive in halting racial harassment as they are with sexual harassment.

Interoffice Dating

Office relationships sometimes develop into romantic relationships. Office romances are natural because the workforce is composed of almost the same percent of each gender. Furthermore, hectic work schedules sometimes don't allow much time outside of work to meet a potential partner. However, office romances can be risky. For one thing, romantic advances might be considered sexual harassment. In fact, repeatedly asking someone for a date after being turned down *is* considered sexual harassment.

Co-workers who are dating can sometimes create uncomfortable situations for other workers. They may think that dating couples are taking advantage of the romantic relationship, by not doing their own work but helping each other, or that they support each other's ideas or actions simply because they are dating. The comfort level with other workers often depends on how closely two dating employees work together. For example, an employee in marketing who dates someone in accounting isn't as likely to create discomfort in other employees as two dating employees who both work in customer service.

An additional problem that can result from co-workers dating is that their attention no longer is focused on their jobs. They might spend too much time talking and not working. Also, they may engage in public displays of affection that make other workers uncomfortable. Such blatant behavior needs to be confronted by the supervisor and monitored to make sure it changes.

Other problems can arise when a couple terminates their romantic relationship. An adjustment period then occurs as the couple attempts to redefine their roles. This can be stressful to one or both parties, resulting in outbursts at each other or other employees. A tension may develop that interferes with work activities. This is when the supervisor must step in. Keep in mind that any action needs to be balanced—otherwise accusations of sexual bias may be raised.

Some organizations have a policy about dating co-workers. Be sure to find out what these policies are and discuss them with your manager before taking any action in dealing with problems caused by an office romance. Also, when employees come from different units in the organization—involving more than one supervisor—cooperative efforts among the organization's management are called for.

Do potential problems mean that office romances should be discouraged? Well, this is actually a policy issue that the organization's management must decide. Research indicates that the benefits of office romances may balance out the detriments. In fact, almost one-third of all romances begin in the workplace and almost half of all those romances result in marriage. Positive relationships, whether a close friendship or a romantic one, help develop a workplace environment that is pleasant and attractive. This in turn helps retain workers and makes it easier to recruit new workers.

Ex-offenders—Workers who are ex-offenders have some difficulties adjusting to the workplace when released from jail or prison. It is important for a supervisor to provide coaching to help ex-offenders remember how to appropriately respond to situations that weren't common while incarcerated. Exercise patience with ex-offenders when they behave in ways that aren't suitable. Keep guiding and encouraging them to improve their actions. Give them simple steps to follow that can be easily achieved. This reinforces their confidence.

Workplace Violence

A rather new phenomenon you will have to deal with in the workplace is violence. Violence has always existed in the workplace, but in recent years it has evolved into a deadly form. There have been many cases where supervisors and employees have been killed by "disgruntled" workers.

241

Types of workplace violence

Workplace violence can range from simple harassment to murder. And murder is becoming more prevalent! Workplace violence seems to be a phenomenon of modern American culture and no organization is immune. When workplace violence does happen, the most common statement from victims and survivors is "I didn't think it could happen here." The greatest number of violent situations in the workplace occur as a result of attempted robberies by nonemployees, primarily in retail stores, fast food restaurants, convenience stores, and service stations. These categories account for about half of all of the homicides in the workplace each year. There are three types of workplace violence:

- **Type 1 violence** both originates and occurs in the workplace. A situation develops in the workplace, often through a series of events that causes an employee to feel like a victim. Typically, the employee feels like he has been treated or disciplined unfairly or terminated without just cause. The employee then decides to seek vengeance or obtain retribution on the people he feels are responsible for the unfair treatment. These people may be supervisors, fellow employees, or anyone who happens to be there when they decide to get revenge. However, many times the people hurt or killed just happen to be in the wrong place at the wrong time and really have no connection with the disgruntled employee. Every violent situation does not necessarily culminate in a shooting, but it may take the form of pushing, shoving, fighting, destruction of company property, or damage to a supervisor's or fellow employee's personal property, like automobiles. Tire slashing is a common way for a disgruntled employee to take out vengeance on other people.

- **Type 2 violence** originates in the workplace but occurs outside the workplace. A worker who has been terminated and wants to seek vengeance for the termination but is not able to get back into the workplace may decide to go to the home of the supervisor to get even with them. In the process, the employee may kill or maim some of the family members of the supervisor. All of these situations do not end in murder but may take the form of destruction of the supervisor's property.

- **Type 3 violence** originates outside the workplace but occurs in the workplace. Often this type of violence is referred to by law enforcement as "spillover" violence and frequently originates from domestic violence. For example, a wife who leaves an abusive husband increases her chances of being harmed by about 75 percent. Frequently the only place a husband knows he can definitely find the wife—if she is employed—is at her workplace. He goes to the workplace, kills her, and most of the time kills himself.

Costs of workplace violence

Workplace violence can be costly not only from the standpoint of human suffering but also from the cost to the organization. The following list illustrates some of the primary costs of workplace violence.

■ **Medical costs** include physical and psychological costs for employees and third-party victims who claim reimbursement for injuries, counseling, and funeral costs.

■ **Lost productivity costs** result from losing productivity during the event and nonproductivity during the time required to make repairs to the facility and equipment.

■ **Property damage** involves costs to facilities and equipment that is damaged or destroyed during the violent event. It also may involve payment for damage to private property of victims.

■ **Lost sales** are incurred because of the event, due to the time the facility must be closed for cleanup and repair, customers avoiding the facility, employees not concentrating on sales efforts, and so on.

■ **Legal fees** to defend against lawsuits brought by victims or their families can be significant, and the actual judgments that come from these suits can be astronomical.

Secondary costs for an organization can arise in any of the following ways.

■ **Medical expenses** may be necessary to provide counseling for employees who were not directly involved in the event, but who have suffered psychological trauma because of the event.

■ **Lower productivity** may occur because employees are fearful, angry, or resent the fact the event happened at their place of employment.

■ **Preventive measures** must be implemented, so the company may approve expenditures for new safety and security procedures to deter future violence.

Causes of workplace violence

One of the primary causes of workplace violence is the threat to an employee's job or the actual loss of the job. Such fear is common today in the midst of "downsizing," "rightsizing," or "reengineering." Many organizations are trimming the fat to become more profitable. Many times employees receive no warning that this is about to happen and they can become quite angry. Poor work

243

performance or the violation of company rules can also result in job loss or at least the threat of it. Since income and job security are basic security needs, the fear of this loss can place immense stress on a marginal employee, or even a good employee who is caught in downsizing.

Another cause of workplace violence can be the autocratic, centralized power structures that delegate very little power to employees. Employees who work for this type of organization are told what to do, when to do it, and how to do it. This management style, while often creating an organization that appears orderly and efficient on the surface, has a negative impact on employees. The employees may compare the actions of their supervisor with those of a dictator and feel they are in an oppressive environment and have no alternative but to strike back at the organization or supervisor.

Employees who commit workplace violence

No common set of characteristics that define a potentially violent employee has been identified. Developing a profile of a potentially violent employee may be counterproductive because it can mislead managers and supervisors, and they might consequently overlook someone that is potentially violent. However, a supervisor can consider some things when attempting to determine whether an employee is potentially violent. The more of these characteristics an employee exhibits, the more you should carefully observe his or her behavior and take preventative measures at the appropriate time. Here are some characteristics of people who have committed acts of workplace violence:

- White males between the ages of 30 and 50 have been the most prominent age group that commits workplace violence.

- A loner who keeps to himself and may be very secretive.

- The person might have a fascination for weapons of all types.

- He or she may have a history of drug and alcohol abuse.

- His medical history may include some type of mental illness.

- She may have a violent past. Past behavior is a very good predictor of future behavior.

- He may be unable to deal with adverse events and circumstances.

Even if an employee has all of the behaviors or history listed here, it is not a certainty, or even a probability that this employee will become violent. However, all of the employees who have committed workplace violence exhibited one or more of these behaviors. If you suspect that you have a potentially violent employee, don't try to handle the situation by yourself. Attempt to get professional help for the employee. Let other managers know about your suspicions so the employee can be monitored. If you are disciplining or terminating an employee whom you suspect to be potentially violent, make sure you have professional help to deal with the situation.

Violence prevention strategies

It should be made clear that violence can't be prevented in every case. However, the potential for violence can be diminished and the amount of injuries and damage reduced. This can be done through environmental designs, administrative controls, and employee training.

Environmental design

A company can take actions to reduce risk of violence through modification of structures and landscaping surrounding the structure.

- Careful planning in the design of buildings can make a difference through access, protection, and security measures.

- Access to and egress from the workplace are important matters to consider. Reduce the number of entrances and exits and that nonemployees or terminated employees can use to gain access to a building.

- Determine areas where attackers could hide and increase lighting, place mirrors, or mount video cameras so that these areas become more visible.

- Keep a well-lighted parking lot and consider how views are obstructed by landscaping.

- Install and regularly maintain alarm systems, video cameras, and other security devices. Panic buttons, noise makers, and cellular phones should be distributed in areas where a violent person might try to access a building.

- Use a closed-circuit video recording for high-risk areas on a 24-hour basis. Public safety should take precedence over privacy in some situations.

- Provide employees with "safe rooms" that can be used in case of an emergency.

245

- Install bright, effective lighting indoors and outdoors.

- Replace burned-out lights, broken windows, or broken locks immediately. Notify law enforcement personnel immediately when doors, windows, or locks have been broken.

- Install metal detectors at building entrances.

- Commonly implemented procedures in retail settings include locked drop safes, carrying small amounts of cash, and posting signs and notices that limited cash is available. Only handle cashless transactions in late night and early morning hours. Provide bullet-resistant barriers between employees and customers.

Administrative controls

Administrative and work practice controls affect the way jobs or tasks are performed. The following examples illustrate how changes in work practices and administrative procedures can help prevent violent incidents.

- **Develop, state, and enforce a policy against violence in the workplace.** This should apply to harassment, verbally threatening a person with violence, touching another employee in any threatening manner, striking or pushing another employee, bringing any weapon into the workplace, or threatening to use a weapon.

- **Report and take action against any employee who violates this policy.** Employees will realize that the organization is serious about enforcement, thus making future violations less likely.

- **Require employees to report all assaults or threats.** They should also report any threat made against an employee, supervisor, or manager. Keep logs and reports of such incidents to help in determining any necessary actions to prevent further occurrences. These records may help identify an employee who is prone to violence.

- **Advise and assist employees, if needed, of company procedures for requesting police assistance or filing charges when assaulted.** Employees need to feel like the company supports their efforts and stands behind them.

- **Set up a trained response team.** This special group will respond to emergencies and establish ways for management to support any response.

■ **Encourage employees who are victims of domestic violence to report this to their supervisors.** When a victim leaves his or her spouse, the supervisor should place management and security personnel on alert. Guards, receptionists, and other employees near an entrance should be alerted to the problem and instructed to call the police immediately, should the person try to enter the building.

■ **Require employees who have been threatened in any manner with violence outside the workplace to report the threat to local police and inform their supervisor.** Follow the same action as described for victims of domestic violence.

■ **Don't allow employees to work alone in an office building at night unless security personnel are posted in the building.** Perpetrators are less likely to commit violent acts if they know security personnel are present.

■ **Establish policies and procedures for evacuation in case of emergencies.** These activities can be coordinated through the emergency response team.

Employee training

Employees need to be trained about the serious nature of workplace violence and encouraged to support administrative controls that have been in place. Following are some tips to keep in mind when training employees to deal with workplace violence.

■ **Train employees in nonviolent behavior and conflict resolution.** This reduces the potential for employees to threaten violence or use violence against other employees.

■ **Provide training that addresses hazards associated with specific tasks or work sites and relevant prevention strategies.** For example, banks normally train tellers in how to respond to a robbery.

■ **Train employees on workplace violence policies, emergency response plans, and programs to reduce violence.** Employees who have practiced and had "drills" in dealing with workplace violence are much more likely to keep their cool in an actual violent situation.

■ **Train employees how to deal with hostile people, including customers and visitors.** Understanding why customers and visitors exhibit violent tendencies can often help the employee diffuse the situation.

247

Summary

Supervisors play a key role in guiding and improving the performance of employees. The organization's workforce is its most important asset and supervisors are vital in the development of this asset. Coaching is a proactive and positive approach to employee development. Supervisors can actively observe and assist employees in improving their performance. Personal problems may sometimes affect an employee's performance. Supervisors need to assist employees with this type of problem by acting as a counselor. Finally, supervisors must sometimes deal with problem employees—whether they want to or not. It is not always easy to do this but it is part of their job; managers expect them to do it and do it well.

Developing Ethical Behavior

Ethics are principles or standards that govern our behavior. Ethical principles usually are set by society. Our communities, organizations, religions, and families establish ethical principles that guide us in our daily actions.

In this chapter, we examine ethical behavior on the job. The supervisor plays a key role in promoting and monitoring ethical behavior in employees. This chapter provides information about ethics from both a conceptual and practical perspective. Supervisors should find this knowledge useful in developing an ethical workforce.

Ethical Problems for Businesses

Businesses are concerned about the ethical behavior of employees for many different reasons.

- **Loss of profits.** Employee theft costs U.S. businesses more than $60 billion each year. In fact, 50 percent of all working students admit stealing from companies, and almost 35 percent said they steal $10 or more a month.

- **Worse than shoplifting.** Employee theft in the retail industry accounts for 41 percent of its losses, compared with shoplifting, which accounts for just 35 percent of their losses.

- **Legal jeopardy.** Employees who copy software illegally can cause an employer to be sued. Violation of copyright laws can result in fines of up to $100,000 and five years imprisonment for each illegal use. Moreover, the Software Publisher's Association targets smaller companies. It's clear that an employee making illegal copies of software can cause major legal problems for an organization.

■ **Information loss.** Employees steal almost $8 billion annually in intellectual property, trade secrets, and computer software and hardware, according to the Technology Theft Prevention Foundation.

■ **Physical danger.** Employees who use drugs on the job are 3.6 times more likely to have an accident. Higher accident rates result in higher worker compensation insurance payments, loss of productivity, and more importantly, injured people.

Unethical behavior is costly to business and causes morale problems. The supervisor can help by developing ethical behavior in employees by responding promptly and appropriately to correct unethical behavior.

Ethical Models

At first glance, behaving ethically seems easy. All a person has to do is "the right thing." However, deciding what is appropriate ethical behavior in every situation is sometimes difficult. In fact, philosophers and ethicists have suggested many basic moral theories, as illustrated in the following sections.

Younger workers—A study conducted by Purdue University of 11 restaurant chains in 1999 found that workers admitted stealing an average of $218. This typically was done by stealing meals for themselves or friends. Younger workers were found to have stolen higher amounts than other workers. It is important for supervisors to inform younger workers about the inappropriateness of this behavior—not all young people are aware that eating food or giving it to friends is wrong. Supervisors in all organizations should be aware that younger workers are not as likely to understand correct ethical behavior.

Take time to discuss this topic with younger workers when they begin the job. When you see them doing something unethical—unless it is a crime or contrary to company policy—warn them, describe the appropriate behavior, get their agreement not to repeat their action, and inform them of the consequences that will occur should it happen again.

Utilitarianism

To judge whether an action is right, utilitarianism asks whether it provides the individual with the greatest amount of happiness or benefits. If society or an organization is expected to maximize happiness, it is necessary to determine what happiness means. Should it be based on happiness as defined by the majority? If so, can society then impose this definition of happiness on everyone? A response to these dilemmas is *preference utilitarianism.* This theory proposes that society should promote conditions that allow every member to pursue happiness in whatever way they choose to define it. However, circumstances still occur that force the happiness of some individuals to be limited in order to provide for the happiness of the greater number of persons. For example, a plant that is old and inefficient should be shut down—even though employees are adversely affected—because building a new plant can increase profits for stockholders, lower prices for customers, and at the same time, provide jobs for other work.

According to this theory, an organization should make decisions that result in the greatest net benefits for society or the least costs. To apply this theory, a supervisor should follow these three steps:

1. Consider all possible options.

2. Determine the utility or value of each option.

3. Select the option with the highest total utility for the organization and all parties involved.

Utilitarianism theory has two major problems. First, it is difficult, if not impossible to identify and measure all possible benefits that may result from a decision. How do you adequately identify and measure benefits or costs that may occur in the future? A second problem is that it is not a just theory. It exonerates a decision that may violate the rights of others or creates an injustice. Nevertheless, utilitarian theory has great intuitive appeal because people perceive happiness as a reasonable basis for morality. It also appeals to the business person who is trained to measure efficiency as the greatest return for the lowest costs. However, efficiency shouldn't be confused with morality.

Respect for Persons

The basic idea behind this theory is that actions should be based on equal respect for each person as a moral agent. The Golden Rule—"Do unto others

251

as you would have them do unto you"—exemplifies this moral theory. Basically, we should treat each person in the same manner we want to be treated. However, this concept is somewhat ambiguous because what one person considers to be fair treatment might be seen as mistreatment by another. The doctrine of rights has been proposed as a way to overcome this problem.

A right is considered to be an entitlement that allows a person to freely act in a certain way. The theory of rights asserts that others cannot block a person from receiving basic treatments and performing basic acts. However, the rights of others may sometimes be superseded to protect the rights of others. Unlike utilitarian theory, however, these rights can't be overridden just to gain more freedom or increase the well-being of others. For example, an organization might fire an employee that won't do the work she is assigned—violating the person's right to physical security. However, this is done to protect the rights of stockholders, managers, and supervisors who might loose their physical security if the business fails—a highly likely outcome when employees don't do their work.

A supervisor who wants to use the theory of rights needs to consider the following points when deciding on a course of action.

- **Is the right I might infringe more basic than the one I'm advancing?** For example, a piece of equipment is so old that it could injure or kill an employee. The right to life is more basic than the property rights that would be lost by the organization because it was required to replace the old equipment.

- **Is it possible to limit a person's right rather than terminate the right?** An example would be deciding to suspend rather than terminate an employee.

- **Is it possible to simply extend or push the limit on a right rather than actually infringing on the right?** This makes the point that simply pushing the right to the limit is far less serious than actually infringing on the right. For example, delaying payment to a vendor is not the same as failure to pay the vendor.

There are two problems with using the rights theory in guiding ethical decisions. First, it is very difficult to balance one right against another. Second, this theory sets such a high standard that it is difficult to apply in some business situations. Many people feel it is unrealistic and simply creates guilt when it can't be achieved. However, the fact that a theory establishes a high level of ethical behavior is a poor reason to reject a moral theory.

Older workers—One of the strengths of older workers is their strong work ethic—according to surveys of managers. They typically have a high level of loyalty, are punctual, very seldom miss work, and are highly productive. Older workers provide good role models for younger workers. Supervisors should consider using older workers as mentors to help younger workers develop a strong work ethic. Older workers can teach younger workers about basic work ethics, encourage them when they do well, and become a role model for them. However, supervisors should first coach older workers about basic mentoring skills. Use older workers for mentors only if they are positive and interested in helping younger workers.

Justice and Fairness

The theory of justice and fairness suggests that decisions should be based on providing fair and comparative treatment to all affected parties. Justice and fairness are somewhat synonymous, but justice is used for situations that are more serious. For example, justice would be the basis for hiring workers who were economically disadvantaged, while fairness would be the basis for stipulating that all employees be allowed a 30-minute lunch break.

The application of this theory by a supervisor involves following some basic principles. Each principle is derived from a different perspective about what constitutes fairness and justice.

- Each employee should be treated equally.

- People should be rewarded for the contributions they make to the organization. There should be comparative equality in the awards given to employees who make a similar contribution.

- Contributions of an employee should benefit only that employee. An employee's work should be rewarded personally. It should not count as part of a group or team's efforts and the group shouldn't receive a reward because of the individual's work.

The justice and fairness theory has some basic problems. First, there are many competing ideas about justice. Capitalism, socialism, egalitarianism, and libertarianism all approach justice differently. It is difficult to know which view is the best one. Since most businesses are based on capitalism, this concept of justice

253

dominates in organizations of the type. However, many social service and government organizations might find that egalitarianism is more applicable. Thus, there is no single basis for determining universal principles of justice. Second, individual concepts of fairness differ greatly. What one employee considers to be fair may conflict with the opinions of other employees.

Moral Development

Lawrence Kohlberg was a clinical psychologist who studied moral development in people. His theory suggests that there are three levels of moral thought consisting of six stages of moral development.

Level 1: Preconventional Thought

- **Stage 1: Punishment and obedience orientation.** People learn to act so as to avoid punishment for disobedience.

- **Stage 2: Instrumental-relativist orientation.** People act in their own interests and are willing to let others do the same when it doesn't interfere with achieving their interests.

Level 2: Conventional Thought

- **Stage 3: Interpersonal orientation.** People act in accordance with what is expected of them in their roles. Your morals are based on what is expected of you.

- **Stage 4: Law and order orientation.** People act out of duty and loyalty. It is necessary to preserve order.

Level 3: Postconventional Thought

- **Stage 5: Social contract orientation.** People act for the welfare of the majority rather than personal or group interests. The person considers moral and legal viewpoints that aren't consistent with their own.

- **Stage 6: Universal ethical principle orientation.** People follow self-chosen principles. Deviation from principles based on law and social contract can be violated when they conflict with the individual's sense of morality.

Welfare-to-work employees—Welfare recipients come from a background of dire poverty. Virtually all recipients have children for which they are responsible. Housing, clothing, and feeding their children are constant concerns. Organizations should consider simple things that can be done to help welfare-to-work employees address this situation. Restaurants and grocery stores could consider modifying policies so that these workers could take home leftover food. Apparel stores could allow workers to have clothes with slight flaws or that need repairs. Supervisors should consider ways that their organization can assist welfare-to-work employees.

Kohlberg believed that individuals go through this moral development progression much like other developmental processes. Stages 1 to 3 are typically reached before adolescence, while people reach stage 4 typically during the teens and early twenties. Most people remain at stage 4 throughout their lives. About 15 percent of the population reaches stage 5 by the age of 35. Few individuals ever progress to the stage 6 level. More middle-class people reach stages 4 and 5 than working-class people. This may be because they are able to focus on higher level needs because more basic needs have been satisfied. There is also a positive correlation between education and moral judgment.

In addition, some basic assumptions about stage development are important to understand. Each stage presupposes understanding or mastery of the previous stage. Unless you've successfully completed the development of stage 3, you aren't able to move forward to stage 4. This means that individuals cannot skip a stage. Once a person reaches a certain stage, this level of thinking will dominate their actions, although they may still frame decisions using beliefs held in earlier stages.

Kohlberg's theory is quite useful in helping supervisors understand ethical behavior. You can often identify the stage that an employee has reached and this provides some insight into how they make their ethical decisions. Use this knowledge to establish ethical guidelines appropriate to the employee's level of development. Supervisors should always try to match their ethical guidelines to an employee's level of development. Trying to force ethical behavior through punishment—a stage 1 moral orientation—is often resented by adolescents and adults in stages 3 and 4. This in turn may result in their making all ethical decisions at the same level. This behavior is not advantageous to most organizations.

Strategies for Promoting Ethical Behavior

Supervisors should be alert to the fact that employees often don't behave in an ethical manner. Studies on employee honesty has found that about 40 percent are honest, 30 percent are situationally honest, and 30 percent are dishonest. Consider the statistics at the start of this chapter about economic losses to organizations. They reveal that employee ethics is a serious problem for most organizations.

An organization should follow some basic principles to establish a strong foundation for ethical behavior.

- **Clearly communicate the organization's mission.** A mission statement establishes a clear purpose for an organization. An organization's purpose helps guide the actions of employees. They see their work as something more than just a way to earn a living. As a result, they are more invested in the organization and less likely to behave unethically in their work. This method fits the development of employees who have reached the law and order orientation stage—Kohlberg's stage 4.

- **Establish an ethics compliance program.** This program should consist of a statement of ethical principles that help guide employees' actions. Employees should be provided training on ethics in the workplace. An ethical compliance program should provide a system that allows employees to report ethical violations—some organizations create a position of ethics ombudsman. This person can provide employees with advice and investigate ethical violations. An ethics program appeals to employees at the interpersonal compliance and law and order orientation stages— Kohlberg's stages 3 and 4.

  The Arthur Andersen group studied companies with ethical compliance programs and found three responses to ethics programs. When ethics programs become part of the organization's culture and are viewed as genuine, employees begin to internalize the values and ethics promoted by the program. When employees find that the program is primarily focused on identifying and punishing violations, it is less successful. When employees think the program's actual purpose is to protect managers and their jobs, unethical behavior actually increases.

- **Model ethical behavior for employees.** Employees who observe honesty and integrity in their supervisors are likely to behave in a similar manner. If you break laws—including organization policies— or ask employees to do so, then you shouldn't be surprised when they behave unethically in other situations.

■ **Be truthful with your employees.** This helps employees feel that they can depend on you. They are more likely to feel a responsibility to treat you in the same way. One exception to this rule is when a confidentiality would be violated. Then, however, don't lie; if possible, explain that you can't discuss the matter further.

■ **Reward employees for ethical behavior.** This should be done even when it may be costly to the organization in the short term. For example, an employee who points out a violation in OSHA safety standards should be rewarded, even though the organization has to pay to bring the standards up to code.

■ **Establish control programs.** Controls shouldn't be used in isolation from other ethical compliance activities. When this happens, employees may develop a siege mentality—it's us against them. It can then become a game to fool management. On the other hand, controls help limit the temptation employees might feel to do something wrong. For example, allowing employees to handle thousands of dollars in cash each day with no controls creates highly tempting circumstances. The reason for controls should be explained to employees. Make the point that controls are protections for employees as well as for the organization.

■ **Discuss ethics with employees on a regular basis.** Let them know that ethics are valued by the organization. Take opportunities to point out ethical dilemmas when they arise and confer with employees about how to appropriately resolve the dilemma.

Immigrant workers–Many immigrant workers come from countries where bribery is common. Nothing is done in business or government unless bribes are given to key people. In fact, workers may bribe supervisors for a good work schedule, promotion, and other job benefits. If an immigrant worker approaches you with a bribe, don't consider it as serious an issue as you would if a naturalized American worker did the same thing. You should report it to your superior to protect yourself. Then discuss the matter with the worker. Explain that this behavior is unacceptable and that organizations in America base promotions, pay increases, and other benefits on merit and performance. Hopefully, this will prevent a repeat of this behavior.

Obstacles to Ethical Behavior

Employees face some common ethical problems on the job. The following sections contain eight specific circumstances where supervisors can assist workers in practicing good ethics.

Favoring friends or relatives

This is a particular problem in a business that deals directly with the public. Many businesses allow employee discounts for immediate family members (father, mother, spouse, brothers, and sisters). However, friends sometimes expect special deals and service. As a result, paying customers do not get proper service because of the attention shown to friends.

Supervisors should inform employees about how to deal with this type of situation. Inexperienced workers—like teenagers—often don't know how to deal with peer pressure when friends ask for free food or other discounts. Having specific rules explained to them allows the employee to use the rules as a way to deflect peer pressure. Supervisors should also closely monitor employees during the first few weeks on the job. Watch how they deal with relatives and friends in the workplace. If you observe inappropriate behavior, coach them on the proper way to act. It is also good to remind employees about the importance of customers and to not be distracted from meeting their needs.

Cheating the employer out of time

An employer pays employees for time spent at work. Some workers cheat the employer out of this time in a number of ways, including the following:

- Breaking for longer periods than is allowed
- Coming to work late or leaving early
- Hiding someplace to avoid working
- Conducting personal business using office equipment
- Goofing around instead of working, such as joking and visiting with other employees when there is work to be done
- Using computers for personal use, like playing games

A relaxed workplace makes a job more pleasant. You want employees to be able to joke and talk. They should be able to have fun when breaks in the work flow make this possible. Employees typically are more productive in this type of situation. However, supervisors should make it clear that a relaxed workplace can't be maintained unless employees fulfill their responsibilities. Immediately inform workers when you see them taking advantage of a relaxed work environment. Tell them what they've done wrong and what they should do to comply with expectations and explain why. Make it clear how company rules and guidelines can also benefit them—when rules are followed, other employees don't resent them, the workload is more evenly distributed, and they are more highly regarded by other employees.

Stealing from the company

Taking money from the cash register or taking merchandise from a store are obvious ways of stealing. However, workers also steal other ways—many times without thinking of it as theft.

- **Money.** Employees who handle cash are in the best position to steal without being caught. However, workers in accounting positions are also able to steal money. Employees who steal money frequently justify it by saying they were just giving themselves a raise or bonus that was really deserved.

- **Merchandise.** Employees may actually steal merchandise by taking it from a store by hiding it in clothes, lunch buckets, briefcases, or backpacks. However, there are more subtle ways to accomplish this task. A stock clerk may damage an item—like food—knowing it will be shared by all employees. A production worker may damage an item known that it will be sold at a steeply discounted price to employees.

- **Supplies.** A U.S. News/CNN poll taken in 1995 found the following results about what percentage of employees think it's okay to take the following items from their organization.

Item	Percent
Pens, pencils	32
Stationery, envelopes	19
Calculators	4
Staplers	4
Tape recorders	3
Telephones	2
Computers	2
Lamps	1
Chairs	1

People often take pens, pencils, paper, paper clips, and other supplies from their employer. It doesn't seem like a big thing because the organization has so many supplies. However, multiplied by all employees, it can cost an organization a great deal of money.

■ **Photocopies.** Many employees use the copy machine for personal use without thinking of it as theft. However, it usually costs a business 2¢ to 5¢ per copy. Making 20 copies may cost $1. If every employee in an organization with 1000 employees did this once a week, it would cost the employer almost $52,000 a year. Small thefts by workers can add up to major expenses for an organization.

■ **Long-distance phone calls.** This is one of the most expensive crimes in business. Telephone companies charge more during business hours. Making personal long-distance calls on the organization's phone system can add up to lots of money.

Disabled workers—A nationwide study done in 1999 by the Hudson Institute found that employees consider the unfair treatment of workers to be the most frequent violation of ethics. Less than 50 percent of the workers surveyed felt that their senior managers were people of high integrity. These results provide supervisors with some important insights. Their ethics are going to be judged by employees based on their treatment of employees. Organizations and supervisors that hire people with disabilities and undertake the effort to help them succeed on the job send all employees a powerful message. The message is, "we care." This is a positive example to workers.

Supervisors should take several steps in dealing with theft. First, make it clear to employees what the organization considers to be theft. For example, some organizations allow a limited use of copy machines and employees are allowed to take discarded supplies and equipment. Second, establish controls that reduce the temptation to steal from the company. Third, take immediate and consistent action when employees are caught stealing.

Software piracy

Computers make it easy to copy a company's software programs. This is known as piracy. It's estimated that over $15 billion in software was pirated in 1995. Some organizations fire employees caught pirating software.

Software is protected by copyright laws, just like books and videos. Sometimes software is made available as freeware or shareware. Freeware means that the program developer allows anyone to freely make copies. Shareware means you can use the software and make copies for others. However, you are expected to pay the program developer if you continue to use the program. Commercial software is purchased, and the right to make copies is restricted.

Have employees follow three basic rules to avoid pirating commercial software. First, allow them to install the program on only one computer. Second, allow them to make only one copy. This copy must be stored and only used if the original is damaged. Third, prohibit them from making copies for anyone else. A much more serious violation is to make a pirated copy and sell it.

Abusing drugs and alcohol

Drinking alcoholic beverages or using drugs on the job is wrong. Taking recreational drugs or nonprescription drugs is against the law. In many organizations, using drugs or alcohol on the job can result in immediate termination. There are three major job problems related to substance abuse:

- **Lower productivity.** Employees produce fewer goods or services.

- **Lower quality.** It's impossible to perform at your best when you are under the influence of alcohol or illegal drugs. Your quality of work will be less than your employer is paying you to provide.

- **Safety hazards.** Substance abuse can cause many safety problems. Since reactions are slowed, workers are more likely to suffer serious or fatal injuries.

Supervisors should make clear that the use of drugs and/or alcohol on the job will not be tolerated. Take immediate action and remove the employee from the work area. Once you've looked after the employee's safety, take the appropriate disciplinary action—following organizational policy. When an employee has drugs in his or her possession, the policy of many organizations is to report the employee to law enforcement officials.

Violating matters of confidentiality

Some employees have access to a great deal of information. If you are in a position to handle such information, don't talk to anyone about it. This includes other workers. Confidential information may include the following:

- **Company information.** Confidential information about a company can cause great harm if it is shared. Trade secrets about products or services can be used by competitors to duplicate products. Financial data can be used by competitors to identify weaknesses and strengths of a business. Customer lists can be used to lure customers away. These and other pieces of information should be shared only with approved people.

- **Customer data.** This could include private information, such as salary, credit history, or employment history. Less critical information like the amount of money spent with the organization, address, and telephone number could still cause harm to someone.

- **Employee data.** This may include salary, personnel records, performance appraisals, or attendance records. Talking about any of this with others could harm the employee's reputation or bring about other problems.

Organizations should limit employee access to information unless it is critical to their jobs. Supervisors should be careful about sharing confidential information with employees. Many organizations keep information in computer systems and access levels are established with passwords. Supervisors shouldn't share their passwords with employees. Monitor employees to ensure they don't share their passwords with anyone else. When employees are found reading information that they shouldn't have, remove it from them and explain why they aren't allowed to have access to the data. Immediately inform your superiors when you discover an employee has inappropriately accessed information or given it to unauthorized personnel.

Contingent workers—It is sometimes tempting to treat contingent workers in a somewhat callous manner. They are only around on a temporary or part-time basis so supervisors know they aren't going to have to work with them on a day-to-day basis. This makes it tempting to assign tasks to these workers that you wouldn't normally expect permanent full-time workers to do. Employees will observe this behavior and feel apprehensive, wondering when and how you might take advantage of them. Supervisors should treat contingent workers in the same manner as all other workers.

Knowing about other employees' unethical behaviors

One of the most difficult ethical dilemmas for employees arises when they discover that another employee has done something unethical. They may find this out because they observe a misdeed, overhear a conversation, or the employee boasts to them about the act. There is a stigma against reporting wrongs committed by someone else—it reminds us of people under an authoritarian regime informing on neighbors and relatives.

Under many circumstances, an employee's misdeeds might not come to light unless they are reported by another employee. Supervisors can increase the possibility of employees reporting the misdeeds of others. Have regular discussions with them about the repercussions that might result if misdeeds aren't reported. Make it easy for employees to report a misdeed—some organizations have hotlines that employees can call anonymously. Don't divulge the name of an employee who reports a misdeed unless it becomes necessary. Once alerted to a problem, try to catch the employee actually committing the misdeed. This protects the identify of the employee who reported the act.

Violating the organization's policies

Many organizations have a set of personnel policies to govern employee behavior. Policies are communicated through a policy manual or in the form of memos. This might be considered organizational law—in some cases, policies reiterate governmental laws. Organizations should enforce policies or eliminate them. Allowing employees to violate policies promotes other unethical behavior.

Supervisors who provide employees with a good orientation can help reduce policy violations. Warning employees when there is the possibility of a violation or on the first infraction is another way to deal with this problem.

Investigating Ethical Violations

Sometimes supervisors must investigate ethical violations. Some reasons that investigations need to be initiated include:

- Control systems indicate that misdeeds are taking place.

- Employees report violations by someone else.

- Customers or vendors report problems.

- Supervisors observe unethical behavior.

- A government official notifies the company that an illegal action may have taken place.

Supervisors should not originate an investigation. They should report the possibility of a violation to managers. Then they can collaborate on the best strategy to pursue. Typically the steps that should be taken are the following:

1. **Gather facts.** Talk with employees, customers, or vendors that might have information about the situation. Review records that might provide relevant information.

2. **Investigate the background of the person making the complaint.** Examine whether a bias might affect his or her perspective of an action. Determine whether the person might have made the complaint because he was motivated by revenge. Consider the reliability of the individual based on past performance and appraisal of other supervisors and employees.

3. **Talk with the employee that has been accused of an ethical violation.** Make it clear that you are not judging his or her guilt or innocence, but simply collecting information.

4. **If it appears the law was violated, contact an attorney.**

5. **Prepare a report on your investigation.** Give the report to your manager and include recommendations for action.

6. **Take appropriate action to correct the situation.**

Supervisors might want at least one other person present when interviewing key people. In addition, it is often good to have someone present when talking to the accused person. These individuals can verify the accuracy of questions and statements you make and responses of the interviewees.

Ex-offenders—Supervisors might expect more ethical problems with ex-offenders than other workers. This isn't necessarily the case. Some studies suggest that workers who have committed more serious crimes like robbery and assault are less likely to repeat this offense than workers who have been convicted of drug and alcohol abuse. This illustrates that common assumptions don't always fit with reality. Consider how workers may be affected by tasks, procedures, and policies. Avoid putting them in situations where they are going to be tempted to commit a crime.

Guidelines for Making Ethical Decisions

The problems illustrated in the preceding sections show the difficulty employees have in making ethical decisions. It is useful when the supervisor provides employees with some practical guidelines they can use when making ethical decisions. In addition, supervisors should be able to use these guidelines in confronting their own ethical dilemmas. The guidelines are in the form of questions that can help direct personal behavior. The more questions a person can answer affirmatively, the more confident she can be that her decision is ethically correct.

1. **Is it legal?** This refers to local, state, and federal laws. Laws express the ethical behavior expected of everyone in society. You should consider whether you could be arrested, convicted, or punished for your behavior. When you do something illegal, your behavior will not be excused simply because you were ordered to do it.

2. **How will it make you feel about yourself?** A good self-concept is one key to doing the right thing. In *The Power of Ethical Management,* Norman Vincent Peale and Ken Blanchard state, "people who have a healthy amount of self-esteem tend to have the strength to do what they know is right—even when there are strong pressures to do otherwise." What you're really asking is this: *Am I at my best?* Most of us want to do our very best. We want to look at ourselves in the mirror without feeling guilt.

3. **How do others feel about it?** You should discuss ethical dilemmas with others. It may be difficult to share the problem with a supervisor. Talk with a co-worker you trust. You can talk to friends, relatives, religious leaders, or anyone whose opinion you respect. Don't just talk to people you think will agree with you. Listen to advice from others, but don't assume that the majority is always right.

4. **How would you feel if the whole world knew about it?** Take the *60 Minutes* test. What if a reporter from *60 Minutes* showed up to broadcast what you are doing? If you don't want co-workers, supervisors, friends, relatives, or the community to know what you are going to do, *don't do it.*

5. **Does the behavior make sense?** Is it obvious that someone could be harmed? Might you harm someone physically, mentally, or financially? Is it obvious that you will get caught? This last question shouldn't be the only thing you consider, but you should keep it in mind.

6. **Is the situation fair to everyone involved?** Ethical behavior should ensure that everyone's best interests are protected. Look at how everyone can benefit, but realize that everyone will not benefit equally by the decision you make. No one should receive a great gain at the expense of someone else.

7. **Will the people in authority at your organization approve?** How does your supervisor feel about the behavior? What would the manager of your department say? Would it be approved by the organization's lawyer?

Find out what those in authority think about the situation. This doesn't guarantee the right decision. Sometimes people in authority support unethical behavior. You aren't necessarily relieved of responsibility because a supervisor approves a certain act. However, asking for approval indicates what behavior is thought to be right by people in authority at your organization.

8. **How would you feel if someone did the same thing to you?** This is the Golden Rule, or "do to others what you would want them to do to you." When applying this principle, look at the situation from another person's point of view. Another way to view this issue was voiced by philosopher Immanuel Kant, who suggested that what individuals believe is right for themselves, they should believe is right for all others. When you make an ethical decision, you should be willing for everyone else to do the same thing that you do. Avoid doing things you think would be unfair to you, because they're probably unfair to someone else as well.

9. **Will something bad happen if you don't make a decision?** Sometimes you may decide to do nothing and it won't affect anyone. You may have good reasons for not wanting to get involved. However, you may be aware of a situation that could result in someone being hurt. Not taking action when you think you should can result in a major problem.

Summary

Ethical behavior in employees is critical to an organization. Several moral theories can help supervisors and employees determine how to behave in an ethical manner. Supervisors can stimulate ethical development in employees through training and coaching. Supervisors are also critical in the implementation and monitoring of control procedures.

Appendix

O*NET Job Descriptions

The U.S. Department of Labor has developed the Occupational Information Network (O*NET) to describe all major occupations in the U.S. economy. We thought it would be helpful to include an appendix with the 25 job descriptions found in the O*NET that specifically pertain to supervisory positions. The following descriptions are meant to be a reference for the reader. You probably don't want to read all 25 descriptions. Instead, you may want to read the one that most closely resembles your job and some related descriptions. Keep in mind that these job descriptions are a composite view of these jobs found throughout the economy. A specific job may differ somewhat from the description found here.

Each description begins with a job title. Notice these are rather broad titles and sometimes use terminology that is awkward. However, you should be able to find a title that generally matches with a specific job title you are looking for. The job title is followed by a one-sentence definition of the job. There are then 6 to 19 tasks that are important in performing the job.

First-Line Supervisors and Manager/Supervisors—Agricultural Crop Workers

Directly supervises and coordinates activities of agricultural crop workers. Manager/Supervisors are generally found in smaller establishments where they perform both supervisory and management functions, such as accounting, marketing, and personnel work, and may also engage in the same agricultural work as the workers they supervise.

1. Determines number and kind of workers needed to perform required work, and schedules activities.

2. Drives and operates farm machinery—such as trucks, tractors, or self-propelled harvesters—to transport workers or cultivate and harvest fields.

3. Confers with manager to evaluate weather and soil conditions and to develop and revise plans and procedures.

4. Directs or assists in adjustment, repair, and maintenance of farm machinery and equipment.

5. Trains workers in methods of field work and safety regulations, and briefs them on identifying characteristics of insects and diseases.

6. Contracts with seasonal workers and farmers to provide employment, and arranges for transportation, equipment, and living quarters.

7. Investigates grievances and settles disputes to maintain harmony among workers.

8. Recruits, hires, and discharges workers.

9. Issues farm implements and machinery, ladders, or containers to workers and collects them at end of the workday.

10. Observes workers to detect inefficient and unsafe work procedures or identify problems, and initiates actions to correct improper procedure or solve problems.

11. Assigns duties, such as tilling soil, planting, irrigating, storing crops, and maintaining machines, and assigns fields or rows to workers.

12. Opens gate to permit entry of water into ditches or pipes, and signals worker to start flow of water to irrigate fields.

13. Requisitions and purchases farm supplies, such as insecticides, machine parts or lubricants, and tools.

14. Inspects crops and fields to determine maturity, yield, infestation, or work requirements, such as cultivating, spraying, weeding, or harvesting.

15. Prepares time, payroll, and production reports, such as farm conditions, amount of yield, machinery breakdowns, and labor problems.

First-Line Supervisors and Manager/Supervisors— Animal Care Workers

Directly supervises and coordinates activities of animal care workers. Manager/Supervisors are generally found in smaller establishments where they perform both supervisory and management functions, such as accounting, marketing, and personnel work, and may also engage in the same animal care work as the workers they supervise.

1. Operates euthanasia equipment to destroy animals.

2. Investigates complaints of animal neglect or cruelty, and follows up on complaints appearing to justify prosecution.

3. Prepares reports concerning activity of facility, employees' time records, and animal treatment.

4. Observes and examines animals to detect signs of illness and determine need of services from veterinarian.

5. Plans budget, and arranges for purchase of animals, feed, or supplies.

6. Directs and assists workers in maintenance and repair of facilities.

7. Trains workers in animal care procedures, maintenance duties, and safety precautions.

8. Monitors animal care and inspects facilities to identify problems, and discusses solutions with workers.

9. Establishes work schedule and procedures of animal care.

10. Assigns workers to tasks such as feeding and treatment of animals, and cleaning and maintenance of animal quarters.

11. Delivers lectures to public to stimulate interest in animals and communicate humane philosophy to public.

First-Line Supervisors and Manager/Supervisors— Animal Husbandry Workers

Directly supervises and coordinates activities of animal husbandry workers. Manager/Supervisors are generally found in smaller establishments where they perform both supervisory and management functions, such as accounting, marketing, and personnel work, and may also engage in the same animal husbandry work as the workers they supervise.

269

1. Transports or arranges for transport of animals, equipment, food, animal feed, and other supplies to and from worksite.

2. Monitors eggs and adjusts incubator thermometer and gauges, to ascertain hatching progress and maintain specified conditions.

3. Inseminates livestock artificially to produce desired offspring and to demonstrate techniques to farmers.

4. Observes animals—such as cattle, sheep, poultry, or game animals—for signs of illness, injury, nervousness, or unnatural behavior.

5. Requisitions equipment, materials, and supplies.

6. Prepares animal condition, production, feed consumption, and worker attendance reports.

7. Trains workers in animal care, artificial insemination techniques, egg candling and sorting, and transfer of animals.

8. Notifies veterinarian and manager of serious illnesses or injuries to animals.

9. Inspects buildings, fences, fields or range, supplies, and equipment to determine work to be done.

10. Recruits, hires, and pays workers.

11. Studies feed, weight, health, genetic, or milk production records to determine feed formula and rations or breeding schedule.

12. Plans and prepares work schedules.

13. Oversees animal care, maintenance, breeding, or packing and transfer activities to ensure work is done correctly, and to identify and solve problems.

14. Assigns workers to tasks, such as feeding and treating animals, cleaning quarters, transferring animals, and maintaining facilities.

15. Treats animal illness or injury, following experience or instructions of veterinarian.

16. Confers with manager to discuss and ascertain production requirements, condition of equipment and supplies, and work schedules.

First-Line Supervisors—Administrative Support

Supervises and coordinates activities of workers involved in providing administrative support.

1. Supervises and coordinates activities of workers engaged in clerical or administrative support activities.

2. Plans, prepares, and revises work schedules and duty assignments according to budget allotments, customer needs, problems, workloads, and statistical forecasts.

3. Evaluates subordinate job performance and conformance to regulations, and recommends appropriate personnel action.

4. Oversees, coordinates, or performs activities associated with shipping, receiving, distribution, and transportation.

5. Verifies completeness and accuracy of subordinates' work, computations, and records.

6. Interviews, selects, and discharges employees.

7. Consults with supervisor and other personnel to resolve problems, such as equipment performance, output quality, and work schedules.

8. Reviews records and reports pertaining to such activities as production, operation, payroll, customer accounts, and shipping.

9. Trains employees in work and safety procedures and company policies.

10. Participates in work of subordinates to facilitate productivity or overcome difficult aspects of work.

11. Examines procedures and recommends changes to save time, labor, and other costs and to improve quality control and operating efficiency.

12. Maintains records of such matters as inventory, personnel, orders, supplies, and machine maintenance.

13. Identifies and resolves discrepancies or errors.

14. Compiles reports and information required by management or governmental agencies.

15. Plans layout of stockroom, warehouse, or other storage areas, considering turnover, size, weight, and related factors pertaining to items stored.

16. Inspects equipment for defects and notifies maintenance personnel or outside service contractors for repairs.

17. Analyzes financial activities of establishment or department and assists in planning budget.

18. Computes figures, such as balances, totals, and commissions.

19. Requisitions supplies.

271

First-Line Supervisors and Manager/Supervisors— Construction Trades Workers

Directly supervises and coordinates activities of construction trades workers and their helpers. Manager/Supervisors are generally found in smaller establishments where they perform both supervisory and management functions, such as accounting, marketing, and personnel work and may also engage in the same construction trades work as the workers they supervise.

1. Assigns work to employees, using material and worker requirements data.

2. Assists workers engaged in construction activities, using hand tools and equipment.

3. Recommends measures to improve production methods and equipment performance to increase efficiency and safety.

4. Trains workers in construction methods and operation of equipment.

5. Records information, such as personnel, production, and operational data, on specified forms and reports.

6. Estimates material and worker requirements to complete jobs.

7. Locates, measures, and marks location and placement of structures and equipment.

8. Directs and leads workers engaged in construction activities.

9. Confers with staff and workers to ensure production and personnel problems are resolved.

10. Supervises and coordinates activities of construction trades workers.

11. Suggests and initiates personnel actions, such as promotions, transfers, and hires.

12. Analyzes and resolves worker problems and recommends motivational plans.

13. Examines and inspects work progress, equipment, and construction sites to verify safety and ensure that specifications are met.

14. Analyzes and plans installation and construction of equipment and structures.

15. Reads specifications, such as blueprints and data, to determine construction requirements.

First-Line Supervisors—Customer Service

Supervises and coordinates activities of workers involved in providing customer service.

1. Supervises and coordinates activities of workers engaged in customer service activities.

2. Plans, prepares, and devises work schedules according to budgets and workloads.

3. Observes and evaluates workers' performance.

4. Issues instructions and assigns duties to workers.

5. Trains and instructs employees.

6. Hires and discharges workers.

7. Communicates with other departments and management to resolve problems and expedite work.

8. Interprets and communicates work procedures and company policies to staff.

9. Helps workers in resolving problems and completing work.

10. Resolves complaints and answers questions of customers regarding services and procedures.

11. Reviews and checks work of subordinates such as reports, records, and applications for accuracy and content, and corrects errors.

12. Prepares, maintains, and submits reports and records, such as budgets and operational and personnel reports.

13. Makes recommendations to management concerning staff and improvement of procedures.

14. Plans and develops improved procedures.

15. Requisitions or purchases supplies.

First-Line Supervisors and Manager/Supervisors— Extractive Workers

Directly supervises and coordinates activities of extractive workers and their helpers. Manager/Supervisors are generally found in smaller establishments where they perform both supervisory and management functions, such as accounting, marketing, and personnel work, and may also engage in the same extractive work as the workers they supervise.

1. Suggests and initiates personnel actions, such as promotions, transfers, and hires.

2. Analyzes and resolves worker problems and recommends motivational plans.

3. Recommends measures to improve production methods and equipment performance to increase efficiency and safety.

4. Trains workers in construction methods and operation of equipment.

5. Records information, such as personnel, production, and operational data on specified forms.

6. Assists workers engaged in extraction activities, using hand tools and equipment.

7. Orders materials, supplies, and repairs of equipment and machinery.

8. Locates, measures, and marks materials and site location, using measuring and marking equipment.

9. Analyzes and plans extraction process of geological materials.

10. Confers with staff and workers to ensure production personnel problems are resolved.

11. Supervises and coordinates activities of workers engaged in the extraction of geological materials.

12. Directs and leads workers engaged in extraction of geological materials.

13. Assigns work to employees, using material and worker requirements data.

14. Examines and inspects equipment, site, and materials to verify specifications are met.

First-Line Supervisors and Manager/Supervisors— Fishery Workers

Directly supervises and coordinates activities of fishery workers. Manager/Supervisors are generally found in smaller establishments where they perform both supervisory and management functions, such as accounting, marketing, and personnel work, and may also engage in the same fishery work as the workers they supervise.

1. Confers with manager to determine time and place of seed planting and cultivating, feeding, or harvesting of fish or shellfish.

2. Observes fish and beds or ponds to detect diseases, determine quality of fish, or determine completeness of harvesting.

274

3. Trains workers in spawning, rearing, cultivating, and harvesting methods, and use of equipment.

4. Plans work schedules according to availability of personnel and equipment, tidal levels, feeding schedules, or need for transfer or harvest.

5. Directs workers to correct deviations or problems, such as disease, quality of seed distribution, or adequacy of cultivation.

6. Oversees worker activities, such as treatment and rearing of fingerlings, maintenance of equipment, and harvesting of fish or shellfish.

7. Assigns workers to duties, such as fertilizing and incubating spawn; feeding and transferring fish; and planting, cultivating, and harvesting shellfish beds.

8. Records number and type of fish or shellfish reared and harvested, and keeps workers' time records.

First-Line Supervisors and Manager/Supervisors— Food Preparation and Serving Workers

Directly supervises and coordinates activities of food preparation and serving workers and their helpers. Manager/Supervisors are generally found in smaller establishments where they perform both supervisory and management functions, such as accounting, marketing, and personnel work, and may also engage in the same food preparation and serving work as the workers they supervise.

1. Inspects supplies, equipment, and work areas to ensure efficient service and conformance to standards.

2. Trains workers in proper food preparation and service procedures.

3. Recommends measures to improve work procedures and worker performance to increase quality of services and job safety.

4. Records production and operational data on specified forms.

5. Observes and evaluates workers and work procedures to ensure quality standards and service.

6. Supervises and coordinates activities of workers engaged in preparing and serving food and other related duties.

7. Resolves customer complaints regarding food service.

8. Specifies food portions and courses, production and time sequences, and work station and equipment arrangements.

275

9. Initiates personnel actions, such as hires and discharges, to ensure proper staffing.

10. Receives, issues, and takes inventory of supplies and equipment, and reports shortages to designated personnel.

11. Analyzes operational problems, such as theft and waste, and establishes controls.

12. Schedules parties and reservations, and greets and escorts guests to seating arrangements.

13. Assigns duties, responsibilities, and work stations to employees, following work requirements.

14. Collaborates with specified personnel to plan menus, serving arrangements, and other related details.

15. Purchases or requisitions supplies and equipment to ensure quality and timely delivery of services.

Forest Fire Fighting and Prevention Supervisors

Supervises fire fighters who control and suppress fires in forests or vacant public land.

1. Directs loading of fire suppression equipment into aircraft and parachuting of equipment to crews on ground.

2. Observes fire and crews from air to determine force requirements and note changing conditions.

3. Trains workers in parachute jumping, fire suppression, aerial observation, and radio communication.

4. Maintains radio communication with crews at fire scene to inform crew and base of changing conditions and casualties.

5. Dispatches crews according to reported size, location, and condition of forest fires.

6. Parachutes to major fire locations and directs fire containment and suppression activities.

First-Line Supervisors and Manager/Supervisors— Helpers, Laborers, and Material Movers

Directly supervises and coordinates activities of helpers, laborers, and material movers. Manager/Supervisors are generally found in smaller establishments where they perform both supervisory and management functions, such as accounting, marketing, and personnel work, and may also engage in the same hand labor as the workers they supervise.

1. Inspects equipment for wear and completed work for conformance to standards.

2. Examines freight to determine sequence of loading and equipment to determine compliance with specifications.

3. Records information, such as daily receipts, employee time and wage data, description of freight, and inspection results.

4. Trains and instructs workers.

5. Observes work procedures to ensure quality of work.

6. Resolves customer complaints.

7. Supervises and coordinates activities of workers performing assigned tasks.

8. Assigns duties and work schedules.

9. Verifies materials loaded or unloaded against work order, and schedules times of shipment and mode of transportation.

10. Quotes prices to customers.

11. Informs designated employee or department of items loaded, or reports loading deficiencies.

12. Determines work sequence and equipment needed, according to work order, shipping records, and experience.

13. Inventories and orders supplies.

First-Line Supervisors and Manager/Supervisors— Horticultural Workers

Directly supervises and coordinates activities of horticultural workers. Manager/Supervisors are generally found in smaller establishments were they perform both supervisory and management functions, such as accounting, marketing, and personnel work, and may also engage in the same horticultural work as the workers they supervise.

1. Prepares and submits written or oral reports of personnel actions, such as performance evaluations, hires, promotions, and discipline.

2. Maintains records of employees' hours worked, and work completed.

3. Confers with management to report conditions, plan planting and harvesting schedules; and to discuss changes in fertilizer, herbicides, or cultivating techniques.

4. Trains employees in horticultural techniques, such as transplanting and weeding, shearing and harvesting trees, and grading and packing flowers.

5. Inspects facilities to determine maintenance needs, such as malfunctioning environmental control system, clogged sprinklers, or missing glass panes in greenhouse.

6. Observes plants, flowers, shrubs, and trees in greenhouses, cold frames, or fields to ascertain condition.

7. Reads inventory records, customer orders, and shipping schedules to ascertain day's activities.

8. Reviews employees' work to ascertain quality and quantity of work performed.

9. Assigns workers to duties, such as cultivation, harvesting, maintenance, grading and packing products, or altering greenhouse environmental conditions.

10. Drives and operates heavy machinery, such as dump truck, tractor, or growth-media tiller, to transport materials and supplies.

11. Estimates work-hour requirements to plant, cultivate, or harvest, and prepares work schedule.

First-Line Supervisors and Manager/Supervisors— Hospitality and Personal Service Workers

Directly supervises and coordinates activities of hospitality and personal service workers. Manager/Supervisors are generally found in smaller establishments where they perform both supervisory and management functions, such as accounting, marketing, and personnel work, and may also engage in the same hospitality and personal service work as the workers they supervise.

1. Informs workers about interests of specific groups.

2. Supervises and coordinates activities of workers engaged in lodging and personal services.

3. Observes and evaluates workers' appearances and performances to ensure quality service and compliance with specifications.

4. Assigns work schedules, following work requirements, to ensure quality and timely delivery of services.

5. Inspects work areas and operating equipment to ensure conformance to established standards.

6. Requisitions supplies, equipment, and designated services, to ensure quality and timely service and efficient operations.

7. Analyzes and records personnel and operational data and writes activity reports.

8. Collaborates with personnel to plan and develop programs of events, schedules of activities, and menus.

9. Resolves customer complaints regarding worker performance and services rendered.

10. Furnishes customers with information on events and activities.

11. Trains workers in proper operational procedures and functions, and explains company policy.

Housekeeping Supervisors

Supervises work activities of cleaning personnel to ensure clean, orderly, and attractive rooms in hotels, hospitals, educational institutions, and similar establishments. Assigns duties, inspect work, and investigate complaints regarding housekeeping service and equipment and take corrective action. May purchase housekeeping supplies and equipment, take periodic inventories, screen applicants, train new employees, and recommend dismissals.

1. Coordinates work activities among departments.

2. Evaluates records to forecast department personnel requirements.

3. Selects and purchases new furnishings.

4. Performs cleaning duties in cases of emergency or staff shortage.

5. Prepares reports concerning room occupancy, payroll, and department expenses.

6. Examines building to determine need for repairs or replacement of furniture or equipment, and makes recommendations to management.

7. Makes recommendations to improve service and ensure more efficient operation.

8. Attends staff meetings to discuss company policies and patrons' complaints.

9. Issues supplies and equipment to workers.

10. Inventories stock to ensure adequate supplies.

11. Establishes standards and procedures for work of housekeeping staff.

12. Conducts orientation training and in-service training to explain policies, work procedures, and to demonstrate use and maintenance of equipment.

13. Advises manager, desk clerk, or admitting personnel of rooms ready for occupancy.

14. Assigns workers their duties and inspects work for conformance to prescribed standards of cleanliness.

15. Screens job applicants, hires new employees, and recommends promotions, transfers, and dismissals.

16. Obtains list of rooms to be cleaned immediately and list of prospective check-outs or discharges to prepare work assignments.

17. Investigates complaints regarding housekeeping service and equipment, and takes corrective action.

18. Records data regarding work assignments, personnel actions, and time cards, and prepares periodic reports.

First-Line Supervisors and Manager/Supervisors— Landscaping Workers

Directly supervises and coordinates activities of landscaping workers. Manager/Supervisors are generally found in smaller establishments where they perform both supervisory and management functions, such as accounting, marketing, and personnel work, and may also engage in the same landscaping work as the workers they supervise.

1. Trains workers in tasks, such as transplanting and pruning trees and shrubs, finishing cement, using equipment, and caring for turf.

2. Directs workers in maintenance and repair of driveways, walkways, benches, graves, and mausoleums.

3. Observes ongoing work to ascertain if work is being performed according to instructions and will be completed on time.

4. Determines work priority, crew and equipment requirements, and assigns workers tasks, such as planting, fertilizing, irrigating, and mowing.

5. Directs and assists workers engaged in maintenance and repair of equipment, such as power mower and backhoe, using hand tools and power tools.

6. Confers with manager to develop plans and schedules for maintenance and improvement of grounds.

7. Keeps employee time records, and records daily work performed.

8. Tours grounds, such as park, botanical garden, cemetery, or golf course to inspect conditions.

9. Assists workers in performing work when completion is critical.

10. Interviews, hires, and discharges workers.

11. Mixes and prepares spray and dust solutions, and directs application of fertilizer, insecticide, and fungicide.

First-Line Supervisors and Manager/Supervisors— Logging Workers

Directly supervises and coordinates activities of logging workers. Manager/Supervisors are generally found in smaller establishments where they perform both supervisory and management functions, such as accounting, marketing, and personnel work, and may also engage in the same logging work as the workers they supervise.

1. Changes logging operations or methods to eliminate unsafe conditions, and warns or disciplines workers disregarding safety regulations.

2. Plans and schedules logging operations, such as felling and bucking trees, grading and sorting logs, and yarding and loading logs.

3. Assigns workers to duties, such as trees to be cut, cutting sequence and specifications, and loading of trucks, railcars, or rafts.

4. Oversees logging operations to identify and solve problems, and to ensure safety and company regulations are being followed.

5. Coordinates dismantling, moving, and setting up equipment at new worksite.

6. Coordinates selection and movement of logs from storage areas, according to transportation schedules or production requirements of wood products plant.

7. Confers with mill, company, and government forestry officials to determine safest and most efficient method of logging tract.

8. Trains workers in felling and bucking trees, operating tractors and loading machines, yarding and loading techniques, and safety regulations.

9. Prepares production and personnel time records for management.

10. Determines methods for logging operations, size of crew, and equipment requirements.

Janitorial Supervisors

Supervises work activities of janitorial personnel in commercial and industrial establishments. Assigns duties, inspects work, and investigates complaints regarding janitorial services and takes corrective action. May purchase janitorial supplies and equipment, take periodic inventories, screen applicants, train new employees, and recommend dismissals. Excludes housekeeping supervisors in hotels, hospitals, educational institutions, and similar establishments.

1. Recommends personnel actions, such as hires and discharges, to ensure proper staffing.

2. Supervises and coordinates activities of workers engaged in janitorial services.

3. Assigns janitorial work to employees, following material and work requirements.

4. Trains workers in janitorial methods and procedures and proper operation of equipment.

5. Confers with staff to resolve production and personnel problems.

6. Records personnel data on specified forms.

7. Inspects work performed to ensure conformance to specifications and established standards.

8. Issues janitorial supplies and equipment to workers to ensure quality and timely delivery of services.

First-Line Supervisors and Manager/Supervisors— Mechanics, Installers, and Repairers

Directly supervises and coordinates activities of mechanics, repairers, and installers and their helpers. Manager/Supervisors are generally found in smaller establishments where they perform both supervisory and management functions, such as accounting, marketing, and personnel work, and may also engage in the same repair work as the workers they supervise.

1. Confers with personnel, such as management, engineering, quality control, customers, and workers' representatives, to coordinate work activities and resolve problems.

282

2. Monitors operations and inspects, tests, and measures completed work, using devices such as hand tools, gauges, and specifications to verify conformance to standards.

3. Recommends or initiates personnel actions, such as employment, performance evaluations, promotions, transfers, discharges, and disciplinary measures.

4. Assigns workers to perform activities, such as service appliances, repair and maintain vehicles, and install machinery and equipment.

5. Examines object, system, or facilities such as telephone, air-conditioning, or industrial plants, and analyzes information to determine installation, service, or repair needed.

6. Patrols work area and examines tools and equipment to detect unsafe conditions or violations of safety rules.

7. Recommends measures such as procedural changes, service manual revisions, and equipment purchases to improve work performance and minimize operating costs.

8. Trains workers in methods, procedures, and use of equipment and work aids, such as blueprints, hand tools, and test equipment.

9. Completes and maintains reports, such as time and production records, inventories, and test results.

10. Requisitions materials and supplies, such as tools, equipment, and replacement parts for work activities.

11. Interprets specifications, blueprints, and job orders; constructs templates; and lays out reference points for workers.

12. Computes estimates and actual costs of factors—such as materials, labor, and outside contractors—and prepares budgets.

13. Establishes or adjusts work methods and procedures to meet production schedules using knowledge of capacities of machines, equipment, and personnel.

14. Directs, coordinates, and assists in performance of workers' activities such as engine tuneup, hydroelectric turbine repair, or circuit breaker installation.

Mates—Ship, Boat, and Barge

Supervises and coordinates activities of crew aboard ships, boats, barges, or dredges.

1. Observes loading and unloading of cargo and equipment to ensure that handling and storage are according to specifications.

2. Supervises activities of crew engaged in ship's activity, such as barging, towing, dredging, or fishing.

3. Supervises crew in cleaning and maintaining decks, superstructure, and bridge.

4. Inspects equipment such as cargo-handling gear, lifesaving equipment, fishing, towing, or dredging gear, and visual-signaling equipment for defects.

5. Assumes command of vessel in the event ship master becomes incapacitated.

6. Supervises crew in repair or replacement of defective vessel gear and equipment.

7. Observes water from masthead and advises navigational direction.

8. Determines geographical position of ship, using loran and azimuths of celestial bodies.

9. Stands watch on vessel during specified periods while vessel is underway.

10. Steers vessel, utilizing navigation devices such as compass and sexton, and navigational aids such as lighthouses and buoys.

Mining Superintendents and Supervisors

Plans, directs, and coordinates mining operations to extract mineral ore or aggregate from underground or surface mines, quarries, or pits.

1. Confers with engineering, supervisory, and maintenance personnel to plan and coordinate mine development and operations.

2. Directs opening or closing of mine sections, pits, or other work areas and installation or removal of equipment.

3. Studies land contours and rock formations to determine equipment needs, specify locations for mine shafts, pillars, and timbers.

4. Directs and coordinates enforcement of mining laws and safety regulations, and reports violations.

5. Studies maps and blueprints to determine prospective locations for mine haulage ways, access roads, rail tracks, and conveyor systems.

6. Reviews, consolidates, and oversees updating of mine records, such as geological and survey reports, air quality, safety reports, and production logs.

7. Inspects mine to detect production, equipment, safety, and personnel problems, and recommends steps to improve conditions and increase production.

8. Calculates mining and quarrying operational costs and potential income and determines activities to maximize income.

9. Negotiates with workers, supervisors, union personnel, and other parties to resolve grievances or settle complaints.

Municipal Fire Fighting and Prevention Supervisors

Supervises fire fighters who control and extinguish municipal fires, protect life and property, and conduct rescue efforts.

1. Confers with civic representatives, and plans talks and demonstrations of fire safety to direct fire prevention information program.

2. Assesses nature and extent of fire, condition of building, danger to adjacent buildings, and water supply to determine crew or company requirements.

3. Evaluates efficiency and performance of employees, and recommends awards for service.

4. Directs investigation of cases of suspected arson, hazards, and false alarms.

5. Trains subordinates in use of equipment, methods of extinguishing fires, and rescue operations.

6. Directs building inspections to ensure compliance with fire and safety regulations.

7. Inspects fire stations, equipment, and records to ensure efficiency and enforcement of departmental regulations.

8. Coordinates and supervises fire fighting and rescue activities, and reports events to supervisor, using two-way radio.

9. Oversees review of new building plans to ensure compliance with laws, ordinances, and administrative rules for public fire safety.

10. Orders and directs fire drills for occupants of buildings.

11. Writes and submits proposals for new equipment or modification of existing equipment.

12. Studies and interprets fire safety codes to establish procedures for issuing permits regulating storage or use of hazardous or flammable substances.

13. Compiles report of fire call, listing location, type, probable cause, estimated damage, and disposition.

14. Keeps equipment and personnel records.

Police and Detective Supervisors

Supervises and coordinates activities of members of police force.

1. Meets with civic, educational, and community groups to develop community programs and events, and addresses groups concerning law enforcement subjects.

2. Trains staff.

3. Prepares reports and directs preparation, handling, and maintenance of departmental records.

4. Prepares work schedules, assigns duties, and develops and revises departmental procedures.

5. Supervises and coordinates investigation of criminal cases.

6. Monitors and evaluates job performance of subordinates.

7. Disciplines staff for violation of department rules and regulations.

8. Directs collection, preparation, and handling of evidence and personal property of prisoners.

9. Assists subordinates in performing job duties.

10. Inspects facilities, supplies, vehicles, and equipment to ensure conformance to standards.

11. Investigates charges of misconduct against staff.

12. Conducts raids and orders detention of witnesses and suspects for questioning.

13. Prepares budgets and manages expenditures of department funds.

14. Requisitions and issues department equipment and supplies.

15. Directs release or transfer of prisoners.

16. Reviews contents of written orders to ensure adherence to legal requirements.

17. Prepares news releases and responds to police correspondence.

18. Cooperates with court personnel and officials from other law enforcement agencies, and testifies in court.

19. Investigates and resolves personnel problems within organization.

First-Line Supervisors and Manager/Supervisors— Production and Operating Workers

Directly supervises and coordinates activities of production and operating workers, such as testers, precision workers, machine setters and operators, assemblers, fabricators, or plant and system operators. Manager/Supervisors are generally found in smaller establishments where they perform both supervisory and management functions, such as accounting, marketing, and personnel work, and may also engage in the same production work as the workers they supervise.

1. Monitors gauges, dials, and other indicators to ensure operators conform to production or processing standards.

2. Maintains operations data such as time, production, and cost records, and prepares management reports.

3. Sets up and adjusts machines and equipment.

4. Reads and analyzes charts, work orders, or production schedules to determine production requirements.

5. Directs and coordinates the activities of employees engaged in production or processing of goods.

6. Plans and establishes work schedules, assignments, and production sequences to meet production goals.

7. Calculates labor and equipment requirements and production specifications using standard formulas.

8. Determines standards, production, and rates based on company policy, equipment and labor availability, and workload.

9. Reviews operations and accounting records or reports to determine the feasibility of production estimates and evaluate current production.

10. Requisitions materials, supplies, equipment parts, or repair services.

11. Confers with other supervisors to coordinate operations and activities within departments or between departments.

12. Monitors or patrols work area and enforces safety or sanitation regulations.

13. Recommends or implements measures to motivate employees and improve production methods, equipment performance, product quality, or efficiency.

14. Interprets specifications, blueprints, job orders, and company policies and procedures for workers.

15. Inspects materials, products, or equipment to detect defects or malfunctions.

16. Demonstrates equipment operations or work procedures to new employees or assigns employees to experienced workers for training.

17. Confers with management or subordinates to resolve worker problems, complaints, or grievances.

First-Line Supervisors and Manager/Supervisors— Sales and Related Workers

Directly supervises and coordinates activities of marketing, sales, and related workers. May perform management functions, such as budgeting, accounting, marketing, and personnel work, in addition to their supervisory duties.

1. Directs and supervises employees engaged in sales, inventory-taking, reconciling cash receipts, or performing specific services such as pumping gasoline for customers.

2. Plans and prepares work schedules and assigns employees to specific duties.

3. Hires, trains, and evaluates personnel in sales or marketing establishment.

4. Coordinates sales promotion activities and prepares merchandise displays and advertising copy.

5. Confers with company officials to develop methods and procedures to increase sales, expand markets, and promote business.

6. Keeps records of employees' work schedules and time cards.

7. Prepares sales and inventory reports for management and budget departments.

8. Assists sales staff in completing complicated and difficult sales.

9. Listens to and resolves customer complaints regarding service, product, or personnel.

10. Keeps records pertaining to purchases, sales, and requisitions.

11. Examines merchandise to ensure that it is correctly priced and displayed, and functions as advertised.

12. Formulates pricing policies on merchandise according to requirements for profitability of store operations.

13. Analyzes customers' wants and needs by observing what sells most rapidly.

14. Takes inventory of stock and reorders when inventories drop to specified level.

15. Prepares rental or lease agreement, specifying charges and payment procedures, for use of machinery, tools, or other such items.

16. Examines products purchased for resale or received for storage to determine condition of product or item.

First-Line Supervisors and Manager/Supervisors— Transportation and Material-Moving Machine and Vehicle Operators

Directly supervises and coordinates activities of transportation and material-moving machine and vehicle operators. May supervise helpers assigned to these workers. Manager/Supervisors are generally found in smaller establishments where they perform both supervisory and management functions, such as accounting, marketing, and personnel work, and may also engage in the same work as the workers they supervise.

1. Assists workers in performing tasks, such as coupling railroad cars or loading vehicles.

2. Repairs or schedules repair and preventive maintenance of vehicles and other equipment.

3. Drives vehicles or operates machines or equipment.

4. Examines, measures, and weighs cargo or materials to determine specific handling requirements.

5. Reviews orders, production schedules, and shipping/receiving notices to determine work sequence and material shipping dates, type, volume, and destinations.

289

6. Computes and estimates cash, payroll, transportation, personnel, and storage requirements using calculator.

7. Inspects or tests materials, stock, vehicles, equipment, and facilities to locate defects, meet maintenance or production specifications, and verify safety standards.

8. Directs workers in transportation or related services, such as pumping, moving, storing, and loading/unloading of materials or people.

9. Maintains or verifies time, transportation, financial, inventory, and personnel records.

10. Explains and demonstrates work tasks to new workers or assigns workers to experienced workers for further training.

11. Resolves worker problems or assists workers in solving problems.

12. Requisitions needed personnel, supplies, equipment, parts, or repair services.

13. Recommends and implements measures to improve worker motivation, equipment performance, work methods, and customer services.

14. Prepares, compiles, and submits reports on work activities, operations, production, and work-related accidents.

15. Plans and establishes transportation routes, work schedules, and assignments and allocates equipment to meet transportation, operations, or production goals.

16. Interprets transportation and tariff regulations, shipping orders, safety regulations, and company policies and procedures for workers.

17. Confers with customers, supervisors, contractors, and other personnel to exchange information and resolve problems.

18. Recommends or implements personnel actions, such as hiring, firing, and performance evaluations.

19. Receives telephone or radio reports of emergencies and dispatches personnel and vehicle in response to request.

Bibliography

Books and Periodicals

American Association of Retired Persons, *America's Changing Work Force: Statistics in Brief.* Washington. D.C., 1998.

American Association of Retired Persons, *American Business and Older Workers: A Road Map to the 21st Century.* Washington, D.C., 1995.

American Association of Retired Persons, *How to Manage Older Workers.* Washington, D.C., 1994.

American Association of Retired Persons, *How to Train Older Workers.* Washington, D.C., 1993.

Bennis, Warren and Burt Nanus, *Leaders: The Strategies for Taking Charge.* New York: Harper and Row, 1985.

Benton, Douglas A., *Applied Human Relations: An Organizational and Skill Development Approach.* Upper Saddle River, NJ: Prentice Hall, 1998.

Blanchard, Kenneth and Norman Vincent Peale, *The Power of Ethical Management*. New York: Morrow, 1988, 47.

Borisoff, Deborah and David A. Victor, *Conflict Management: A Communication Skills Approach*. Boston: Allyn and Bacon, 1998.

Bridges, William, *Jobshift: How to Prosper in a Workplace Without Jobs*. New York: Addison-Wesley, 1994.

Boyett, Joseph H. with Boyett, Jimmie T. *Beyond Workplace 2000*. New York: Dutton, 1995.

Broadwell, Martin M. and Broadwell Dietrich, Carol, *The New Supervisor,* 5th edition. Cambridge, MA: Perseus, 1998.

Capozzoli, Thomas and R. Steve McVey, *Managing Violence in the Workplace*. Del Ray Beach, FL: St. Lucie Press, 1996.

Cohany, Sharon R., "Workers in Alternative Employment Arrangements: A Second" *Monthly Labor Review*. November 1998, 3-21.

Cribbin, James J., *Leadership: Strategies for Organizational Effectiveness*. New York: Amacom, 1981.

DuBrin, Andrew J., *Human Relations: Interpersonal, Job-Oriented Skills,* 6th edition. Upper Saddle River, NJ: Prentice Hall, 1997.

Farr, J. Michael and LaVerne L. Ludden, *Best Jobs for the 21st Century*. Indianapolis: JIST, 1999.

Franklin, James C., "Industry Output and Employment Projections to 2006," *Monthly Labor Review*. November 1997, 39-57.

Flynn, Gillian, "Get The Best from Employees with Learning Disabilities," *Personnel Journal*. January 1996, 76.

Henderson, George, *Human Relations Issues in Management*. Westport, CT: Quorum Books, 1996.

Howard N. Fullerton, Jr., "Labor Force 2006: Slowing Down and Changing Composition," *Monthly Labor Review*. November 1997, 23-38.

Hughes, Richard L., Robert C. Ginnett and Gordon J. Curphy, *Leadership: Enhancing the Lessons of Experience*. Chicago: Irwin, 1996.

Judy, Richard W. and Carol D'Amico, *Workforce 2020*. Indianapolis: Hudson Institute, 1997.

Kayser, Thomas A., *Team Power: How To Unleash the Collaborative Genius of Work Teams*. New York: Irwin, 1994.

Knowles, Malcolm, *The Adult Learner: A Neglected Species*. Houston: Gulf Publishing, 1984.

Langdon, Michael, *Where Leadership Begins*. Milwaukee: ASQC Quality Press, 1993.

Lissy, William, "Employee Theft," *Supervision*. May 1, 1995; 17.

Lussier, Robert N., *Supervision: A Skill Building Approach*. Homewood, IL: Irwin, 1989.

McCormick, Ernest J. and Daniel Ilgen, *Industrial and Organizational Psychology*, 8th edition. Upper Saddle River, NJ: Prentice Hall, 1985.

Meilinger, Phillip, "The Ten Rules of Good Followership," *Military Review*. August 1, 1994; 32.

Mink, Oscar G., Keith Q. Owen and Barbara P. Mink, *Developing High-Performance People: The Art of Coaching*. Reading, MA: Addison-Wesley, 1993.

Murphy, Emmett C., *Leadership IQ*. New York: John Wiley and Sons, 1996.

Nahavandi, Afsaneh, *The Art and Science of Leadership*. Upper Saddle River, NJ: Prentice Hall, 1997.

Nelson, Debra L. and James Campbell Quick, *Organizational Behavior: Foundations, Realities and Challenges*, Alternate edition. New York: West Publishing, 1995.

Newstrom, John W. and Keith Davis, *Organizational Behavior: Human Behavior at Work*, 10th edition. New York: McGraw-Hill, 1989.

Robbins, Stephen P. and David A. DeCenzo, *Supervision Today*, 2nd edition. Upper Saddle River, NJ: Prentice-Hall, 1998.

Robey, Daniel, *Designing Organizations*. Homewood, IL: Irwin, 1991.

The Secretary's Commission on Achieving Necessary Skills, U.S. Department of Labor, *Learning a Living: A Blueprint for High Performance, a SCANS Report for America 2000*. Washington, D.C.: Government Printing Office, 1992.

Sheehy, Gail, *New Passages: Mapping Your Life Across Time*. New York: Random House, 1995.

Schultz, Duane and Sydney Ellen Schultz, *Psychology & Work Today: An Introduction to Industrial and Organizational Psychology*, 7th edition. Upper Saddle River, NJ: Prentice Hall, 1994.

Steingold, Fred S., *The Employer's Legal Handbook*. Berkley, CA: Nolo Press, 1998.

Stewart, Greg L., Charles C. Manz and Henry P. Sims, *Teamwork and Group Dynamics*. New York: John Wiley and Sons, 1999.

Stuart, Lisa and Emily Dahm, *21st Century Skills for 21st Century Jobs*. A report of the U.S. Department of Commerce, U.S. Department of Education, U.S. Department of Labor. National Institute for Literacy and Small Business Administration, 1999.

Tichy, Noel M. and Mary Anne Devanna, *The Transformational Leader*. New York: John Wiley and Sons, 1986.

Tobias, Paul H. and Susan Sauter, *Job Rights & Survival Strategies: A Handbook for Terminated Employees*. Cincinnati: National Employee Rights Institute, 1997; distributed by JIST.

Wellins, Richard S., William C. Byham and Jeanne M. Wilson, *Empowered Teams*. San Francisco: Jossey Bass, 1991.

Yukl, Gary, *Leadership in Organizations*, 4th edition. Upper Saddle River, NJ: Prentice Hall, 1998.

Related Internet Sites

America's Learning Exchange
http://www.alx.org

Bureau of Labor Statistics
http://www.bls.gov

Center for the Study of Work Teams
http://www.workteams.unt.edu

The Corrections Connection
http://www.corrections.com

From Welfare to Work in the Federal Government
http://wtw.doleta.gov/ohrw2w/index.htm

Immigration and Naturalization Service
http://www.ins.usdoj.gov/graphics/aboutins/repsstudies/index.htm

Internal Revenue Service
http://www.irs.gov

Job Accommodation Network
http://janweb.icdi.wvu.edu/

National Alliance of Business: Welfare-to-Work Web Site
http://www.nab.com/workforcedevelopment/welfarereform/introduction/

President's Committee on Employment of People with Disabilities
http://www50.pcepd.gov/pcepd/

Safe Work/Safe Kids—U.S. Dept. of Labor
http://www.dol.gov/dol/esa/public/summer/sw-sk.htm

SCANS 2000—The Workforce Skills Web site
http://www.scans.jhu.edu

Small Business Administration
http://www.sba.gov

Training SuperSite
http://www.trainingsupersite.com

Welfare to Work Partnership
http://www.welfaretowork.org

Workforce Investment Act
http://usworkforce.org

Index

303